Psychology and Crime

Psychology and Crime
Understanding and tackling offending behaviour

Francis Pakes and Jane Winstone

WILLAN
PUBLISHING

Published by

Willan Publishing
Culmcott House
Mill Street, Uffculme
Cullompton, Devon
EX15 3AT, UK
Tel: +44(0)1884 840337
Fax: +44(0)1884 840251
e-mail: info@willanpublishing.co.uk
website: www.willanpublishing.co.uk

Published simultaneously in the USA and Canada by

Willan Publishing
c/o ISBS, 920 NE 58th Ave, Suite 300,
Portland, Oregon 97213-3786, USA
Tel: +001(0)503 287 3093
Fax: +001(0)503 280 8832
e-mail: info@isbs.com
website: www.isbs.com

First published 2007

Hardback
ISBN 978-1-84392-260-5

Paperback
ISBN 978-1-84392-259-9

British Library Cataloguing-in-Publication Data

A catalogue record for this book is available from the British Library

Project managed by Deer Park Productions, Tavistock, Devon
Typeset by GCS, Leighton Buzzard, Bedfordshire
Printed and bound by T.J. International Ltd, Padstow, Cornwall

Francis Pakes
To my children Katie Rose and Anna Daisy Pakes

Jane Winstone
To my mother Rita Watts and my children, Jon, Andrew and Beth

Contents

About the authors

Francis Pakes is a principal lecturer at the University of Portsmouth. He studied psychology at the University of Groningen in his native Netherlands. His PhD (from Leiden University) was on the decision making by Dutch public prosecutors in criminal cases. He moved to the UK in 1998, where he has lectured at the University of Portsmouth ever since. Francis coordinates a number of MSc programmes at the Institute for Criminal Justice Studies, including an MSc in criminology and criminal psychology. His other books include *Comparative Criminal Justice* (Willan 2004), *Community Justice* (co-edited with Jane Winstone; Willan 2005), and *Applying Psychology to Criminal Justice* (Wiley 2007), co-edited with David Carson, Becky Milne, Karen Shalev and Andrea Shawyer.

Jane Winstone is a principal lecturer at the University of Portsmouth. She studied social science and then psychology with the Open University and qualified as a probation officer before joining the University of Portsmouth, Institute of Criminal Justice Studies, in 1998, to coordinate the new training arrangements for probation officers. Jane's main research interests are in the management of mental health in the criminal justice system and in youth crime. She is currently completing her PhD in youth penology, and her latest publications include *Community Justice* (co-edited with Francis Pakes; Willan 2005) and a co-authored chapter (with Francis Pakes) in *Applying Psychology to Criminal Justice* (Wiley 2007).

Aaron Pycroft (responsible for Chapter 8, 'The Psychology of Addiction') is a senior lecturer at the Institute of Criminal Justice Studies, University of Portsmouth. Prior to taking up this post he worked for 15 years in the non-statutory sector as a practitioner, and operational and senior manager within the field of substance abuse. He has worked extensively with Drug Action Teams, Primary Care Trusts, housing associations, criminal justice agencies and local authorities in developing and providing services. His main research interests are alcohol and drug issues, multiple needs and multiagency working.

Introduction

Today's society is fascinated by crime. Crime and deviance have taken on a cultural significance they never previously had. As a result, crime is a hot topic in the media and one that leads people to be continually exposed to criminal events, portrayals of those who commit them, and the suffering of victims. Most of the crime we experience, we experience vicariously. But the bias in crime reporting is such that it is easy to get the wrong idea about the reality of crime. Most crime is neither violent nor morbid; most offenders are not psychopaths; and although prison does not work, there may well be other, less punitive but more constructive interventions that are actually quite effective. This book seeks to expose some of the most prevalent myths about crime and criminal behaviour, and provide the reader with accurate and up-to-date knowledge of crime, offending behaviour and interventions.

In addition, we can say that we live in a psychological society. Concepts such as frustration, repression and self-esteem were once the province of psychologists and counsellors but have now become part and parcel of everyday parlance. Further to that, there is a widespread misconception that psychology is primarily for counselling and therapy in order to further the understanding of ourselves. Instead, psychology is an empirical science seeking to gain useful knowledge about people and human behaviour in general.

In this book, we seek to apply the latter, sound knowledge of human behaviour, our understanding of crime, criminal behaviour and criminal justice policy. We have devised a number of chapters that look at crime generally, at specific types of offences, or at specific phenomena in the area of crime and justice.

Chapter 1 deals with causes of crime. These can apply to the individual, such as a low level of frustration tolerance, or to the family, as in domestic abuse. Other causes are sociological, such as disorganised neighbourhoods or social inequalities. We will argue that we need to look at such risk factors in conjunction in order to understand properly the emergence of crime and antisocial behaviour. Finally, we look at resilience as a factor in avoiding the trappings of a life of crime.

Chapter 2 examines the largely mythical 'criminal mind'. It looks at how offender profilers make use of crime scene information in order to make statements about an offender's personality, background and life circumstances, and we briefly explore how mental illness might link to serious offending (although we will see in Chapter 6 that the answer to that query must be: not very strongly).

Juvenile offending is the topic of Chapter 3. It looks at a variety of risk factors that help predict which youngster in which circumstances is disproportionately at risk of becoming delinquent. It also looks at official responses to youth crime, from imprisonment to Antisocial Behaviour Orders (ASBOs), and assesses their likely impact upon preventing young people from embarking upon long-term criminal careers.

Chapter 4 focuses upon aggression and violence and looks at the role of a number of factors known to inhibit or facilitate it, including social learning, alcohol, testosterone, and the effects of television violence and violent video games. It also presents a general aggression model that puts these findings into a coherent framework.

Chapter 5 debates the extensive area of sexual offending and looks at the prevalence of sex offending in England and Wales. It explores how the development of typologies has identified the different motivations underpinning sex offences and child molestation and presents the current research in this area. The chapter also has considerable focus on the assessment and treatment of sex offenders, as currently takes place in prison and as carried out by the probation service, and the strengths and weaknesses of these approaches.

Insanity, mental health and mentally disordered offending are debated in Chapter 6. We briefly outline various types of mental illness, and we look at the link between mental illness and crime. The main conclusion must be that those with mental health difficulties are more likely to be a danger to themselves than to others, and that most individuals with mental health problems who come into contact with the criminal justice system are more in need of adequate medical and social support – which is far more likely to reduce incidents of offending behaviour than time spent in a prison environment.

Chapter 7 aims to debunk the myth that stalking victimisation is something that typically befalls celebrities. In fact, young women at university are disproportionately at risk from this type of harassing behaviour. The chapter also emphasises that stalking is far from a harmless, inadequate expression of affection, as the behaviour of many stalkers sooner or later escalates to become threatening and violent.

Chapter 8 is written by Aaron Pycroft. It explores the phenomenon of addiction and the ambivalent attitudes in society that relate to it. In order to understand the inherent complexity of this subject, he proposes a trans-theoretical model of change (TTM), and he introduces complexity theory and looks at issues such as relapse prevention and self-efficacy.

Chapter 9 attempts to dispel various misconceptions in the area of date rape, or, as it is often termed, 'acquaintance rape'. It looks at prevalence and at a form of date rape that is the focus of much concern despite the fact that until recently good evidence of its prevalence was very scarce, that of date rape by means of so-called date rape drugs. We will conclude that while there are typical date rape drugs, in most cases where date rape allegations have been made, the substance found in the victims' system is, in fact, alcohol. Prevention of sexual violence in a dating context and how to be safe, are also discussed.

Chapter 10 focuses upon prisons. It has been well established that prison produces poor results from the perspective of reoffending rates, and this chapter will examine why that is, with particular focus on the psychology of imprisonment. This discussion will include reference to Zimbardo's prison study experiment, role orientations of both prisoners and those who detain and care for them, and what happens when relationships become dysfunctional.

Finally, Chapter 11 looks at victims and fear of crime, and establishes two things. The first is that victims are not always who you assume them to be: we know, for instance, that those who have committed crimes are particularly at risk of becoming victims, and the same is true for mental health patients. In addition, we find that those who are most afraid of crime are not always the groups most at risk. The intricate nature of the relationship between fear of crime and risk of victimisation will be discussed here, as well as the concept of designing out crime, by introducing a concept called 'defensible space'.

Although crime and justice have become highly politicised, we have focused upon the psychology of crime. That is not to say that the book is insular. Where relevant and appropriate, we have discussed legislation and sociological theories, and we bring political rhetoric and social movements in to our debates. There is no doubt that crime and criminal policy can be properly understood only if these processes are given their due weight. We do think, however, that the sound application of psychological methods of research and psychological knowledge are vital in understanding the individual offender and in evaluating structured interventions. Psychology does not have all the answers, but it does have much to offer to our understanding of the area of crime, justice and community safety.

Chapter 1

Why do people offend? psychological and sociological explanations

Introduction

On 10 July 2006, the British news media reported on a 40-year-old man from Newcastle who walked into a police station carrying a large bag. Calmly, he told the receptionist that he had shot and killed four people. The man was immediately overpowered and arrested. His bag was found to contain a range of weaponry. When police entered the man's house, the four victims were discovered. They were relatives, a man and a woman in their seventies and two men in their forties, all shot dead from close range (*Daily Mail* 10 July 2006).

Why did this happen? What is it that brings a man, on a quiet Sunday, to kill two relatives with a handgun with a silencer, and then to wait quietly for the two other residents to come home, and to shoot them as well? The newspaper made much of the fact that the man had fought in the Gulf War in 1991 and speculated whether that was a contributing factor.

In September 2005, the BBC ran the story of a man on the Isle of Man who was sent to prison for three months for taking part in a 'happy slapping' incident. He was with two others when he assaulted a man in Douglas, Isle of Man, and the assault was filmed on a mobile phone. The offender admitted the assault after footage was shown and also admitted that he had been drinking. However, he could not explain why he became involved in the violent attack (BBC News 8 September 2005).

Crime can be incomprehensible stuff. It is difficult if not impossible to creep into offenders' minds and establish with any degree of certainty just why they did what they did. In cases where offenders are prepared to talk about their crime, the reasons they give are often unsatisfactory. Happy slapping is allegedly carried out for fun. 'Fun' is hardly an explanation. Similarly, the claim that sex offences are carried out for sexual gratification offers some sort of explanation, but not one that is very enlightening. We can see that that is the immediate motive, just as material gain explains why theft or fraud might occur, but it fails to establish other facts: Why was this particular victim chosen? Why at that point in time? Why do other people with the same problems not resort to crime?

Wilson and Seaman (1990) documented accounts of individuals convicted of murder, who often gave rather trivial reasons for their crimes. Norman Smith said he acted out of boredom when he shot Hazel Woodard while she was at home watching television. The students Nathan Leopold and Richard Loeb said that they committed a murder simply as a challenge. They killed a 14-year-old boy. Ruth Steinhagen invited a baseball player into her hotel room in Chicago and then shot him. When asked why, she said that she wanted the thrill of murdering him (Wilson and Seaman 1990).

These accounts illustrate that asking 'why' is not necessarily the right question. To understand offending behaviour so that we can predict or prevent it requires a different type of analysis. That is what this chapter is about. Before he became prime minister, Tony Blair launched a famous slogan when he said that New Labour would be 'tough on crime, tough on the causes of crime' (Blair 1993). In order to start our enquiry, we must develop ideas about what we actually mean when we talk about the causes of crime. After that, this chapter will outline various biological, psychological and social explanations of crime. Biological factors include genes, hormones, and brain injury or dysfunction. Psychological factors include personality, a factor known as self-control, and the concept of sensation seeking. We will also examine the role of the family. Sociological factors include poverty, subcultures and a concept called strain. In the end, we examine factors that might prevent people from committing crime.

Understanding causes of crime

When psychologists or criminologists talk about offending behaviour, they are often talking about causes of crime rather than motives. We do not necessarily need to know what the offender was thinking at the time of the offence. It is anyway doubtful whether that is where reliable answers can be found. After all, we can only uncover that by asking the offender, and it is very possible that the answer will be influenced by demand characteristics (that is, the expectation of what the interviewer wants to hear) and concerns of self-presentation (that is, the desire to leave a particular impression of oneself); for example, Douglas and Olshaker (1997) argue that asking such questions often brings about well-rehearsed self-serving answers, rather than anything nearer to the truth.

Instead, psychologists and criminologists are usually concerned with what the social and psychological factors are that contribute to the offending behaviour. Thus, when we talk about the causes of crime, psychologists and criminologists tend to look at general factors that apply to offending and offenders in a way that is disproportionate. If most offenders share a characteristic which non-offenders do not, that might be identified as a possible correlate of crime. Whether that characteristic is anything to do with actually producing crime is a different matter. That is a key question when deciding to call a factor a *cause* of crime.

There are other ways of understanding crime, of course. One way is by life stories; in criminology, this is called narrative individualism (Bretherick 2006). The method is in-depth case study: we describe the life of notorious criminals, and in their past we seek to identify certain key events or circumstances that might have driven them to offend. When Ressler and Shachtman (1992) interviewed serial killers in US prisons, they found that many offenders would pinpoint a certain event that set them off on the path to destructive violence. Such watershed events often involve being subjected to sexual or physical abuse. Alternatively, witnessing violence in the home might also act as a later trigger.

On the other hand, the 'defining moment' can be something relatively trivial or unexpected. The long running British soap *Coronation Street* at one point featured a serial killer called Richard Hillman. Viewers were offered the suggestion that his motivation may have had something to do with the fact that he was infertile. His inability to father children may have been the initial trigger that brought about the subsequent destructive tendencies. Criminologists and psychologists would not call this a cause of crime: for that, we would have to establish in real life that men who cannot father children are significantly more likely to commit crimes than others. Such a study does not exist. We therefore do not say that infertility causes crime.

3

A cause of crime, therefore, is a factor or circumstance that applies significantly more to offenders than to non-offenders and that potentially has a direct, but not necessarily immediate, link to crime. Factors such as alcohol dependence or drug abuse are commonly understood to have a potential bearing on people's behaviour. It is hardly controversial to think of those as causes of crime. The extent to which societal factors such as poverty or social exclusion can cause crime is more hotly debated. Equally, the role of biology, via genes, hormones or brain dysfunction is a factor of concern. Not only is the extent to which people's biological make-up affects their propensity to offend a controversial factor, but also the question of how to use such knowledge is another factor for which there are no easy answers. Later in this chapter, we will discover that we are most concerned with a certain type of cause of crime: the type that we can change. After all, as men are more prevalent offenders than women, we could focus on gender as a cause of crime. However, as gender, by and large, tends to be fixed, that knowledge does not help us much in trying to prevent crime. It is therefore more fruitful to look at circumstances that we can influence. Thus, in this chapter, we seek to identify causes of crime with an eye to prevention.

Biology

Understanding criminal behaviour from a biological perspective seems deceptively easy. You simply assume that what causes crime lurks within criminals: there is something wrong with them. Whether it is a faulty gene, or too much or too little of a certain hormone, or the fact that they fell on their head as babies, the assumption is that offending behaviour is the result of some sort of pathology. Cesare Lombroso (1911) was one of the first to advocate this. He was an Italian army doctor in the nineteenth century who examined criminals and concluded that they are degenerate, not fully developed as human beings. Criminals in this view are Darwinian failures, a lesser, more primitive version of *Homo sapiens*. Their offending behaviour is an expression of inferior desires and decision-making. Lombroso argued that although these people do manage to survive in civil society they are actually more equipped to live in the wild. Incapable of telling right from wrong, they are unable to sustain meaningful social relationships, and are biologically predisposed to a life of crime. Importantly, Lombroso argued that you could tell criminals by their physical features. Dwyer (2001) summarises these as follows:

- a narrow, sloping brow;
- a prominent jaw;
- high cheekbones and large ears;
- extra nipples, toes or fingers. (Dwyer 2001)

Later in his career, Lombroso softened his views and conceded that maybe only a subset of all criminals subscribed to this typology (Lombroso 1911). Nevertheless, Lombroso's name is synonymous with the approach that regards criminals as subhuman degenerates.

It must be appreciated that within the scientific and social world of the nineteenth century, this was not such an outrageous position. Lively research took place that sought to establish the racial superiority of whites. Much of this was achieved via the measurement of the skull (or the brain) of various races. Usually, the conclusion that these European researchers sought to reach was that white people were more intelligent and civilised (e.g., Gould 1981). This line of enquiry has long been since discredited as biased and often racist in nature.

Lombroso's work fits this tradition. Differences between races or between groups of people such as criminals and non-criminals were explained in terms of how evolved these groups were. Science soon moved away from this approach, but it dominated popular debates on crime long after. In a way, Lombroso's research is a skeleton in criminal psychology's cupboard. Today, it is a source of embarrassment, rather than of knowledge. His work was methodologically sloppy and biased, and his ideas tended to be misguided.

A methodologically more promising way to study the relation between genetics and crime is via so-called twin studies. The rationale underlying twin studies is simple. Monozygotic twins are identical twins with an identical genetic make-up. Therefore, any differences in their behaviour can be ascribed to the environment. Dizygotic twins are fraternal twins. These non-identical twins are genetically as similar to each other as other siblings. Studying the behaviour of twins can therefore provide valuable clues as to the extent to which criminal behaviour is affected by nature or by nurture.

Twin studies are a classic paradigm in criminal psychology. Early examples include a study by Lange in 1931. Lange looked at 13 monozygotic and 17 dizygotic twins. He did find a very high level of concordance, that is, similarity, between identical twins: if one twin had a conviction leading to imprisonment, there was a 77 per cent chance that the other twin had the same. It was only 12 per cent for the non-identical twins. However, the sample size was so small that it was difficult to draw unequivocal conclusions. These findings may not generalise easily from his sample to the general population.

More recent twin studies have been carried out in Scandinavia, and they tend to find results that go in the same direction. However, the concordance for monozygotic twins does not tend to be as high as in Lange's early study. Christiansen examined no fewer than 3,586 pairs of twins from Denmark. He found a concordance for male identical twins of 35 per cent (13 per cent for fraternal twins), whereas, for women, it was lower still, 21 per cent and 8 per cent, respectively. That would suggest a rather modest role for genes, as the results for identical twins suggest that when one twin has a criminal record, that does not mean that the other twin will have one too.

A number of points need to be made. Firstly, as we said, twin studies have improved in that the samples have become larger, and are put together in a more systematic fashion. In addition, the measurement of offending behaviour has improved as well. Lange looked at imprisonment, which is a crude factor that will only take into account serious crime, and only the crimes for which participants have been caught and convicted. As much crime goes officially undetected, that measure certainly has its limitations. Christiansen looked at criminal records generally which is less crude but still not as accurate as self-report data might have been. In addition, we must ask to what extent similarities between twins are brought about by nature or nurture. After all, identical twins usually share not only genes, but also much of their environment. They usually grow up in the same household, in the same place of residence, and they might attend the same school, and share a group of friends. In other words, their environment might be highly similar as well. Thus, any similarities can be explained by both their genes and the similarity of the environment. Thus, these twin studies might suggest a modest effect of genetic build-up, but still cannot provide conclusive answers. A study that looks at identical twins brought up separately would be able to provide clearer answers, but, unfortunately, in criminology such a study does not exist.

An ambitious longitudinal twin study is currently taking place in the UK. It is called the Twins Early Developments Study (see Jaffee et al. 2005, for an overview). The study follows the development of 1,116 twins and their families over time to look at various factors in their development. Some of these factors, such as intelligence and attention deficit hyperactivity disorder (ADHD), may have an impact on crime.

The research group recently published a paper in which they assessed how behavioural problems had come about as a function of both adverse circumstances and maltreatment in conjunction with certain genetic vulnerabilities. These genetic vulnerabilities were factors such as impulsivity and hyperactivity. They found that a genetic vulnerability to problem behaviour had a big impact on the degree to which maltreatment produced behavioural problems in 5-year-olds (Jaffee *et al.* 2005). A genetic vulnerability does not inevitably lead to problems, but is likely to make the effects of abuse or maltreatment much worse.

Recent research has moved away from looking at nature–nurture from an either–or perspective, but is investigating the ways in which genetic vulnerabilities and adverse life circumstances might bring about a variety of problem behaviours in childhood. Some children who display this type of problem conduct early are most likely to acquire a criminal lifestyle when they grow up (Moffitt 1993; Moffitt and Caspi 2001).

Modern types of research seek to explain certain types of offending from a biological perspective. There is some evidence that, in rare cases, genetics can have a strong impact on impulsive and violent behaviour. In Chapter 4 on aggression, we will discover that biological factors such as levels of testosterone or certain types of brain injuries may also have an influence. Thus, it does not seem safe to ignore biology and genetics as factors altogether. However, it is only in interaction with much more potent factors that they affect criminal behaviour. By themselves, their role is, at most, very modest.

Personality

Personality is an elusive thing. We cannot observe it directly, but must infer it from a person's behavioural patterns over the course of time. The assumption is that those patterns hang together in a meaningful way, are relatively stable over time, and vary from individual to individual. Personality is closely linked to a person's identity and self-perception. Personality is usually measured via questionnaires in which respondents answer questions about themselves, agree or disagree with certain statements, or indicate how they would behave in a variety of situations.

Hans Eysenck is credited with formulating the most famous personality theory within criminal psychology. His personality dimensions are broad and basic and closely linked to temperament.

In his view, personality is shaped by subtle individual differences – 'particularities', in his own words (Eysenck and Gudjonsson 1989; 247) – in the brain and nervous system that, in interaction with the environment produce certain behavioural preferences or tendencies.

Eysenck's extroversion–introversion dimension is well known. Every individual is more or less extrovert or introvert. Extroverts are outgoing, sociable, and impulsive. They need more stimulation, are more easily bored, and are more likely to be the life and soul of any party. Introverts tend to be shy, to keep themselves to themselves, and to be better able to give meaning to their existence in solitude. They do not require constant stimulation or thrills. Eysenck's second dimension is stable versus unstable. The two dimensions can be combined to form four types: stable introvert, stable extrovert, unstable introvert, and unstable extrovert (the stability dimension was originally called neuroticism (Eysenck and Eysenck 1976). Those who score high on the neuroticism or stability scale tend to display traits such as anxiousness, depression, and low self-esteem. Finally, the third dimension is psychoticism or the tendency to have a mental breakdown or suffer from psychotic mental health problems. Knust and Stewart (2002) call this dimension also 'tough-mindedness'. Associated traits are aggression, egocentricity and coldness to others.

If we look at these dimensions, it probably is no surprise that those who are extrovert, unstable or neurotic, and high on the psychoticism scale are more likely to offend than others (Eysenck and Eysenck 1985). When Knust and Stewart administered Eysenck's personality questionnaire among prison inmates, they indeed found that inmates scored high on extroversion on the psychoticism scale. Although Hans Eysenck died in 1997, the instrument that he developed with his wife Sybil, the Eysenck Personality Scale (Eysenck and Eysenck 1975), is still frequently used.

A trait related to extroversion is thrill or sensation seeking. Zuckerman (1994) is generally credited with coining the term 'sensation seeking', in his words:

> a trait defined by the seeking of varied, novel, complex and intense sensations and experiences, and the willingness to take physical, social, legal and financial risks for the sake of such experience. (Zuckerman 1994: 27)

This trait consists of four subtraits. The first is *thrill and adventure seeking*, and it refers to legal ways of thrill seeking such as sports and other activities. The second, *experience seeking*, refers to the desire to explore, as by travelling. The third, *disinhibition*, is linked with criminality and alcohol and drug abuse. The fourth subtrait is *boredom susceptibility,* the extent to which people are easily bored. In their research, Knust and Stewart (2002) found imprisoned offenders to score particularly high on the so-called unsocialised personality dimensions, psychoticism, extroversion and susceptibility to boredom.

There are other personality traits associated with offending or, the other side of the coin, with being able to withstand the seductions and rewards of criminal activity. After all, it must be appreciated that many types of crime can be very tempting. Property crime is tempting from a material gains perspective; sexual crime might have sexual gratification as its reward, violence might get respect from peers, and, on top of all that, committing crime can be very exciting. Gottfredson and Hirschi (1990) therefore argue that the question is not why certain people commit crimes but why so many people do not. Their key concept is self-control. In their view, much crime involves short-term gains, but long-term risks and losses. Those who go in for the exhilaration and short-term gain of shoplifting, or stealing a mobile phone have a different perspective on life than those who look for rewards in the longer term. Self-control is the required trait to overlook the short-term gains and to stay focused on what is good in the longer term.

How is self-control acquired? Gottfredson and Hirschi (1990) argue that it is acquired usually via good parenting. A child raised in a nurturing and structured environment grows up realising that certain behaviours are allowed or rewarded, whereas others are not. When the child is growing up, such rules become internalised, and the locus of control shifts away from parents or carers to the self. Children learn to control their own behaviour because norms, values and ideas about appropriate behaviour become part of their identity. That self-control is the strongest antidote to the seductions of crime (Katz 1988). Other controls are social bonds, which are external and will be discussed later.

The family

The family can be studied from two angles. The first is to look at family structure. From that perspective, we can ask questions such as, is growing up in a single-parent household a risk factor for delinquency? Or, is having many siblings a protective factor against crime? The other perspective is to look at family interactions and investigate whether parenting styles and other circumstances bear on the children's development or future delinquency.

Talk about the family and crime has often focused on divorce and single mothers. 'Kids need a father' is an often heard cry. In the past, coming from a broken home has indeed been identified as a risk factor for offending behaviour. A key research study in this regard was by Glueck and Glueck from 1950. However, divorce rates were much lower at that time, and there was more stigma attached to divorce than there is today. Thus, the children from those families probably suffered more negative effects in their social environment than they would today. Loeber and Stouthamer-Loeber (1986) argue that any increased risk is primarily an issue of supervision. After all, two pairs of eyes see more than one, so that it might be easier to get up to mischief undetected as a child in a single-parent family. A similar explanation has been given for the fact that having a large number of siblings has been identified as a risk factor (Farrington 1991). Exposure to delinquent siblings might be another factor, but it is also possible that families with many children are financially less well off and possibly more chaotic.

When we discuss crime and divorce, it is important to stress that it is not the divorce per se, or the absence of a father figure that accounts for any elevated risk of delinquency. Rather, it is the stress and discord prior to separation that has been identified as the operating factor. Family harmony is therefore more important than family make-up (McCord 1979). Rutter (1971) accordingly found that single-parent families due to the death of one parent do not represent a risk factor for criminality.

Although they are difficult to pinpoint, parenting styles have been extensively studied in their relationship to future delinquency. Harsh physical punishment, especially when inconsistently applied, has been identified as a risk factor. Equally, psychological abuse in the form of constant criticism, neglect or verbal abuse can be quite harmful, according to some even more so than certain forms of physical abuse.

Sadly, having a stepfather has been identified as a risk factor for sexual abuse in the home. Thus, family make-up does correlate with risk of victimisation. Finkelhor (1993) found that girls were most at risk, in pre- or early adolescence age, living without a natural parent, having a stepfather, having a mother with learning difficulties and witnessing family conflict. According to Finkelhor, class and race are not of much importance. It generally is safe to say that it is family interactions and dynamics that are more important in helping to shape children's skills, attitudes and outlook on life, as well as providing a safe and nurturing environment.

Family studies have been utilised to assess whether crime, as it were, runs in the family. The unsurprising finding is that it does. The so-called Cambridge Study (see Farrington and West 1990) followed a group of boys who were born in London's East End in 1953. Using data from that longitudinal project, Osborn and West (1979) found that criminal parents are significantly more likely to have criminal children. Only 13 per cent of non-criminal children had a father with a criminal record, whereas 40 per cent of criminal children did so. Thus, having a father with a criminal record is a strong predictor for acquiring a criminal record yourself.

There are many ways in which we can explain this relationship. Criminal fathers might serve as a role model for their sons, so that we can explain the crimes of their sons as the result of social modelling (see Chapter 4, in which we discuss this process). It is also conceivable that the homes in which these children grow up are poorer and more chaotic, or that the parenting styles of criminal parents are relatively poor. Those factors are likely to affect a child's development as well. Conceivably, sons of criminal fathers are statistically more likely to have criminal peers. Perhaps alcohol or drugs problems are also more prevalent in these homes. Finally, we might mention genetic transmission. However, as there is a large variety of potential explanations, we cannot say that the findings from the Cambridge Study support the 'nature' argument over the 'nurture' argument.

Nevertheless, the Cambridge Study is a key study in criminal psychology. On the one hand, it did demonstrate the link between criminal records regarding father and son, but it also showed the prevalence of offending behaviour. One in five East End boys had a criminal conviction at age 17. This figure went up to one in three by the age of 25. Police contacts were much more frequent still. It highlights the statistical 'normality' of a certain level of offending among young males (Farrington 1991). Another key finding that is that only 6 per cent of boys accounted for no less than 50 per cent of all offending behaviour. Thus, in short, many people commit some crime, but a few commit many. That is worth knowing, from the angle of crime prevention. Further scrutiny reveals that these latter boys displayed a catalogue of social and psychological problems from a young age onward. That included impulsivity at age 10, aggression at age 14, drink problems and delinquent peers at age 18, and a variety of social problems with relationships, mental health, housing and substances at age 32. Moffitt argues that the problems of this subset of boys, which she estimates to be in the order of 5 per cent of all young boys, are such that their delinquency is likely to start at an earlier age, and is more likely to persist into adulthood; thus it is this group that finds it difficult to 'grow out of' crime (Moffitt 1993).

Environmental factors: bonds, gangs and society at large

Taking the environment argument a few steps further allows us to look at the wider environment and society as a whole as factors impinging on offending. In turn, we discuss social bonds, structural strain and subcultures. After that, we will move on to look at the position taken by so-called critical criminologists.

Our wider social environment contains both risk and protective factors for offending behaviour, but, of course, not for everyone in equal measure. We know that having delinquent peers is a risk factor for offending. That is hardly surprising, but how can our social environment work to reduce the chances of offending behaviour? Gottfredson and Hirschi (1990) stress the importance of social bonds. Social bonds are the factors that make you realise how much you depend on other people and other people on you. Offending and other deviant behaviour put those bonds at risk. In the long term that is usually not a good option. Social bonds are, you could say, protective factors against crime. Without them, most if not all of us would not be able to refrain from crime. Hirschi (1969) discusses four types of social bonds. The first is *attachment*. It reflects the extent to which people feel connected with and loved by others. A secure family upbringing is seen to be crucial to attachment. In Chapter 9, we will revisit attachment theory to find that many stalkers have attachment issues. People with a high level of attachment tend to agree with statements such as 'My parents are good role models', and 'In times of need, there is always someone to turn to'. *Commitment* is to do with having a stake in a conformist lifestyle: having a partner, a job, and a mortgage. It reflects the extent to which a person is bound by society's regular institutions. Offending behaviour would put all that at risk, as a criminal conviction might ruin a professional career and reduce the chances of becoming a homeowner. *Involvement* is the extent to which your regular social and professional activities keep you busy. If you have a demanding job, a commute, children to look after, a garden to tend, and an elderly neighbour to go grocery shopping for, there will be little time or energy for crime or antisocial behaviour. A high level of commitment usually brings about a high level of involvement, so that these bonds work together to reduce the opportunities and temptations of crime. Finally, there is *belief*, the degree to which people believe that they should be law-abiding. It is common for individuals with high levels of social bonds to internalise these convictions, and that is what belief refers to.

Social bonds work together to enhance self-control. Most people do not need to be deterred by CCTV or the threat of prison. Instead, we deter ourselves. Carroll and Weaver (1986) demonstrated this in their so-called shoplifting study. They asked experienced shoplifters and so-called novices, people that might have thought about it but never actually shoplifted, to think aloud while walking through a shop assessing the shoplifting possibilities. Experienced shoplifters turned out to be thinking about opportunities to commit their crime. In contrast, the novices spent most of the time worrying about getting caught.

The other side of the coin is a situation in which you are attached to people who frequently commit crimes. This is the realm of *subcultures* such as gangs. Any group can engender a subculture, that is, a set of values and beliefs that are different from the majority. Criminal subcultures are characterised by subversive values and ideas. In today's terms, that means that if you 'hang around' with people with different ideas about crime, it is likely that both your beliefs and your actions will be influenced by that. Sutherland (1974) calls this differential association. Rather than acquiring prosocial attitudes via parents and peers, subcultures can foster the acquisition of antisocial values.

It can, however, be questioned how deeply internalised those antisocial values are. Do those in juvenile gangs honestly believe that stealing is normal and violence appropriate? According to Sykes and Matza (1957), a technique is utilised that is known as neutralisation. It helps to generate justification for crimes and other antisocial behaviours. There are five neutralisation techniques. They are as follows, to paraphrase McGuire (2004):

- denial of responsibility: e.g., 'it wasn't my fault';
- denial of injury: e.g., 'they'll just claim it on their insurance and shops make a lot of money anyway';

- denial of victim: e.g., 'women actually want to be raped';
- condemning the condemners: e.g., 'all cops are corrupt, so they are no better than me';
- appeal to higher loyalties: e.g., 'if someone insults my sister, they must suffer for it'.

The use of such neutralisation techniques suggests that even hard-core criminals, at some level, like to regard themselves as honourable. In addition, they also seem to be keen to be seen to be honourable, even if that is in a fashion that is not altogether regular. Perhaps, then, the difference in values between criminals and non-criminals in reality is smaller than we sometimes tend to assume (Sykes and Matza 1957).

There has been a fair bit of research into establishing the nature of the relation between poverty and crime. It is generally understood that poverty per se is not a strong risk factor for crime. 'It would be misleading to equate crime with absolute poverty. The great majority of poor people are law-abiding citizens and the poor do not steal because they lack food or clothing' (Giddens 2001). But it is important to qualify this. First there is a difference between absolute and relative poverty. *Absolute poverty* is failure to satisfy basic needs such as food, clothing and shelter. *Relative poverty* is more difficult to define. By definition, it is being poor relative to the wealth in society and therefore relates to the distribution of wealth. Relative poverty is often understood to be poor to the extent that you cannot fully take part in society (Giddens 2001).

Relative poverty is therefore linked to social exclusion, and social exclusion can be said to cause strain. The UK government has established a Social Exclusion Unit (SEU) (see www.socialexclusionunit.org.uk). It describes social exclusion as follows.

> Social exclusion happens when people or places suffer from a series of problems such as unemployment, discrimination, poor skills, low incomes, poor housing, high crime, ill health and family breakdown. When such problems combine they can create a vicious cycle. (Social Exclusion Unit 2006a: no page number).

Social exclusion can easily cause resentment. In sociology, that is often discussed in terms of structural strain. Robert K. Merton argued that 'some social structures exert a definite pressure upon certain persons in society to engage in non-conforming rather than conforming conduct' (1957: 132).

In Merton's view, the motivations for crime lie in the strains imposed by an unequal society. The goals that we should strive for are clear: life is about success. It is about doing well in school, excelling in arts or science, or becoming a medal-winning athlete. The dream is making lots of money, and acquiring the good things in life, both material and otherwise. However, people with poor social and verbal skills, and low intelligence who suffered a chaotic or abusive upbringing will find it difficult to achieve this. Upon growing up, that is something that the individual must come to terms with. Not everybody will be successful in life, and many will feel that society in fact does not offer a level playing field. How do people cope with that strain?

Merton argues that there are four ways of coping with strain. Some of these are more likely to lead to crime than others. The first is *confirmation*. It is choosing to live your life in socially acceptable ways and accepting that you simply cannot have it all. The second is *innovation*, which involves seeking alternative ways to achieve society's goals that bring the good things in life. That might be private enterprise, but it might also be white-collar crime: it is achieving the same things, but in different ways. *Ritualism* is focusing on daily activities but losing sight of the bigger picture. It evokes images of people sitting behind grey desks in nondescript office blocks, completing mindless administrative tasks. Finally, there is *rebellion*, in which both society's goals and the accepted means to achieve them are rejected. You may think of environmental protesters, for instance, or radical cultural or religious movements. It is fair to say that most people, influenced by their social bonds, choose conformity. Of course, nonconformity does not necessarily mean crime, nor does conformity guarantee that no crimes will be committed. It is no doubt true that some of the most conformist and successful people will commit white-collar and other crimes that involve millions of pounds and more often than not get away with it.

Merton gives the influence of society upon the individual a central position in his explanation for crime. We must always remember that crime is a social construction and defined by those in power. In that light, we must appreciate that the perceived nature of an offence is often influenced by who commits it and in what context. Take the following example.

At the annual Wimbledon tennis championship, the tournament provides towels for the players in the traditional green and purple colours to use during matches. They are the property of the All England Club that organises the annual tournament. These towels are stolen in large numbers by the players, most of whom receive large sums of prize and sponsorship money anyway, as *The Daily Telegraph* reports. Wimbledon winner Roger Federer freely admits, 'I do take a few. I have a big collection stacked up back home – they make a good gift'. Doubles player Bob Bryan said, 'These towels have been a long tradition at Wimbledon and players make a habit of stealing as many as they can get their hands on' (Iggulden 2006). Apparently the total value of towels stolen amounts to some £60,000 a year.

Stealing a towel worth £20 from the All England Club might not seem that big a deal. However, stealing a similarly priced towel from your local department store is likely to be looked upon rather differently. It might involve store security personnel, a prosecution, and a court appearance. After all, theft is a serious crime, but maybe not if you are a Wimbledon tennis player. It does illustrate that certain 'crimes' by certain people are less likely to be perceived as 'proper crimes' than similar actions by others.

Critical criminologists would argue that this small example actually represents the reality of criminal justice: the force of the law is used against the working-class shoplifter, but not against the rich and famous who commit offences. It perhaps tells us something disturbing about society if the small crimes of the poor worry and anger us, but we shrug our shoulders when the rich and powerful engage in the same behaviours or worse. It reminds us that we should think critically about what crimes are, and who decides that.

In conclusion, 'a crime is a crime is a crime' does not apply. How a crime is perceived depends on who commits it and in what context. In addition, criminal definitions change over time. Marital rape has only become an offence in the last 30 years. Stalking is also a newly defined type of crime. In addition, there are behaviours that are regarded to be wrong by many, but are not criminal offences. That might include the conduct of large companies regarding environmental waste or health and safety provisions. It shows that the relation between criminal definitions and the degree of social harm that certain behaviours cause is sometimes rather weak. Perhaps criminal psychology should be concerned more with the question of what 'makes' a crime in the first place.

Conclusion

In this chapter we have explained that the psychology of crime is primarily concerned with identifying causes and correlates of crime.

It is easy to think of correlates of crime, such as low intelligence, a criminal parent, issues with aggression and anger, and drug and alcohol problems. In fact, being a male makes you far more likely to be in trouble with the law as well, as does being young and outgoing. But we must distinguish between correlates and causes. Correlates of crime are factors that statistically relate to offending behaviour. On the other hand, we think of causes as factors that have an impact on offender behaviour and that we, at least in theory, might be able to address. Drug abuse is a good example: we know that those with drug problems are much more likely to commit a variety of crimes. We also can assume that if we could deal with these drug problems, the crime problem might be (partly) solved as well. It therefore makes sense to think of drug abuse as a cause of crime (and, of course, depending on the type of drug, a criminal activity itself).

Those who work with offenders in order to prevent them from reoffending would call such a circumstance a criminogenic need. This is a novel approach compared with the more traditional distinction between static and dynamic risk factors. Static risk factors tend to be demographic or criminal history variables that are not open to manipulation. If teenagers have been violent in the past, they are more likely to behave violently in the future. That is a static risk factor: the fact that they were violent in the past is something we cannot change. In contrast, dynamic risk factors are, at least in theory, changeable. Dynamic risk factors are considered criminogenic needs only if there is evidence that any improvement in those needs will reduce reoffending. Psychotherapy, for instance, may well benefit a troubled youngster, but has not been proven to reduce reoffending. Criminogenic needs therefore are those risk factors that we know affect offending behaviour and that we think we know how to tackle. Working with offenders in the UK is based on criminogenic need.

McGuire (2004: 116) summarises the following major factors with a clear link to risk of crime. Some of these could be addressed with specific interventions.

- antisocial attitudes, beliefs, or cognitive-emotional states;
- association with pro-criminal peers;
- a number of temperamental and personality factors, including impulsivity, egocentrism and poor problem-solving skills;
- a varied history of antisocial behaviour;
- family history of criminality;
- low levels of personal, educational, or financial achievement.

These factors are obviously generic and predict future offending in general. It is worth keeping in mind, as is the fact that most offenders are generalists likely to commit a variety of offences (Gottfredson and Hirschi 1990; Moffitt 1993). However, certain types of crime have different pathways of causality and a different set of risk factors associated with them (e.g., Armstrong 2005). For example, when discussing the nature of aggression, we examine violent television and video games as potential contributing factors. For certain types of sex offending, we need to look into issues of victim empathy and cognitive distortion (e.g., Marshall *et al.* 2001). Thus, although these generic factors are powerful explanatory factors, specific offence types will require specific risk factors to be considered.

Obviously, we should not take these factors to be deterministic. No single factor inevitably leads to crime. Instead, most people are influenced by a constellation of protective and risk factors whereas other circumstances such as opportunity have a role to play as well. Furthermore, many life circumstances change: most juvenile offenders grow up and might leave their criminal lifestyle behind, often without any specific intervention by the criminal justice system. Thus, a focus on risk factors for crime should not give the impression of doom and gloom.

In fact, recent research is increasingly focused on identifying the factors that make young people transcend the most adverse circumstances. Some people have suffered a great deal of mental, physical and sexual abuse, but they manage to beat the odds to become highly successful people. What these people often have in abundance is resilience (Luthar 2003). Social scientists at present are probing to find its constituents (e.g., Olsson *et al.* 2003).

Initially, resilience was seen as an extraordinary capability, associated with the heroism of certain individuals in overcoming enormous adversity. It is increasingly thought that a certain level of resilience sits within all of us. Unlocking it might hold great promise, not only in resisting the lure of crime, but also in areas such as mental health, education and acquiring a sense of well-being and self-worth (Luthar 2003). Thus, whereas much research on the causes of crime focuses on problematic circumstances, a positive theme is emerging at last.

Chapter 2

The criminal mind: understanding criminals from their scene of crime

Introduction

In Chapter 1, we discussed what it means to understand criminal behaviour. We explained that psychology's efforts are often not steered toward understanding what moves an individual to commit an offence. Instead, we are looking for causes of crime at an aggregate level: we want to know about factors influencing criminal behaviour that apply to many people, rather than to one or a few individuals. That knowledge helps us to identify risk factors that we can subsequently hope to influence. In that fashion, we can hopefully reduce the risk of reoffending and prevent crime in the first place.

However, there is an important exception to this: sometimes the specific motivation of an individual offender is of crucial importance, as when an offence has been committed and the culprit is still at large. With a killer or a rapist on the loose, we have a pertinent interest in the specific motivations of this one individual. After all, we need to catch them and the sooner the better. Understanding why and how they operate is likely to enhance our chances of apprehension.

In order to achieve that, we need to gain whatever information that can help us. Evidence might come from various investigative efforts: eyewitness accounts of rape victims might be obtained; police or security officers might look at CCTV images from the area in which the crime was committed. The crime scene will be carefully investigated by scene of crime officers, and they will be looking for a variety of physical traces. These can include footprints, fingerprints, fibres from clothing, objects left behind and biological traces.

Physical traces (blood, semen, or hair) on the victim or the crime scene are routinely subjected to DNA analysis, often called DNA fingerprinting or DNA profiling (Townley and Ede 2004). If offenders have been apprehended before, their DNA might have been taken on that occasion and stored. The technique will then yield a match and the identity of the 'owner' of the DNA has been established. It has been called the 'greatest breakthrough in forensic science since fingerprinting' (Townley and Ede 2004: 8; Williams and Johnson 2005: 545).

Since 1995, we have had the UK National DNA Database. This investment has resulted in the UK having the world's largest DNA database (NDNAD) of over three million people, 4.5 per cent of the UK population, covering the majority of the active criminal population. In addition, there are over 200,000 DNA profiles obtained at crime scenes of crimes yet unsolved (Williams and Johnson 2005). This is a wealth of information, and it is being used to good effect. Since 2001, over 130,000 suspects have been identified by a match of their DNA with DNA in that database. In a typical month, DNA intelligence matches will link suspects to 15 murders, 45 rapes and 2,500 other crimes (Mennell and Shaw 2006). A crime as a result of which DNA is recovered is almost twice as likely to be solved as a crime from which no DNA is obtained. We can therefore hardly overstate its importance, although we must acknowledge civil liberty and privacy issues associated with the technique (Williams and Johnson 2005).

Offender profilers look at crime scenes with different eyes. Whereas police officers look at crime scenes as places where physical evidence is to be secured, offender profilers tend to focus on, as it were, psychological evidence. That requires a different way of looking. In this chapter, we will explain what profiling is, and how profilers work, and provide some evidence as to the success of their methods. Moreover, we widen our discussion to debate whether there is such a thing as 'a criminal mind' in the first place. The term is often used in relation to serial killers, particularly in the USA. Our discussion will also touch upon issues such as psychopathy and antisocial personality disorder.

Offender profiling

The imagery invoked by the term 'offender profiling' is vivid. This picture involves horrific crimes, such as bizarre, ritualistic murders involving unspeakable sexual sadism. We are reminded of films such as *The Silence of the Lambs*, featuring Anthony Hopkins as Hannibal Lector, possibly the quintessential example of this type of mythical creature, and Jodie Foster playing the FBI agent seeking to uncover his knowledge. You might also think of television series such as *Profiler*, or Robbie Coltrane in *Cracker*.

Two separate myths dominate these images. The first is that the offenders chased by the profilers are unspeakably bad with a dose of mad thrown in for good measure, but coupled with that is a high level of cold-blooded intelligence, which makes these offenders almost impossible to catch. The second is the mythical status of the profilers themselves: experienced, clever, and in possession of knowledge and intuition that makes them the only people equipped to track down these offenders and bring them to justice.

People can be forgiven for assuming that that is the reality of offender profiling. These myths are seductive and persistent. However, as we will see, the reality of profiling is much more mundane (Gudjonsson and Copson 1997; Ainsworth 2000). Profilers are more likely to liaise with police teams, rather than to work completely independently of them; the offenders they profile rarely, if ever, fit the Hannibal Lector stereotype, and, surprisingly often, profilers do not even produce a profile at all. That makes it pertinent to start from the beginning by defining profiling. Jackson and Bekerian (1997) define it as follows.

> A profile is assumed to involve the construction of a behavioural composite – a social and psychological assessment. A profile is based on the premise that the proper interpretation of crime scene evidence can indicate the personality type of the individual(s) who committed the offence. It is assumed that certain personality types exhibit similar behavioural patterns and that knowledge of these patterns can assist in the investigation of the crime and the assessment of potential suspects. (Jackson and Bekerian 1997: 3)

It must be noted that, while the term 'profiling' is seemingly ubiquitous in the media, usage of the term is actually in decline in the field itself. Apart from offender profiling, the same processes, more or less, are referred to by terms such as 'criminal profiling', and 'psychological profiling', whereas there are types of profiling that are called 'personality profiling' and 'geographic profiling', and other profilers call their work 'investigative psychology' or 'behavioural science analysis'. The key, though, is that they use information from the crime and the way in which it was committed to make predictions about the offender who carried it out. Often these crimes will be serious offences such as rape, murder or extortion. It has also been said that the crime needs to be of a certain emotive nature. Crimes that are purely acquisitive, such as burglary or bicycle theft, would not be suitable, as the offenders do not display any sort of individualised behaviour when committing them (Ainsworth 2000).

Profiling can be done in various ways, and the distinction commonly made is between the US and the British approaches to profiling (Brewer 2000). The former is associated with the work and teaching carried out the Behavioral Science Unit at the FBI facility at Quantico, Virginia. This is where many profilers, from the USA and elsewhere, have received training. It is associated with a process of induction (Turvey 2002), including looking at a crime scene, interpreting the information available, and using heuristics to derive a description of the likely culprit.

The British approach, mostly embodied by David Canter, is more statistical in nature and goes along the following lines. Information about a great number of offences is gathered and analysed. That produces patterns of behaviour that occur more or less frequently in the commission of certain crimes by certain types of offenders. This can be seen as a detailed body of knowledge about the commission of certain crimes, and that knowledge can be used to arrive at a profile when new unsolved crime is tackled.

Criminal profiling at the FBI

There is a strong tradition of profiling at the FBI, which has resulted in many publications (e.g., Hazelwood 1983; Hazelwood and Burgess 1995). The best-known are memoirs of FBI special agents (e.g., Ressler and Shachtman 1992; Douglas and Olshaker 1997), but there have been other publications as well. From those memoirs, a compelling picture emerges of the methods used by these profilers. A key skill is that of perception. To the layperson, any crime scene of a serious offence is likely to be shocking and overwhelming. The information contained in it is something we are not used to, so that we would probably overlook certain telling signs. Profilers, in contrast, have a keen eye for the information that is of relevance to them. In particular, they will seek for signs of planning and control by the offender. The exact location of the offence will yield valuable clues, as will the type of weapon used, and any signs of victim resistance. A good example is in fact provided in a British profiler, Paul Britton, who can be said to use a similar methodology. That goes to show that we cannot generalise and say that all FBI profilers do their profiling in one fashion and all British profilers in another. In fact, Britton's and Canter's approaches, although both are British, differ diametrically.

Britton's main profession is that of a psychologist specialising in sexual dysfunction. That gives him an expertise that he is able to use when producing profiles. Britton's celebrated debut case was his involvement in the murder case of Caroline Osborne in Leicester in 1984. She was brutally murdered in a park area near a railway when she was walking her dog.

The crime scene was rather puzzling, as there were aspects that did not seem to make sense. For instance, the victim was bound with twine, but no signs of robbery or sexual assault were found. The murder occurred at a place and time when many people were in the vicinity, but there were no witnesses to the event. At a loss, the investigating team contacted Britton (Britton 1997).

Despite the absence of any overt signs of sexuality, Britton decided to approach the murder as sexually motivated. He provided the following description:

> Caroline Osborne's murder was an expression of corrupt lust. The bindings, control and choice of victim suggested a killer whose sexual desire had become mixed with anger and the need to dominate. (Britton 1997: 49)

Furthermore, Britton argued that the murder had been planned, but not with any sophistication. The location, out in the open at a busy time, was highly risky. This led Britton to conclude that killer and victim were not well acquainted. However, Britton deemed it very likely that the killer lived nearby: 'This is his territory' (Britton 1997: 51). He also predicted, 'I think you're going to find knives, pornography, and a lot of black magic paraphernalia … that sort of thing' (57).

The profile turned out to be very accurate. Tragically, though, the killer, Paul Bostock, was arrested only after he had struck again, some 14 months later. Bostock, who was 19 years old and from Leicester, was an almost exact match to Britton's profile. He lived less than a mile from the crime scene, and knives, pornography and items relating to black magic were found in his bedroom.

We can see that Britton utilised his specialist knowledge to infer the type of offender that committed this crime. He selected the information relevant to him, and used heuristics and specialist knowledge to make predictions about this offender. In this case, he turned out to be quite accurate, bringing him a reputation of success.

A celebrated example in former FBI special agent John Douglas's experience as a profiler was the 'he must have a speech impediment' statement he made about the Trailside Killer in the San Francisco Bay area. Numerous hikers had been killed alongside heavily wooded trails in that area. The killer did turn out to have a stutter. Douglas explained what details from the crime he used for this inference:

> The secluded locations where he wasn't likely to come into contact with anyone else, the fact that none of the victims had been approached in a crowd or tricked into going along with him, the fact that he felt he had to rely on a blitz attack even in the middle of nowhere – all of this told me we were dealing with someone with some condition he felt awkward or ashamed about. (Douglas and Olshaker 1997: 156)

Thus, the location has certain characteristics that make certain offender characteristics more or less likely. Douglas subsequently retracted slightly, and said that the characteristic need not be a speech impediment, but might also be acne, polio, or a missing limb. Thus, it is arguable that the speech impediment statement was the combination of deduction and a lucky guess.

Organised and disorganised offenders

A key distinction made by these profilers is that of organised versus disorganised offenders, two categories of offenders whose ways of working as well as general persona are very different. The ability to decide whether a crime scene looks like the work of an organised or a disorganised offender is a key skill. An organised crime scene suggests a high level of planning and control by the offender, who must have thought about how to commit the offence, who may have brought items to facilitate it, and who will have taken measures to avoid detection, recognition and leaving traces. In contrast, a disorganised crime scene is chaotic, and it seems that the offender was not always on top of the situation and in control of the victim. There are signs of opportunism, and ad hoc and haphazard behaviour, pointing to an offender who probably is less able to exercise full control. That will be reflected by the way in which the crime was committed.

To juxtapose both types (thus, for the moment, ignoring the evidence (e.g. Canter 1994; Turvey 2002) that the two are not necessarily opposites), disorganised offenders do not choose victims in a logical way, they are less consciously aware of a plan, and their crime scenes display haphazard behaviour. The attacks are unplanned and of a spontaneous nature. Ressler *et al.* (1988) point out that 'The disorganisation may be the result of youthfulness, lack of criminal sophistication, use of drugs and alcohol and/or mental deficiency'.

Box 2.1   The organised offender (Ressler *et al.* 1988)

(a)   He appears to plan his murders.
(b)   He targets his victims.
(c)   He displays control at the crime scene.
(d)   He often uses a con or a ruse to gain control over a victim.
(e)   He is adaptable and mobile, and learns from crime to crime.
(f)   He will often use restraints and rape kits.
(g)   He will use his own weapon and takes it away after he has finished, to avoid fingerprints.
(h)   He will attempt to wipe away fingerprints and blood from the crime scene; sometimes this need to avoid detection means that the suspect leaves the victim nude or decapitated.
(i)   He will take 'trophies' from the scene. These trophies are taken as an incorporation of the suspect's post-crime fantasies and as acknowledgement of his accomplishments.
(j)   He will seemingly live a normal life. He may be reasonably attractive and gregarious and feel superior to almost anyone.
(k)   He will stage the crime to confuse the police. He will deliberately mislead the police by leaving false trails at the scene.

The disorganised offender picks victims at random, selecting by means of opportunity, for example, at a location near his or her residence or employment. The victim essentially becomes a casualty because he or she is in the wrong place at the wrong time. The weapon will be one of opportunity, obtained at the scene, and it often will be left there. There is little attempt to remove evidence and no attempt to conceal the body. Generally, elements that suggest planning or control on behalf of the offender are lacking and indicative of social and mental inadequacy. Disorganised offenders are often socially inept and have severe issues of self-esteem, with poor educational records and often no permanent job. They are relatively likely to be homeless, and lonely.

Lacking the skills to meet victims in public places, disorganised offenders use the blitz style of attack on a victim. There is a prevalence of attacks from behind and there is minimal use of restraints. The crime scene will appear sloppy, and there will be little attempt to hide the body. The suspect in this category will invariably be a loner and an underachiever.

David Canter discusses this distinction in terms of the *continuity hypothesis*. He argues that the skills that an offender possesses to get through life in general are the same skills used to commit the offences. Thus, an offender who has good social and verbal skills, and is good-looking, and professionally successful, will have an armoury of skills that facilitate offending. Such an individual will find it possible to meet female victims in places like pubs and clubs, befriend them, and attack only once they are in a secluded or private location. His life skills will enable him to do that. In contrast, an offender who lacks these skills, because, for instance, he suffers from mental health problems, is homeless and cannot present himself as a regular or interesting person, will have to resort to other means. An offender with those characteristics would be more likely to ambush a stranger in a park. Thus, the strengths and weakness that an offender possesses might be discerned via analysis of the crime scene, which will provide clues as to his social position, intelligence, and verbal and social skills; possibly his type of profession; and so on.

However, Canter (1994) and Turvey (2002) are highly critical of the organised–disorganised dichotomy, as well as other classifications, suggesting that they are merely 'shorthand summaries' for groups of offenders who have characteristics in common. The latter even goes as far as to call it a false dichotomy. Canter argues that the very broadness of their content and the potential for slippage of a particular behaviour from one category to another make them little more than descriptions of crime scenes, with little predictive value.

There are other interpretative frameworks that seem to be widely in use. One is the distinction between modus operandi (MO) and signature. The latter term was coined by Douglas and Olshaker (1997). MO is learned behaviour. It is what a person does to commit a crime, and it might be expected to improve with each crime because the offender learns from each crime, and is subsequently able to plan and prepare better for the next one.

Signature, on the other hand, 'is what a person has to do in order to fulfil himself. It is static: it does not change'. Douglas and Olshaker go on to describe an example:

You wouldn't expect a juvenile to keep committing crimes the same way as he grows up unless he gets it perfect the first time. But if he gets away with one, he'll learn from it and get better and better at it. That's why we say that MO is dynamic. On the other hand, if this guy is committing crimes so that, say, he can dominate or inflict pain on or provoke begging and pleading from a victim, that's a signature. It's something that expresses a killer's personality. It's something he needs to do. (Douglas and Olshaker 1997: 249)

The difference between MO and signature is particularly important when linking crimes. The notion that the former is likely to develop over time, whereas the latter is not, may be very helpful in that respect. The signature sheds more light on the 'why' of killings; MO is particularly concerned with the 'how'. Two examples that Douglas and Olshaker describe illustrate the point further.

The difference between MO and signature can be subtle. Take the case of a bank robber in Texas who made all of his captives undress, posed them in a sexual position, and took photographs of them. That's his signature. It was not necessary or helpful to the commission of a bank robbery. In fact, it kept him there longer and therefore placed him in greater jeopardy of being caught. Yet it was something he clearly felt a need to do.

Then there was a bank robber in Grand Rapids, Michigan […]. This guy also made everyone in the bank undress, but he didn't take pictures. He did it so the witnesses would be so preoccupied and embarrassed that they wouldn't be looking at him and so wouldn't make a positive ID later on. This was a means towards successfully robbing the bank. This was MO. (Douglas and Olshaker 1997: 252)

The final example is the distinction between posing and staging. It is relates to post-offence behaviour, particularly in murder cases. Posing is the behaviour of arranging a crime scene so as to make a point; for instance, to taunt the police or to make a point about the victim. In particular, when a killer seemingly targets a specific group, such as prostitutes, grotesque acts of posing are sometimes observed. Staging is the rearrangement of a crime scene for a different purpose. Here the objective is to confuse police and forensic investigators. A typical example would be for a murder to look like a case of suicide. Despite the reservations about the dichotomy, both posing and staging would be associated with an organised offender, someone who remains calm and focused immediately after the commission of the crime. An opportunistic, disorganised offender who is primarily concerned about fleeing the scene to avoid detection will spend no time at all on such activities.

Statistical profiling

Whereas individualistic profilers deduce offender characteristics from individual crime scenes, the statistics approach is altogether different. It is heavily associated with David Canter's investigative psychology approach. In this approach, it is more important that the profiler has sound statistical skills than experience in criminal investigation. Canter and Heritage (1990) were among the first to apply this technique, in the area of stranger rape. They collected data from 66 rape offences and looked at 33 types of behaviours that did or did not occur during the rape. They were able to assess this via case files, mostly by analysing the statements victims made to the police. All these behaviours were taken as separate variables. Their analysis consisted of two stages. The first involved looking at the relative frequency of certain offender behaviours. Secondly, the analysis concerned establishing patterns of co-occurrence of certain behaviours.

Canter and Heritage (1990) found that binding and gagging the victim often go together: if a rapist does one, he is likely to do the other as well. On the other hand, some behaviours are unlikely to occur in one and the same rape. The confidence approach of 'being friendly and sociable to a victim before attacking them', and the blitz attack, 'as it were pouncing out of a dark alley', do not easily go together. Similarly, an apologetic attitude and wearing a disguise do not naturally seem to happen at the same time either. Thus, certain behaviour may happen often or not, and certain behaviours are more likely to happen within the same offence than others.

The latter findings have given Canter and Heritage the opportunity to look at behavioural patterns of rapists and thereby identify 'themes' in rape. John House (1997) in Canada adopted this technique, and it has resulted in interesting findings. In an analysis of 90 rape cases he identified four themes in stranger rape, but only two out of three instances of rape could be themed as such. The largest group were rapes with an 'intimacy' theme. This reveals a distorted attempt on the part of the offender to establish some twisted form of intimacy with the victim. It involves behaviours such as apologising to the victim, asking personal questions, attempting to kiss the victim, and asking the victim to participate actively in the rape (House 1997).

The second most frequent theme was aggression. It involves physical, verbal and often gratuitous violence against the victim, that is, violence beyond the level required to control the victim to enable the offence to take place. The third theme that emerged was that of criminality, and it involves the display of forensic awareness, and stealing something from the victim, often personal items, as trophies, but also money and other goods. Use of a weapon is prevalent here as well. The fourth and least frequently occurring theme is sadism, as characterised by behaviours such as sodomy, torture and gagging.

House went on to determine whether those who commit rapes with a certain theme differ in their criminal record from other rapists. It turns out, for instance, that those who commit 'intimacy' rapes are most likely to have a criminal past that includes fraud or deception. On the whole, however, it is important to note that most stranger rapists have extensive criminal records, in which property and violent crime feature more heavily than sexual crime per se (Davies and Dale 1995; Davies 1997; House 1997).

What House, and Canter and Heritage have done with rape, Canter and Fritzon (1998) achieved with arson. A detailed study of the characteristics of 175 instances of arson and of the characteristics of those who carried them out led to the identification of interesting distinctions. Arson behaviour can be either expressive or instrumental. Expressive acts of arson can be directed at either objects (such as schools) or people (often the arsonists themselves), whereas instrumental arson can occur to destroy evidence or to take revenge. The characteristics of expressive object-orientated arsonists are rather different from those with an 'instrumental-person' orientation. This research offers empirical support for the idea that arson has a number of rather different psychological origins. Practically, different types of arson are often committed by rather different people, and this, in turn, may help focus police enquiries into arson, serial arson in particular.

The success of profilers

At first sight, it seems easy to establish when a profile is a good profile: if it matches the offender, it is good; if it fails to do so, it is not. When Copson (1995; see also Gudjonsson and Copson

1997) set out to uncover the success rate of profilers in the UK, he found that it was not so simple. First of all, there was the public perception, furthered in many autobiographical accounts of profiling, that profilers are pretty much infallible, due to a combination of selectivity, hindsight bias, and the tradition of self-congratulation in such books. They continue to reinforce the almost magical nature of the profiling process.

Gudjonsson and Copson's findings are rather at odds with that image. They looked at 184 instances of profiling in the UK, mostly murders (61 per cent) and cases of rape (22 per cent). Their analysis was hampered by the fact that, on many occasions, profilers did not seem to have produced a written profile. That inevitably hampers any evaluation. The second problem they encountered was that many points of advice were not verifiable. Descriptions tended to involve offenders' fantasies, and cognitive distortions. Even after apprehension, it would be very difficult to establish independently whether these are accurate or not. It turned out that statistical profilers, such as Canter, offered more verifiable points of advice than others. Across the board, though, they found that about two out of three points of advice had been technically accurate, whereas one-third was not.

While this provides some measure of quality in profiling it does miss a vital point: was the profile actually useful? Did it help the police to apprehend the offender? Gudjonsson and Copson asked the investigative teams that dealt with a profiler a number of simple questions that elicited rather revealing answers. Table 2.1 shows the respondents' answers regarding the utility of the profilers' input.

Thus, it seems that although the profiler's advice did not often help a great deal in solving the crime directly, it was considered to be operationally useful most of the time. When asked how it had been useful, respondents answered as in Table 2.2.

Table 2.1 Responses on the utility of profiling

Question	Yes	No
Did the advice assist in solving the case?	14.1%	78.3%
Did the advice open new lines of enquiry?	16.3%	82.1%
Did the advice add anything to information supplied?	53.8%	38.6%
Did the advice prove operationally useful?	82.6%	17.4%

Source: Gudjonsson and Copson 1997.

Table 2.2 How the advice was useful

How the profiling advice would be useful	Positive responses (%)
Led to the identification of the offender	2.7
Furthered understanding of case/offender	60.9
Expert opinion reassured own judgement	51.6
Offered structure for interviewing	5.4
Other	2.3
Not useful	17.4

Source: Gudjonsson and Copson 1997.

The information from Table 2.2 shows that profilers are not typically providing a breakthrough in any case. Profilers do not solve cases on their own. Instead, what the police teams seem to value is not necessarily the profile itself, but the presence of an independent expert who can offer a second opinion, even if that only validates the views already held by the police. In an unsolved murder case, which, for many investigative teams is not a common thing, such a reassurance from an experienced expert may be welcome, particularly when pressure is felt because of coverage of the investigation and its lack of success in local and national news media. Thus, when we think about success in profiling, we should steer our focus away from the profile, that is, the product. Rather it is the *process* of engagement with the profiler that police officers value. Gudjonsson and Copson (1997) describe that as follows:

> Success in British profiling is very difficult to determine, but seems to have little to do with high rates of accurate prediction, directly assisting in solving cases, or leading to the identification of offenders. Instead, it seems to be to do with the introduction of new thoughts, arising from an intelligent second opinion, and the development of investigative philosophy – formulating and testing theories about the case and the offender – through the process of consultation and debate with the profiler. (Gudjonsson and Copson 1997: 90)

Psychopathy and antisocial personality disorder

Is there a criminal mind? Is there a way in which a person's brain can be wired such that they will, inevitably, offend again and again? The short answer is 'no'. However, there are mental health problems (see Chapter 6) that sometimes link to offending behaviour, and Chapter 4, on aggression, offers an interesting but rare genetic example. It is sometimes thought that we can tell 'real', incorrigible criminals from opportunistic offenders because the former are psychopaths and the latter are not. However, let us first of all stress that the link between mental illness and crime, as we explain in Chapter 6, is not as strong as might be imagined. Most people who suffer from a mental illness are more a risk to themselves than to others. But there is concern regarding 'psychopathy', although that is an ill-defined and overused term. The image it invokes is that of the seemingly well-adjusted person, living a normal life by day while committing atrocious acts of cruelty and destruction under the cover of darkness. The protagonist in Brent Easton Ellis's novel, *American Psycho*, appeals to such depictions.

McCord and McCord (1964) have defined the psychopath as 'an asocial, aggressive, highly impulsive person, who feels little or no guilt, and is unable to form lasting bonds of affection with other human beings' (5). Robert Hare (1991) has developed a psychology checklist, which examines the extent to which the following characteristics apply to an individual:

- glibness/superficial charm;
- grandiose sense of self-worth;
- need for stimulation, with proneness to boredom;
- pathological lying;
- cunning and manipulating behaviours;
- no sense of remorse or guilt;
- a very shallow emotional affect – they display emotions they do not really feel;
- a lack of empathy for others;
- they are parasitic – they live off others;
- they are impulsive, and show poor control over their behaviours;
- they tend to be promiscuous;
- their behaviour problems start early in life;
- they cannot form long-term plans that are realistic;
- they are impulsive and irresponsible;
- they do not accept responsibility for their actions – another caused it;
- marital relationships are short, and many;
- they display juvenile delinquency;
- they violate probation often;
- their criminality is diverse (Hare 1991; 1993; 1996).

It is not difficult to imagine that people who possess such qualities are not unlikely to engage in offending behaviour. The link between psychopathy and crime is well established (Hare 2002). Similarly, psychopathy is increasingly seen as a risk factor for reoffending. Monahan *et al.* (2001) found psychopathy (as measured by Hare's checklist) to be the strongest risk factor for violent recidivism in a group of over 1,000 civilly committed psychiatric patients. Serin *et al.* (1990) also found that psychopathic offenders generally reoffend more than non-psychopathic offenders after release from prison. The difference was starkest for violent offenders: psychopathic offenders were four times more likely to reoffend. It must, however, also be appreciated that scoring high on Hare's checklist sometimes almost constitutes admitting to criminal behaviour. Thus, the fact that it correlates with criminal behaviour should not surprise us: it is, as it were, almost built in. In addition, the fact that the psychopathy checklist consistently relates to offending propensity does not qualify it as a mental illness.

However, we must note that the 'criminal mind' as possessed by creatures such as Hannibal Lector, or ascribed to real criminals such as Jeffrey Dahmer, does not necessarily fit perfectly with psychopathy. Two key concepts relating to psychopathy are impulsivity and a shallow (or empty) emotional life. Impulsivity does relate to opportunistic crime, but does not sit well with the assumed coldness and sophistication required for more elaborate patterns of offending. We can therefore wonder whether psychopathy as a concept furthers our understanding of such individuals very much.

Conclusion

To conclude, we would re-emphasise that the very concept of a criminal mind is tenuous. It is true that certain temperamental and personality characteristics make offending behaviour more likely. But we also know that other factors, such as drug misuse and a damaging childhood, are more potent predictors of future offending. We must therefore wonder whether the concept of the criminal mind primarily leads us to acquire a seductive yet spurious understanding of criminals. It invites the idea that they are fundamentally different from us, as if the vast majority of 'normal' people go about their everyday life with the odd monster lurking among us, hiding in the thicket and ready to jump out to bite our throat. The fact that we are invited to regard them as less human than ourselves can subsequently serve as justification for draconian measures against them.

The UK government has recently decided to provide at least 300 secure detention spaces for people deemed to be suffering from dangerous and severe personality disorder (DPSP, see www.dspdprogramme.gov.uk). That is not a psychiatric term, but a legal one. They are intended to keep dangerous offenders off the streets, and this, of course, is one of the aims of criminal justice and a duty of the government. It is obvious that people with a mental health problem who pose acute danger to others (or themselves) need to be controlled. Secure mental hospitals such as Broadmoor indeed perform an important function, but the major point remains that most people with a mental health problem are not dangerous criminals. The DPSD project seems to open the door to preventative detention, seemingly justified by the risk posed, but not by offences committed (Fennell 2000).

The DSPD project should therefore be critically evaluated in light of the extent to which it succeeds in avoiding attaching that stigma to mental health patients generally and those with personality disorders in particular. The project fortunately involves research into the causes of personality disorders and avenues of successful treatment, and that is a positive outcome, as it is widely acknowledged that knowledge in this area is lacking (Blackburn *et al.* 2000; Blackburn 2004).

Our final comment is that the continuing emphasis on the linkage between mental health and crime is unfortunate. That is the case not only for those mental health patients who are in trouble with the law, but even more so for the hundreds of thousands of mental health patients in the UK who live law-abiding lives, but nevertheless experience fear and distrust on a daily basis while having done nothing to deserve it.

Chapter 3

Pathways into crime: understanding juvenile offending

Introduction

How and why do young people become criminals and what can be done about it are the questions that have preoccupied society since the label of 'young offender' first came into legal, social and political use in the eighteenth century. This is especially important if it is borne in mind that persistent and long-term criminal lifestyles are widely acknowledged to be established in youth.

Approaches to the management of youth crime have swung between the welfare-orientated and punishment, an uneasy marriage of philosophies that has resulted in a plethora of sometimes contradictory legislative policies. What is apparent from this tension in intervention is that the social contexts of pathways into crime cannot be ignored when considering the causes of crime in young people and that to take a purely psychological or individualist approach focused on blame is unlikely to be an effective response. As France and Homel (2006) state, 'In studying the actions of individuals within changing social environments it is important to make a distinction between *individual developmental pathways* and *societal access routes*' (295).

This chapter will look at the research evidence regarding pathways into crime and explanations of youth offending, and consider the question of whether current responses sufficiently recognise that requiring young people to change their antisocial behaviour cannot be done in isolation of the contexts in which such behaviour occurs.

Background

Until around 1776, there was no clear policy regarding sanctions for youth delinquency, and youth crime was not seen as conceptually different from crime committed by adults, nor was youth crime identified as requiring particular social or political attention. However, by 1776, the term 'disorderly youths' (Muncie 2006) had been coined in England, reflecting social and political concern regarding the behaviour of young people. Youth crime was increasingly being perceived as requiring specific attention and a dedicated approach, and by 1810, in England and Wales, the prosecution of juveniles was being actively pursued.

In 1828, the House of Commons Select Committee of Inquiry noted that education is not sufficient to check 'juvenile depravity' and that it would be expedient to create a separate prison for the correction of young offenders. The advantages of prompt summary punishments and plans for the compulsory employment of young vagrants were agreed (House of Commons 1828: ix).

Thus, by 1828, the term 'young offenders' was in the political and social domain, and the ensuing debates were preoccupied with the provision of appropriate detention facilities and ensuring that sentences for young offenders would fulfil a corrective function that would embrace the ideals of both punishment and rehabilitation centred on education and training – thus, the welfare versus punishment dispute was established, and it has persisted to this day.

Youth offending in England and Wales – key statistics

Before we embark on further debates around the issues, it is useful to look at the profile of youth offending in England and Wales in order to establish the extent of the problem.

- Around 5 per cent of 10–17-year-olds will come into contact with the criminal justice system through arrest for a notifiable offence in a year.

- Over a quarter of a million (287,883) offences by 10–17-year-olds resulted in a disposal of some sort (cf. 268,480 in 2003).

- Around 20 per cent of disposals resulted in a detention in custody (cf. 7,500 in 2003).

- The top three offences in 2004 were motoring offences (23 per cent); theft and handling stolen goods (16.9 per cent) and violence against the person (14.1 per cent).

- 83.5 per cent of offences were committed by males and 16.5 per cent by females; nearly three-quarters of offenders are between the ages of 15 and 17 years.

- 84 per cent of offences were committed by white young people. Ethnicity was not recorded in 4 per cent of cases, and 12 per cent of offences are committed by black and other minority ethnic young people.

- The 1-year reoffending rate was 41.3 per cent across all disposals (2004).

- The reconviction rate for young people sentenced to custody was approximately 80 per cent within a 2-year period after release (Audit Commission 2004; Youth Justice Board 2004; Whiting and Cuppleditch 2006).

In spite of the difficulty in interpreting data, which mainly centres on issues of what is actually being measured – for example, rates of arrests, charges and criminal convictions do not always provide an accurate picture of the actual rates of youth crime or of changes in those rates – it is possible to state some broad conclusions about youthful criminal activity. The majority of offenders in the youth justice system (YJS) are white males aged 15–17 with only 14.1 per cent of offences falling within the violent category posing high risk of harm. While some adolescents engage in some forms of illegal activity (such as underage drinking, and illegal drug use), the majority do not engage in criminal activity serious enough to warrant attention by the YJS. It is important to bear this in mind when considering some of the net-widening civil solutions to dealing with perceived youth infringements of the social norms, such as the antisocial behaviour order (ASBO).

Correlates and causes of youth crime

Empirical work undertaken by psychologists and criminologists over the past two decades or so has made a significant theoretical contribution to the debate on pathways into crime based on sophisticated cross-sectional and longitudinal studies of the factors associated with youth antisocial behaviour. Empirical studies are obviously important in terms of wider generalisation, and longitudinal studies for their potential to yield information about the causes of antisocial activity.

Much of this research has taken place in North America. The key publications which have informed the work of the Youth Justice Board (YJB) in England and Wales are such as those provided by Graham (1988), Lipsey (1995), McGuire (1995), Utting (1996), Sherman *et al.* (1997), Andrews and Bonta (1998), Ross *et al.* (1998), Loeber and Farrington (1998), Rutter *et al.* (1998), Hoge (2002), and Farrington (1996; 2000). Further work is being conducted by a conglomerate of universities funded by the Economic and Social Research Council, and their preliminary findings will be reported here.

Delinquent youth groups

> The young always have the same problem – how to rebel and form at the same time. They have now solved this by defying their elders and copying one another. (Crisp 1968: no page no.)

Le Blanc *et al.* (1988) and Tremblay *et al.* (1992) have shown that youths who associate with antisocial peers demonstrate aggressive-egocentric personality traits and fail to embrace positive social values. These young people are at the highest risk of serious conduct disorders. These findings are supported by a recent Home Office study (Sharp *et al.* 2006), which is consistent with the known statistics on youth offending in England and Wales.

Sharp *et al.* (2006) used multivariate analysis to demonstrate that around 6 per cent of those aged 10–19 could be classed as belonging to a delinquent youth group, and that these young people are 26 per cent more likely to have committed at least one notifiable offence in the last year when compared to their non-member counterparts. The pattern remains when examining individual offence types (the only exception to this is robbery which was low for both members and non-members at 1 per cent). However, it would be a mistake to think that all delinquent group members are engaged in the commission of multiple serious offences. The results show that of the 34 per cent who had committed one serious offence, only 7 per cent had six or more convictions for repeat serious offending. With regard to less serious infractions of the law, 28 per cent of members had committed six or more offences in the past year. If we summarise the findings in terms of the pattern and frequency of offending behaviour, there appears little doubt that this study points to the significantly higher rates of offending of delinquent group members than non-group members, suggesting that 6 per cent of individuals who are members of a delinquent youth group are responsible for around a fifth (21 per cent) of all notifiable offences committed by 10–19-year-olds.

Sharp et al. (2006) further demonstrated that while young people who were not members of delinquent groups stated that they had carried weapons, including a knife (4 per cent) and a gun (less than 1 per cent), young people in a delinquent group were more likely to put themselves in risky situations by carrying weapons: 13 per cent had carried a knife and 1 per cent a gun. Drug use was also statistically far more common in delinquent groups; for example, 45 per cent had used an illegal drug in the past year, and 11 per cent had used a class A substance. This is significantly higher than for non-members (15 per cent for any drug and 3 per cent for class A drugs). Furthermore, delinquent group members most likely to engage in a pattern of serious and frequent offending and drug use were also more likely to have non-group membership friends who were also offenders.

Clearly, being a member of a delinquent gang and having friends outside the gang who also offend places the individual young person at high risk of offending, but what makes it likely that a young person will join such a gang or become involved in individual or peer group acts of delinquency? In the Sharp et al. study, the factors most strongly associated with group membership were having friends in trouble with the police; having run away from home; commitment to deviant peers; having been expelled or suspended from school; and being drunk on a frequent basis (Sharp et al. 2006). These findings support the research of Farrington (1986), Andrews and Bonta (1998), Hoge (2002), Loeber and Farrington (1998), and Rutter et al. (1998), among others, that risk factors (a term first used by Andrews et al. 1990) that place a young person at risk of offending can be grouped into categories.

Risk factors

Family risk factors
Prenatal and perinatal factors around the time of birth have been linked to a range of later problems for children. Children born to young mothers are also at increased risk of low achievement in school; antisocial behaviour; and early initiation into smoking, alcohol and illegal drugs (Furstenberg et al. 1987). Research demonstrates

(Patterson *et al.* 1998) that poor parental supervision and discipline, and harsh, inconsistent or neglectful parenting are contributory factors to later youth involvement in delinquent behaviour.

Family conflict, as opposed to types of family structure, is a strong indicator of an increased risk that children will offend. Family conflict involves the difficulties caused by the economic stress resulting from divorce or breakdown of the parental relationship, and the impact of family breakdown upon the quality of the child's relationship with one or both parents (Farrington 1986; Graham and Bowling 1995). A family history of criminal activity, that is, having a convicted parent or sibling by the age of 10, is a risk factor for later-onset delinquency (Farrington 1986). This can be understood alongside parental attitudes that condone antisocial and criminal behaviour. While this is difficult to separate from other risk factors such as poor parental supervision, this risk factor is relevant to drug use and can be linked with negative social modelling, whereby children learn antisocial behaviour modelled by significant others such as parents or carers (Hawkins *et al.* 1992).

Drawing upon a wide range of research, the YJB (2001) concluded that children from low-income families are more likely to become involved in crime than those from more affluent backgrounds. However, it is acknowledged that the links between conventional family measures of social and economic class, based on occupational status, and criminality have generally been weak compared with more specific measures of poverty (Utting *et al.* 1993) and educational achievement of parents (Wadsworth 1979).

School/educational risk factors

Low achievement, beginning at primary school (Maguin and Loeber 1996), and aggressive behaviour, including bullying (Loeber and Hay 1996) have been shown to be risk factors. The YJB (2001) also demonstrated links between delinquency and lack of commitment to school. However, they pointed out that the cause-and-effect pathway is by no means straightforward, for while truancy can lead to delinquency, it is likely that delinquency also leads to truancy (Graham 1988). Graham (1988) demonstrated that school disorganisation is a contributory factor to delinquency in a study that showed that secondary schools that have the highest proportions of juvenile offenders among their students tend to be characterised by low levels of achievement and high rates of truancy and disruption. Linked to this are inadequate teaching skills, poor relations between pupils and staff, failure to offer praise and rewards, labelling of less academic pupils as failures, and inconsistent enforcement of school rules. Rutter *et al.* (1998; cited in YJB 2001: 15) found that while there is evidence that individual schools do exert an influence over antisocial behaviour, there remains an explanatory gap about the particular circumstances in which this occurs.

Community risk factors
A range of studies have demonstrated that children who grow up in disadvantaged neighbourhoods, typically economically deprived areas with poor living conditions and high rates of unemployment, have an increased risk of involvement in crime, including violence (YJB 2001: 15). Community disorganisation and neglect have also been shown to be a risk factor. This draws together research showing that higher rates of youth offending and drug problems occur in neighbourhoods with a poor physical environment, often marked by extensive vandalism and an inconsistent police presence (Sampson 1986; 1997; Power and Tunstall 1997; Dean and Hastings 2000). Research demonstrates that there is also a significant link between the availability of drugs and alcohol in a community and increased risk that young people will use them illegally (Hope 1996).

Personal/individual risk factors
Rutter *et al.* (1998; cited in YJB 2001: 18) demonstrated that ADHD and impulsivity are significant triggers at the start of a developmental sequence that can lead some children to become persistent and violent offenders. However, it is associated with poor social functioning generally and interrelated cognitive impairment rather than criminality alone. Low intelligence and cognitive impairment continue to be a predictor for youth offending even after variables such as low family income and large family size have been controlled for (Farrington 1989; 2000).

Young people are more likely to be drawn into offending behaviour if they feel that the rules and values of society have limited relevance to them; for example, if they feel excluded from opportunities, hold generally hostile attitudes, and feel a limited sense of responsibility for others (Hawkins *et al.* 1987; cited in YJB 2001: 19). This is validated by the weighty body of evidence that attitudes and behaviour are strongly linked (McGuire 2002). It is therefore unsurprising that attitudes in young people that condone offending and drug misuse are strong indicators of early involvement in crime and drug misuse and that friendship groups are established around these behaviours. Peer group influence (Warr 1993; cited in YJB 2001) can then be shown to be linked to young offenders committing delinquent acts in small groups rather than alone and the early onset of offending. The latter is an important indicator of young people at risk of even greater, long-term problems and an entrenched pathway into an adult criminal lifestyle. This is one of the differences between 'adolescence-limited' and 'life-course persistent' antisocial behaviour (Moffitt 1993).

Continued membership of a delinquent peer group has also been shown subsequently to play an important part in a young person's choice of cohabitation or marriage partner, when antisocial values are shared, militating against ceasing offending behaviour after adolescence (West 1982). Finally, the fact of being born male is a static predictor of later involvement in delinquent behaviour, statistics consistently demonstrating that young men commit more offences than young women.

A theoretical comment

Cultural criminology and study of the social contexts in which youth crime occurs are currently making a mark in research and analysis. This recognises 'hybridity, difference and diversity' (Muncie 2006: 202) in youth cultural practices and challenges the explanation of subcultural theory as 'idealist' and 'romanticist' (Young 1986; in Muncie 2006: 187). The criminal justice response, however, relies heavily upon the framework of cognitive and behavioural theory to explain many of the findings in respect of how young people learn to behave antisocially.

Based on the assumption that it is learning that underpins observable behaviour, both cognitive and behavioural theory attempt to describe the processes by which individuals learn. Behavioural theories, first espoused by John B. Watson in the 1940s, arise from the premise that people learn through being conditioned by external events to respond in specific ways to situations, via the process which has come to be known as *stimulus–response* linked to the conditions that are operating, or *operant conditioning*. Cognitive theory has its roots in a critique of behaviourism, which was perceived as an over-deterministic explanation by a school of thought that came to be closely associated with social learning theory (Bandura 1977). Social learning theory suggests that learning is mediated through cognitive (thinking/reasoning) processes, so that the resulting observed behaviour based on learning is thus a proactive response to external stimuli, as opposed to a conditioned response. It is therefore important where and when learning occurs and who is seen as significant in setting a model to be adopted, and to understand what sustains the behaviour – if an undesirable pattern is to be broken. It is a short leap from harsh and/or neglectful parenting to perceiving that if young persons find their stability and role models in a delinquent group, then this is the behaviour that will be valued and copied – perhaps and most especially if similar antisocial attitudes are also observed in adults in the family environment.

However, risk factors can be both symptoms and causes of pathways into crime. For example, antisocial behaviour can be both a cause and a consequence of heavy alcohol consumption (Farrington 1996). No single factor can be specified as the 'cause' of antisocial or criminal behaviour; rather, it should be understood as triggered by a multiplicity of factors that cluster together and interact in the lives of some children, while important protective factors (see below) are absent (Utting *et al.* 1993; Farrington 1996). In addition, the literature does not provide a full understanding of the way in which the variables interact with one another. Moreover, the dynamic processes underlying the variables remains unexplained in some cases (Hoge, n.d., accessed 2 August 2006). For example, gaps still remain in our understanding of exactly how parenting practices affect the development of conduct disorders. The role of genetic factors in affecting the development of personality and behaviour traits is also not fully understood (Hoge, n.d., accessed 2 August 2006). Nevertheless, the identification of variables linked with youthful criminal activity is important from the point of view of understanding the phenomenon, developing tools for assessing the risk of criminal activity, and developing prevention and treatment programmes (Hoge, n.d., accessed 2 August 2006).

In an attempt to respond to the gaps in knowledge between known risk factors and pathways into crime, a 5-year funded study has been undertaken by a conglomerate of universities headed by Cambridge University (UK). The preliminary findings, released in December 2005, call into question some commonly held views about risk indicators and why young people become involved in crime, such as the imprisonment of a criminal parent. This has been shown to be a respite for some youngsters from what may have been a chaotic home life (Home Office Press Release 2005). The early results also cast some doubt on the inevitability of the link between drug use and crime, showing that this is indeed a complex relationship, in which offending, in terms of risk to the public, may cease even though some kinds of drug use may continue. The findings also confirm research that young people most often experience crime as victims and witnesses, but of this group there is a statistically higher percentage who are the most likely also to be involved in criminal behaviour – thus challenging notions of the 'ideal' victim.

Key factors in the findings of why young people offend have been shown to be where they live, their knowledge and understanding of the difficulties of managing their lives in a deprived neighbourhood and the strategies that they employ to survive in such an environment (Kemshall *et al.* 2006). Kemshall *et al.* (2006) further comment that this research suggests that young people can be very resilient in developing coping skills and resisting potential labels, but external support in the form of, for example, changing schools, is required to aid children's own reconstruction of themselves and to establish positive interaction with opportunities and choices.

Offender profiling and assessment

The risk factors outlined above are widely accepted as being reliable, even if gaps remain in understanding the causal and correlational pathways. These risk factors form the body of research evidence that has underpinned the development of actuarial tools for assessing individual risk of offending. ASSET is the name of the current statistical tool used in the YJS for England and Wales. This is a form of offender profiling that has, since its implementation, changed the language of the criminal justice system, being associated with terms such as 'risk management' and 'prevention', and has expanded the role of psychological assessment in juvenile justice (Hoge 1999). It is not to be confused with forensic offender profiling, such as that carried out by the FBI (see Chapter 2).

In terms of risk management and prevention, the statistical tool allows a 'risk/need' classification to be performed. The 'risk' part of this assigns scores to prioritise those aspects shown by the research evidence base to predispose the individual, in terms of attitude, behaviour and circumstances, to engage in antisocial/criminal acts.

In terms of prevention, the concept is closely aligned to Newton's law that every force has an opposite and opposing force, and, although this concept is most often cited within the natural sciences, criminology has adopted (possibly unconsciously) a similar idea in attempting to redress risk factors. Risk factors constitute a force in the direction of crime and antisocial behaviour, whereas protective factors can be seen as providing a pull away from it.

Prevention is linked to the 'need' analysis (known in full as 'criminogenic need'), which is performed as part of the actuarial assessment, and identifies those aspects of the individuals' profile that are indicators of delinquent behaviour that could, by intervention, be changed. Prevention thus targets the risk indicators that could be changed into what are labelled 'protective factors'. Protective factors are almost the opposite of risk factors and, like risk factors, when clustered together, form what can be described as an envelope of psychological protection that militates against the likelihood that any risk factors that may be present will ultimately manifest themselves in antisocial behaviour.

This follows the reasoning of social learning theory that if behaviour has been learnt, it can be unlearnt and replaced with positive pro-social attitudes. The need aspect also identifies gaps in, for example, basic skills and employability, thus attempting to identify the results of an individual risk factor (poor schooling, achievement, etc.) and, through intervention, turn it into a protective factor.

Research (Garmezy 1985; Radkey-Yarrow and Sherman 1990; Werner and Smith 1992, Farrington 2000; cited in Youth Justice Board 2001) has demonstrated that when protective factors are already in place in a young person's life, that person is less likely to become involved in criminal behaviour. These protective factors are as follows:

Social bonding

A strong bond of attachment with one or both parents, characterised by a stable, warm, affectionate relationship has been shown to protect children who would otherwise be at high risk of offending or illegal drug use. This has been extended to include the quality of relationships between children and teachers in educational settings that facilitate positive, constructive behaviour in individuals and groups.

Clear standards for social behaviour

Prevailing social attitudes across a community as well as the views of individual parents can help to protect children from the risk of offending.

Consistent parenting

Consistent parenting is parenting that does not send mixed messages; the particular family rules are consistently and constructively reinforced. 'No' never means 'yes' or 'maybe'.

Secure residence with parent/significant other

The research demonstrates that children who have a long-term home with a parent, or with someone with whom they have formed a loving and secure relationship, are protected against the risk of juvenile delinquency. Conversely, children with disrupted home lives, who have spent periods in local authority care, and who have been the subject of the *at risk* register, are more likely to become involved in offending behaviour as young people.

Pro-social attitudes

Pro-social attitudes are family attitudes that promote pro-social behaviour and respect for authority, such as the authority of teachers and police, as well as that of the parents.

Opportunities for involvement

Children who are involved in organisations such as Cubs, Scouts and Brownies, or organised activities such as dancing classes, music classes, and sports; or school productions; or community projects for the elderly, are less likely to become involved in offending behaviour.

Social/learning skills

Resilient children appear to display a repertoire of social problem-solving skills and a belief in their own self-efficacy. This includes an ability to plan ahead, foresee consequences, and find positive solutions to problems.

Recognition/praise

Children who are appropriately praised, receiving recognition for good behaviour, and for demonstrating good social skills, effort at schoolwork, and participation in activities (meaning not level of success, but level of personal achievement), are less likely to become involved in offending. Individual characteristics showing that protective factors are present are a resilient temperament, sense of self-efficacy and positive and outgoing disposition. These are the psychological indicators that an individual will be less likely to become involved in criminal activity or that such activity would be sustained over any significant period of time (Garmezy, 1985; Radkey-Yarrow and Sherman 1990; Werner and Smith 1992, Farrington 2000).

Once an offender actuarial assessment has been performed, appropriate interventions are then modelled on the psychological profiling and an assumed level of 'risk' (Muncie 2006: 276). However, the limitations of this approach should be recognised. Firstly, statistics predict patterns of behaviour but cannot predict individual outcomes. The best that research can offer is a framework of indicators: stereotyping or labelling individuals on the basis of this is only likely to lead toward, rather than away from, delinquent behaviour. Secondly, some risk factors are static; that is, they are known to predispose the young to criminal behaviour, but they cannot be altered. The best known of these are gender and age; for example, age of onset of criminal activity and the fact that young males are more likely to be involved in some form of criminal behaviour than any other group in the population or at any other time in their lives. Thirdly, the research evidence base is incomplete, as the theoretical comments above indicate. This could partly account for what are known as 'false positives' and 'false negatives', whereby the results of actuarial assessment contradict clinical assessment and observation. Fourthly, as with most forms of offender profiling, the emphasis is upon explanations that focus on the individual.

As the risk factors already demonstrate, individual delinquent behaviour can only be fully understood in terms of the social contexts within which it arises, whereas the risk/need assessment focuses primarily upon the individual requirement to change rather than the individual's circumstances. The current political emphasis upon 'responsibilisation' is just one example of the contribution of this form of profiling to the lexicon that has developed under the umbrella of 'risk management' and 'prevention'. It also demonstrates the tensions that exist between recognised social need, which is indicative of a welfare-orientated approach to ameliorate the impact of structural inequalities and criminogenic need, which points the way to a more punitive and control-orientated, individualistic response to youth crime.

Responses to youth crime

Obviously, the development of a 'risk/needs' assessment tool is for the purpose of targeting resources and policy in order to respond to youth crime. The concept of 'prevention' is therefore one which targets primary, secondary and tertiary contexts in which dynamic risk factors (those which can be changed) are known to be present.

Primary crime prevention is a long-term strategy. The aim is to improve overall life opportunities, focusing upon intervention in aspects that have been demonstrated to be contributory factors in the emergence of criminality. Resources are targeted at high-crime neighbourhoods, and situational strategies are implemented, such as target hardening and increased surveillance (McGuire 2002; Muncie 2006).

The aim in secondary crime prevention is to prevent involvement with delinquency through targeting identified, 'at-risk' populations, such as children playing truant or experimenting with drugs (YJB, 2001). Tertiary crime prevention is the domain of the penal services, such as prisons, probation and the YJS. The focus is upon adjudicated (sentenced) offenders with the aim of reducing the risk of the commission of a further similar offence through the implementation of, for example, behavioural change programmes modelled upon research that has demonstrated effective practice strategies (Bottoms *et al.* 2001). 'Effective practice' is the term in current use in the criminal justice system and the YJS to describe practice, modelled on research evidence, that can be demonstrated to have a positive impact on reducing offending behaviour.

The research findings suggest that resources to promote protective factors should be primarily targeted on young men, should be delivered by pro-social modelling to exemplify the new behaviours and attitudes to be adopted, and should employ effective, evidence-based practice.

The Youth Justice Board (YJB) for England and Wales is the body set up to oversee the YJS and to implement strategies to respond to youth crime. The board was established in September 1998 under the Crime and Disorder Act to drive up standards and promote good practice. The aim was to reform the YJS and bring greater coherence to what had been politically perceived as a fragmented and uncoordinated delivery. The remit of the YJB is to prevent crime and the fear of crime, identify and deal with young offenders, and reduce reoffending. It is therefore the body that oversees the activities of youth service delivery by the police, Youth Courts and the multiagency Youth Offending Teams (YOTS), with responsibility for intervention in the custodial settings of Young Offender Institutions, Secure Training Centres and Local Authority Secure Homes.

The YJB has undertaken its role by using the research evidence base to inform strategies for intervention. Primary and secondary crime prevention has focused upon multiagency partnerships. The YJB has targeted strategies and resources by using an index of multiple deprivation to identify those areas where marginalised youths are most likely to be at risk of becoming involved in criminal activity. The index of multiple deprivation consists of ward level indices around six domains:

- income;
- employment;
- health and disability;
- education, skills and training;
- housing;
- geographical access to services.

The types of protective measures that the YJB has supported come under the broad headings of:

- positive activities for young people
- Safer School Partnerships
- Youth Inclusion programmes
- Youth Inclusion and Support panels
- Splash Cymru
- Positive Futures
- mentoring programmes
- parenting programmes.

These are typically in the form of prenatal services, family support by home visiting, parenting information and support, pre-school education and after-school clubs, family literacy schemes, reading schemes, reasoning and social skills education, youth employment with education schemes, strategies to prevent truancy and school exclusion, further education for disaffected youth, and youth work. The YJB also promotes early diagnosis and medical support for carers with children who are suffering from ADHD or cognitive impairment, to complement parenting information and maximise the potential of the young child.

Housing management initiatives, community mobilisation, community policing, and peer-led community programmes and strategies to improve school organisation, including teacher training and antibullying initiatives in schools, all form part of the package that the YJB has developed in recognition that the prevention of youthful antisocial behaviour requires an individualist, welfare-orientated approach that also addresses the social and geographical context, structural deprivation, and the known social and environmental causes and correlates of the onset of criminal behaviour.

A series of measures is also in place to try to ensure that young people who come to the attention of the law for misdemeanour behaviours have a range of opportunities to address this before facing the full weight of prosecution. These include the Acceptable Behaviour Contract, Local Child Curfew, Child Safety Order, Reprimand, and Final Warning Scheme, all designed as diversions of graduated intensity, to keep children out of the courts. Failing to comply with the terms can lead to the imposition of an ASBO, a civil measure that can be used for anyone over 10 years of age who is behaving in a manner that causes distress or harassment. Breach of any part of the requirements of an ASBO, such as entering a proscribed geographical area, even if the behaviour is not offensive, can be prosecuted and may lead to imprisonment. Thus, while the underlying intention of diversion is laudable, the result of these schemes can, in actual practice, mean that repeated misdemeanours may rather swiftly lead to entry into the criminal justice domain.

In the management of tertiary crime prevention and adjudicated offending, a number of conceptually separate areas of research have been drawn together in an attempt to provide a constructive and coherent response. These include:

1) research evidence of risk and protective factors and pathways into crime;

2) the development of actuarial tools to identify those most at risk of reoffending and to identify areas where preventative strategies require addressing;

3) meta-analysis research evidence informing 'what works' models;

4) the use of the actuarial tools to identify suitable individuals and target them in 'what works' type interventions.

The 'what works' paradigm arises out of a body of research based on meta-analysis (Lipsey 1995), which has demonstrated that the delivery of a grouping of strategies is more likely to reduce offending. These principles have come to be known as 'risk, need, responsivity and integrity', as exemplified in the following:

• programmes designed to improve personal and social skills;

• programmes that match individual level of risk and identified individual criminogenic need (risk and need);

- structured programmes focused on changing behaviour (based upon a cognitive behavioural approach);

- programmes that match the learning style of the offender (responsivity);

- multiple service (multimodal) programmes combining a number of different approaches (Lipsey 1992; 1995);

- community-based programmes (Lipsey and Wilson 1998) to facilitate situational learning;

- the active involvement of researchers in design and implementation of programmes to ensure *integrity* of programme delivery.

Age, ethnic background and previous criminal history were shown to have a modest effect, and, overall, older juveniles with longer criminal records showed larger reductions in delinquency with interventions based on these groupings of programmes than did young offenders and lower-risk groups. It was claimed that if the principles were followed and delivered to an accurately targeted group, net reductions in recidivism rates of up to 20 per cent could be achieved (Lipsey 1995; Ross *et al*. 1998; YJB 2001; McGuire 2002).

Approaches modelled upon these principles that have been implemented in both custodial and community settings by the YJB include JETS (Juvenile Enhanced Thinking Skills) and PRISM (a one-to-one programme for juvenile substance abusers). However, of all the interventions that have been researched, the one with the most promising results as a positive treatment for antisocial behaviour in young people, with several studies producing consistent beneficial effects, is functional family therapy (FFT) (Harrington *et al.* 2005). Perhaps this is unsurprising, as FFT is community based and targets not only the individual/personal risk factors but also the family risk factors. However, whereas family therapy skills and training are widely available within community and adolescent mental health settings, they are not available, as yet, within youth justice settings.

Despite the fact that the 'what works' model has been enthusiastically embraced for both adjudicated youth and adult offenders, a note of caution needs to be sounded. It is not the only type of programme that can work with offending behaviour, as FFT demonstrates, and resources and research need to be actively targeted at identifying the broadest range of treatment options possible. As Muncie (2006: 276) states, 'what works' types of provision can be successful only 'at reducing *some* reoffending for *some* offenders at *some* times', and where there are complex social and environmental influences at work in a young person's life, treatments which target the individual alone are unlikely to have positive, long-term outcomes.

Sentencing and legislation: prevention, punishment or net-widening?

A plethora of Acts and political activity have marked the past 20 years, focusing on increasingly punitive responses to perceived youth delinquency. The rate at which legislation has been passed to deal with young offenders is unprecedented in modern criminal justice history. This has resulted in an expansion of settings in which young offenders can be dealt with and also an expansion of the range of sentences that can punish behaviour that might previously have been understood as youthful misdemeanours and high spirits – or as problematic circumstances that would have been dealt with by the Social Services. These Acts include:

- Criminal Justice Act 1988, which replaced both the Detention Centres and Youth Custody Centres with Young Offenders Institutions (YOI);

- Criminal Justice and Public Order Act 1994, which prefaced the opening of Secure Training Centres (STC);

- Crime and Disorder Act (1998) attempted to modernise the Juvenile Justice system (Goldson 2002a) by:
  - establishing the Youth Justice Board to oversee the youth justice system;
  - creating multi-agency youth offender teams (YOTS);
  - abolishing separate sentences and replacing these with a generic detention and training order (DTO) for 15–17 years and for 12–14 years considered persistent offenders;
  - introducing a rehabilitative component of the DTO with half of sentence served in detention and half under supervision of YOTS;
  - introducing a custodial sentence of detention (without training) for grave crimes for those of 18–21 years of age;
  - introducing the Anti-Social Behaviour Order (ASBO) as a civil offence with conditions that had legal force, to deal with nuisance behaviours.

- Youth Justice and Criminal Evidence Act 1999, which introduced key restorative justice initiatives including establishing Youth Panels and introducing Referral Orders for Youth Offenders to Youth Panels;

- Powers of Criminal Courts Act 2000, which provided that children and young people aged 10–17 years can be detained in either a Local Authority Secure Unit or YOI for longer than the maximum of 2 years at the discretion of the Home Secretary;

- Criminal Justice and Police Act 2001, which extended the condition to be met for a custodial remand from *'protecting the public from serious harm'* to *'preventing commission of future imprisonable offences'*;

- Anti-Social Behaviour Act 2003, which strengthened provisions for the ASBO and parenting orders, amongst a range of other initiatives.

With the introduction of the ASBO, it is argued that the boundaries between crime prevention and crime control are becoming blurred (Smith 2003: 61) at one end of the spectrum, while, at the other end, the conditions for putting young people into a secure setting and keeping them there have been relaxed. This is known as net-widening. For the YJB, therefore, an apparent tension exists between meeting the requirements (and results) of punitive political responses to win public approval, and the development of strategic responses solely based on the research evidence that preventative measures and dealing on a broad front with needs should be the basis of intervention. In addition, the welfare philosophy and associated diversionary strategies appear to have suffered a decrease in popularity with the advent of the 'what works' paradigm accompanied by a political rhetoric that has demonised the behaviour of young people (Muncie 1999; 2006). One thing that is clear is that public tolerance of incivility has lowered while the fear of young people has increased (Young and Matthews 2003).

The individualist theoretical aspects of cognitive behaviourism, particularly behaviourism as part of the 'what works' evidence base, have made their own contribution to a political revival of punitive responses to the young offender. These include the following principles of:

- *Inevitable and inescapable.* The effects of punishment require that the offender has no means of avoiding punishment; it is certain to follow the occurrence of undesirable behaviours. It must challenge the thinking that lies behind the 'I can get away with it' attitude that supports risk-taking.

- *Immediacy ('celerity').* Punishment should follow the undesired behaviour rapidly, so that the two are temporally connected in the offender's nervous system. There are significant moves to reduce the length of bail and remand, particularly for young offenders, as a reflection of this.

- *Severity.* Unless punishment is applied at maximum or very high intensity, its effects are likely to be uncertain. Community sentences and diversion schemes have been perceived as a 'soft option' and are attacked for this reason.

- *Alternative responses available.* To reduce or eliminate any negative goal-directed behaviour, alternative means of achieving the goal should be available to the individual. An example is the use of diversionary schemes as a way of making amends without going through the full legal process.

- *Comprehensibility.* For the meaning of punishment to be clearly communicated, the reason for its use and the justification for it must be understood by the recipient. This may be one of the reasons why it is argued that unpaid work (and its predecessor, community service) is such a successful sentence. Here there is a clear relationship between hard work, loss of freedom and punishment.

There is a wide range of punitive community disposals available of graduated intensity, including surveillance. In addition, the Referral Order and restorative justice initiatives are at the forefront of victim inclusion strategies; they aim to restore a positive relationship between the individual offender, the victim and the community through mediation and reparation. Despite the fact that it is claimed that there is a significantly lower rate of reoffending recorded for those subject to restorative justice approaches than for those sent to youth custody (Hughes *et al.* 1998), the welfare versus justice tension is never more in evidence than with the problems posed for the YJB by the numbers of young people being incarcerated.

Over the past 10 years, custodial rates for youths have increased by 90 per cent (Muncie 2006) rising to 7,600 in 2003 (NACRO 2003).

Child prisoners are more likely to come from the marginalised and impoverished families and neighbourhoods identified in the YOI index of multiple deprivation than from any other grouping (Goldson 2002; Goldson and Coles 2005). Goldson (2006: 146) also notes that 'approximately half of the children held in penal custody at any one time will be, or will have been, "open cases" to statutory child welfare agencies as a result of neglect or other child protection concerns'. Again, this supports the evidence that these children are operating in an environment that, through no fault of their own, has increased their risk of offending. It is already well documented that prison is one of the most social exclusionary settings, has a negative impact on the physical and mental well-being of children (Goldson 2002; Nellis 2005; Muncie 2006), and inhibits rather than promotes pro-social learning while cutting young persons off from whatever family ties and networks of support they might have relied upon. HM Chief Inspector of Prisons (1999: 3) has noted that penal custody often marks 'just one further stage in the exclusion of a group of children who between them have already experienced almost every form of social exclusion on offer'.

It is unlikely that, as the situation is at present, Youth Offender Institutions (YOIs) can provide the positive experience that will lead to rehabilitation. Goldson (1997: 83) reported that conditions are 'unsuited to guaranteeing basic standards of safety and welfare, and each day is characterized by a culture of bullying, intimidation and routine self-harm'. The response to such environmental distress can be seen in the rates of suicide, with 134 suicides in prison committed by 15–21-year-olds, most within one month of reception, in 1999–2000 (Goldson 2002). The Commission of Racial Equality (2003) also reports high levels of intimidation, discrimination and failure to protect black prisoners. Perhaps one of the most distressing examples of this was the murder of Zahid Mubarek, an Asian teenager, at Feltham YOI in 2000, when Mubarek, just hours from release, was placed in a cell with a known white racist, who beat him to death. An inquiry (Keith 2006) catalogued a history of racist abuse at Feltham YOI, in which prison officers were implicated, and the inquiry heard that three white officers had previously been disciplined for an attack on an ethnic minority inmate. During the attack, officers handcuffed him to the bars of his cell, removed his trousers, and smeared black boot polish on his buttocks.

There is absolutely no evidence that such attitudes or such difficult environments produce the desired outcome. The conclusion of HM Chief Inspector of Prisons (1999) was that intervention cannot be expected to change individual behaviour and develop victim awareness until these young people have had the opportunity to experience a positive environment and a proactive concern for their welfare.

Conclusion

The punitive philosophy arising out of public demand and resting its case upon individualist psychological theoretical perspectives appears to have exponentially infiltrated the sentencing process. The outcome is that we have a system for young people that draws them inexorably through a series of stepping stones into the network of criminal proceedings under the veil of attempting to address welfare and justice needs. Unfortunately, once in the meshes of the sentencing process, it is apparent that prison, the form of punishment used with increasing frequency, is the one most likely to lead to reconviction.

In 1816, as fears that young people were out of control escalated, the Society for Investigating the Alarming Increase of Juvenile Delinquency in the Metropolis published a report addressing the rise in juvenile crime (Goldson 2002). The report found that there were three principal 'causes': lack of education, lack of employment and inadequate parenting. Two further 'auxiliary causes' were identified: defective policing and the overseverity of the criminal code for children. The latter was responsible for capturing young people in the criminal justice system, resulting in what was seen in 1820 as a juvenile crime wave. Very little appears to have changed in the twenty-first century. Despite the knowledge base that now informs our understanding of the psychological and social causes and correlates of pathways into crime, the legislative climate continues to pursue a popular punitive rhetoric that creates tension with evidenced-based strategies to combat youth crime.

Chapter 4

Aggression and violence

Introduction

Feelings of anger, frustration and hostility are regular occurrences in modern life. It is easy to be irritated by an individual jumping a queue, incessant noise emanating from a neighbouring apartment, or the invasion of personal space in a train or shopping centre. These feelings are probably common to all of us. We can understand, perhaps sometimes even condone, violence in circumstances of provocation or injustice. However, some violence seems senseless and defies comprehension.

The psychological understanding of aggression and violence is indeed far from straightforward. We know of various factors that impinge on it, and we are aware of the situations in which violence is most likely to occur. But what do we know about notoriously violent people? Do they differ from others in genetic make-up, or do they view other people and their behaviour differently? Is it something they have learnt, from parents, peers or television or is it the case that all of us are capable of violence in certain circumstances?

According to statistics from the British Crime Survey (Home Office 2005), the total number of violent offences in England and Wales in 2004/5 was 2,412,000. These include:

- 401,000 incidents of domestic violence;
- 828,000 incidents where the offender was an acquaintance;
- 836,000 incidents where the offender was a stranger;
- 347,000 incidents of mugging.

Violent crime has fallen by 43 per cent since its peak in 1995 and has remained relatively stable since 2000. In 2004/5, 3.6 per cent of people experienced violent incidents, 50 per cent of which resulted in injury (www.crimestatistics.org.uk; Nicholas *et al.* 2005).

Behind every statistic lies a story. The case of Thompson in Worcester is one that typifies a great many cases in courtrooms up and down the country. Thompson, 19 years old, had been drinking in the early evening. He subsequently barged into a 14-year-old and threatened him in the street. He then went on to head butt and punch the boy. The victim ran off, but was pursued by Thompson. He fled into a McDonald's restaurant, but Thompson caught up with him there to continue the assault. Thompson, who had previous convictions for drink-related incidents, was sentenced at Worcester Magistrates' Court to 10 weeks in a Young Offenders Institution (This is Worcestershire 2003).

Violence is easily associated with certain contexts and events. Typical are pub brawls, so-called turf wars between criminal gangs, and violence by football hooliganism. The emergence of 'happy slapping' is also a pertinent development. This is a novel variety of so-called senseless violence that involves beating up innocent people in the street 'for a laugh' as the assault is filmed or photographed on mobile phones. Much 'violence talk' relates to such incidents. Newspapers may be full of stories about people who have experienced random acts of stranger violence; in contrast, research suggests that much of the world's actual violence is interpersonal and takes place behind closed doors between people in an intimate relationship (e.g. Stanko 2000).

Violence can occur for many reasons, and in a variety of contexts. This offers a challenge to psychology: how can we make sense of such a destructive and yet widespread phenomenon? Is there an effective way of both predicting and preventing it?

This chapter focuses on the causes of violence, and why it is that certain individuals seem to have a higher propensity for it than others. We could have decided to take an even wider stance on the subject and take warfare, weapons of mass destruction and genocide into account. However, as that would bring us into the world of politics and international relations, and away from psychology, we have decided to limit ourselves to interpersonal violence.

In what follows, we will examine a number of factors that have been assumed to cause aggression, including frustration, testosterone, alcohol, and certain types of brain damage or injury, as well as heat, and violent television and video games. We will subsequently look at the role of cognition and social information processing. After that, we will seek to put all these findings into a more comprehensive framework, using Anderson and Bushman's (2002) general aggression model.

It is first important to provide definitions. According to Anderson and Bushman (2002), aggression is

Any behaviour directed toward another individual that is carried out with the proximate (immediate) intent to cause harm. In addition, the perpetrator must believe that the action will harm the target and that the target is motivated to avoid the behavior. (28)

Frustration and aggression

The link between frustration and aggression seems straightforward enough. When an individual has a certain goal and finds that that goal cannot be achieved, frustration ensues. That frustration becomes a cue for aggressive behaviour. The typical example is the air passenger who abuses airline staff when refused entry to the plane. Another example is the football player who commits a foul after conceding a goal.

Dollard *et al.* (1939) have been credited with formulating the so-called frustration–aggression hypothesis. Their theory has been subsumed into a wider framework proposed by the influential researcher Berkowitz. It is, rather unattractively, called the cognitive neoassociation theory (Berkowitz 1990; 1993). He recognised that, apart from frustration to do with failed goal attainment, anger and aggression can arise from other unpleasant feelings as well. These are often brought about by events perceived to be unpleasant and that state of mind is called negative affect (Berkowitz 1993).

Negative affect describes feelings, memories and notions of both anger and fear. Our bodily response is one of arousal, in order to either fight or flight. The appraisal of the event, the negative emotions that that triggers, and the body's physiological response all make aggression and violence more likely. In addition, subsequent events are more likely to be interpreted in a way that is congruent with these feelings, further strengthening the cognitive position already taken and exacerbating the likelihood of aggressive behaviour (Berkowitz 1993). Thus, negative affect is a result of negative events, but it also influences the perception of future events in such a way that it becomes enhanced.

In this framework, frustration does indeed cause aggression, but non-confrontational unpleasant moods or states can do that as well. One of these states is depression. Although depression is usually associated with lethargy and passivity, it is interesting to note that Monahan *et al.* (2001) actually found a link between depression and violence in a sample of psychiatric patients discharged after voluntary admission. Berkowitz's cognitive neoassociation theory would help us understand that apparently counter-intuitive finding: the concept of negative affect might link depression to aggression.

In a similar vein, we can appreciate the effect that heat seems to have on aggressive behaviour. Readers might recall the film *Falling Down* (Schumacher 1993), in which the protagonist, played by Michael Douglas, gets stuck in a traffic jam in the soaring heat. He leaves his car, frustrated by the fact that the traffic will cause him to miss his daughter's birthday party. He ends up going on a violent rampage, and the heat forms a compelling backdrop to these events.

The idea that heat affects us is what the so-called heat hypothesis postulates (Anderson 2001). In a real-life study, Kenrick and MacFarlane (1984) found that aggressive use of the claxon increased on hot days, but only for drivers in cars without air conditioning, in the US state of Arizona. In a simulated setting, Vrij *et al.* (1994) in The Netherlands found that when Dutch police officers dealt with a re-enacted burglary in hot weather they were more likely to view the burglar as aggressive and threatening and more likely to use their weapons. Anderson *et al.* (2000) estimate that an increase in temperature of 2°F (just over 1°C) accounts for an increase in the US murder rate by 4.5 per 100,000.

The heat effect fits Berkowitz's cognitive neoassociation theory, as heat might produce negative affect. Anderson's explanation is compelling:

> Heat-induced discomfort makes people cranky. […] A minor provocation can quickly escalate, especially if both participants are affectively and cognitively primed for hostility by their heightened level of discomfort. A mild insult is more likely to provoke a severe insult in response when people are hot than when they are more comfortable. This may lead to further increases in the aggressiveness of responses and counter-responses. (Anderson 2001: 34)

The so-called excitation-transfer theory helps us to understand displaced aggression. The typical example is when feelings of hostility are induced by a source against which retaliation is not possible, as when that source is a person of high authority. It is sometimes tempting to react aggressively against innocent others, so as to take it out on them. In Zillmann's experiments (Zillmann *et al.* 1972; Bryant and Zillmann 1979), participants were subjected to a provocation (to which they cannot retaliate) and to a stimulus that heightens arousal, such as loud noise or physical exercise. These situations are compared to situations in which the increased arousal is present but without the initial provocation. The findings were invariably that increased arousal did produce increased aggression, but only if there had been a provocation. When an individual has been provoked, and negative affect has been the result, increased bodily activity does increase the chance of violent behaviour. Zillmann's findings augment Berkowitz's model, in the sense that it is not only negative affect that causes the body to prepare physically for violence. Any other form of physical arousal, even from a pleasant activity, can precipitate a violent response more quickly (Zillmann *et al.* 1974).

Testosterone, brain injury and a genetic defect

It is often assumed that young males' aggressive behaviour is to do with levels of the hormone testosterone. Testosterone occurs in both men and women and is mainly produced by the male testes and the ovaries in women. It is important for a host of functions, including muscle build and sexual development, and it is also associated with dominance behaviours and aggression. However, the relationship between testosterone and aggression is not as simple as might be assumed. Injecting testosterone into people does not produce increased aggression, so that the straightforward link of more testosterone equals more aggression does not seem to apply (O'Connor *et al.* 2004). Similarly, Archer (2005) describes studies involving boys in puberty, during which their levels of testosterone naturally increase but without an accompanying increase in aggressive behaviour.

Testosterone levels predictably rise in response to sexual stimuli. They also increase in anticipation of competition (often measured in the context of sport), when winning, and in particular when winning or losing is connected with status. The same is true for passionate sports fans, whose testosterone levels are higher immediately after their favourite team has won than after a defeat.

Increased levels of testosterone can be adaptive from an evolutionary perspective: it does enhance aggression, but only in certain types of competitive situations. Male dominance behaviours are about acquiring high status to enhance the chances of mating. The link between aggression and testosterone is indirect and mediated by this dominance behaviour. It is therefore no surprise that the link between testosterone and aggression is modest, as Archer (2005) concludes: 'Testosterone levels showed a low but positive correlation with measures of aggression and higher correlations with dominance, variously measured by leadership, toughness, personal power, and aggressive dominance' (Archer 2005: 344).

Aggression is occasionally associated with a certain type of brain injury or dysfunction. This has been observed by Lishman (1968) in British war veterans and by Grafman *et al.* (1996) among Vietnam veterans. From their literature review, Brower and Price (2001) conclude that a certain type of injury or dysfunction of the frontal lobe is associated with aggressive behaviour, particularly with aggressive dyscontrol. The aggression that these patients display is primarily impulsive and not premeditated. However, perhaps contrary to expectation, strong links with crime were not found. The latter finding puts the results of this research in context in two ways. Firstly, behavioural control of any desire to behave antisocially can be weakened by brain injury or dysfunction, but that does not seem to cause excessive offending. However, it does relate to impulsivity and aggression. Secondly, such dysfunctions are quite rare. As a generic explanation for aggression, therefore, this explanation fails to carry substantial weight: it might explain the behaviour of a certain few individuals but is insufficient as a basis for understanding aggression and violence in society (Brower and Price 2001).

This is not to discount the famous finding by Brunner and colleagues, who studied a Dutch family in which a gene defect was genetically transmitted through the family. Only the males were affected, and they displayed a variety of problems, including increased aggression. The type of aggressive and problem behaviour varied, from rape to arson to exhibitionism. Women who carried the gene defect did not show increased aggression or any other effects produced by the gene. This shows that genetic defects, in rare cases, can produce increased impulsive aggression. These findings demonstrate that, whereas, in the bigger picture, genetics might not be helpful to our understanding of aggression, at the same time we cannot discount the role that genes may play (Brunner *et al.* 1993).

Social learning

It has long been feared that violence on the screen (both television and cinema) influences those who choose to watch it. That assumption underlies the regulation of violent (and sexual and commercial) content of films and television programmes. Let us start this investigation by looking at a time-honoured experiment involving children. You might assume that children are more easily influenced than adults, so it would be interesting to examine to what degree their behaviour changes after having observed violence. The Bandura *et al.* (1961) experiment did just that. It exposed children to violent behaviour to see whether the children subsequently displayed more aggression themselves. The simple answer is that they did, and as the experiment was quite complex and a seminal study in psychology, it is worth exploring it in some detail.

Bandura *et al.* recruited 36 boys and 36 girls enrolled in the Stanford University Nursery School. They ranged in age from 37 to 69 months, with a mean age of 52 months. Initially, all the children had been slightly aroused so as to facilitate a certain level of aggressive behaviour. This was achieved as follows. They were placed in a waiting area where they were left to play with attractive toys, such as a fire engine. After about two minutes, these toys were taken away, and the experimenter explained that they were special toys. The children were no longer allowed to play with the toys, as they were reserved for other children. Bandura *et al.* called this mild aggression arousal, and we might also say that that would induce negative affect.

These children were then left in a room to play with potato prints and picture stickers (the experimenter remained present in a passive capacity). Subsequently brought into the room was an adult (the 'model'), who played in a different corner with a number of toys, including a 5-foot, inflated Bobo doll. With children in the non-aggressive condition, the model played with the various toys but ignored the Bobo doll. In the aggressive condition, the model started playing with the other toys but soon turned to the Bobo doll and showed violence toward it both physically (kicking, punching, and sitting on it), and verbally ('Throw him in the air', 'Kick him').

A further condition involved the gender of the model. If we disregard control groups for the moment, which saw no model at all, we are left with eight experimental groups. Four groups consisted of boys; one set observed a male model playing aggressively; another

63

saw that male model play non-aggressively, whereas two other groups witnessed a female model. For one of these groups, the female behaved aggressively, and in the remaining male group she played non-aggressively. Similarly, there were four experimental groups involving the girl participants. That makes this, in psychological research jargon, a 2 × 2 × 2 design, yielding eight different experimental groups (but remember that all children underwent the experiment individually).

The children who watched the model display aggression against the Bobo doll showed much more aggression toward the doll itself when left to play with it. In addition, boys showed more physical imitative aggression than girls. Furthermore, boys displayed more 'novel' aggression toward the doll, if they had observed aggressive play earlier. Interestingly, the data seem to suggest an interactive effect of gender of the child with gender of the model: boys were most aggressive when having observed a male model, whereas girls were more affected by a female aggressive model, at least as far as imitative aggression is concerned. A female aggressive model did not seem to engender the same levels of aggression in boys. Non-imitative aggression was also affected by the gender of the model: girls displayed this most after watching a female model, and boys after watching a male model.

Table 4.1 Aggression scores for boys in girls in Bandura *et al.*'s (1961) so-called Bobo doll experiment

Responses	Experimental groups			
	Aggressive model		Non-aggressive model	
	Female model	Male model	Female model	Male model
Imitative physical aggression	5.5 (girls) 12.4 (boys)	7.2 (girls) 25.8 (boys)	2.5 (girls) 0.2 (boys)	0.0 (girls) 1.5 (boys)
Imitative verbal aggression	13.7 (girls) 4.3 (boys)	2.0 (girls) 12.7 (boys)	0.3 (girls) 1.1 (boys)	0.0 (girls) 0.0 (boys)
Non-imitative aggression	21.3 (girls) 16.2 (boys)	8.4 (girls) 36.7 (boys)	7.2 (girls) 26.1 (boys)	1.4 (girls) 22.3 (boys)

Source Bandura *et al.* 1961.

The data are of interest for a number of reasons. Firstly, they show that simply observing aggression can be a measurable influence on aggressive behaviour. That has potential ramifications for the effects of violent television and video games, and also of witnessing domestic violence. It demonstrates rather convincingly that social learning is a factor of significance. However, it must also be said that Bandura and colleagues created a setting in which imitation of aggression was most likely to occur: after all, actual play soon followed observation of the model, and negative affect was induced to enhance the probability of such behaviour. In looking to generalise from such a laboratory setting into real-life situations, the size of the likely effect might be debated. However, it seems beyond debate that there is such a thing as observational or vicarious learning of aggression.

Finally, it must also be noted that the Bobo doll study is not so much an experiment as a paradigm. The same set-up has been used to investigate whether the effects would be lessened if children observed the model not live but on video (Bandura et al. 1963). In a further study, Bandura tested whether it mattered whether the children would observe not only the model's aggressive behaviour but also the consequences of that behaviour; that is, whether the model would be punished or rewarded for that behaviour (Bandura 1965). He found that punishment did decrease the level of aggression displayed by the children, but there was no difference between reinforcement and a neutral response to the model's aggression. Bandura's work remains highly influential, as it established something that today we find rather self-explanatory: that of modelling, or social or vicarious learning.

Television and video games

The step from Bandura's pioneering work to the effects of television violence is easily made: if we have established that children are more aggressive after watching violent behaviour, what does television violence do to society's levels of aggression and violence? Television violence and its effects on people, in particular children and youngsters, have been extensively studied. Some interesting findings have emerged. The general conclusion is that television violence is one factor contributing to the development of aggression (Huesmann et al. 2003). Huesmann et al. distinguish two types of effects of television violence. The first is a short-term effect: children and youngsters might be inclined to act out what they see on television immediately afterward. This is the realm of Bandura's studies. The other is longer term, and involves the acquisition of cognitions and attitudes that facilitate aggression. On the latter, Huesmann *et al.*'s conclusions are unequivocal: 'Both males and females from all social strata and all levels of initial aggressiveness are placed at increased risk for the development of adult aggressive and violent behavior when they view a high and steady diet of violent TV shows in early childhood.' The effect is not equally strong for all who are exposed to television violence. The level of identification with aggressive same-sex characters is a factor of significance, as is the perception that television violence is realistic and true to life. They also found that the more children watch television in general (regardless of what type of programmes), the more likely they are to display violence as adults.

There are various ways in which these relationships can be explained. The viewing of aggressive behaviour might lead to the acquisition of aggressive scripts for social problem solving. It might also be associated with desensitisation, at it were, getting used to violence so that its negative emotional impact is reduced. Finally, there is the justification hypothesis: children who 'like' aggression might be attracted to aggressive television because it makes them feel 'normal', on the one hand, and it enriches their aggressive behaviour repertoire on the other hand.

Key to many of these long-terms effects is social information processing. It is the generic term for all the processes and decisions that help us understand and interpret social situations. After all, many social situations can be ambiguous and difficult to understand. What do other people want? What will people think if I say something? Would Kellie like it if I asked her out? Why is John walking away? These types of questions arise in social situations, and we seek to answer them by deploying our social cognition. In doing this, there are a number of stages that can be identified. Although they might seem more or less obvious, it is useful to distinguish them, as it helps to pinpoint stages at which violent individuals might differ from others. Crick and Dodge (1994) describe them as follows. The first stage is encoding of social cues. The second is the interpretation of those cues into a mental representation of the social situation. The third is the assessment and clarification of goals and outcomes. The fourth stage concerns considering possible courses of action, or responses, in the situation. After that, there is the phase of response selection, and the final stage is the evaluation of what went on before. Crick and Dodge do emphasise that the stages need not take place in a discrete fashion, but can happen simultaneously, and are no doubt heavily influenced by our prior knowledge of our social world, embodied in scripts and schemas.

Akhtar and Bradley (1991) found that aggressive children tend to perform worse than non-aggressive children at each stage of Crick and Dodge's social information-processing model. McGuire (2004) summarises their findings as follows.

Frequently aggressive children:

- encode a narrower range of cues;
- selectively attend to aggressive cues;
- attribute hostile intent to others, especially in ambiguous situations;
- generate fewer potential solutions to problematic social situations;
- select action-oriented rather than reflective solutions;
- possess a more limited range of interactive skills;
- display more often an 'egocentric' bias.

Aggressive children are more likely to attribute hostility to others: the person who bumps into you in a shop is, in their eyes more likely to have done that on purpose, rather than by accident. Similarly, a joke is less likely to be friendly banter than a 'wind up'. This phenomenon is called the *hostile attribution bias.* It is often researched via scenarios in which people behave pro-socially, ambiguously or hostilely, and the subject is asked to gauge the actual motives of those people. Aggressive children are often found to be – slightly – more inclined to rate ambiguous behaviours as hostile (Palmer and Hollin 2001; Palmer 2003).

McGuire emphasises that although television viewing habits make a difference, we can only properly understand their impact if it adds into the equation what happens inside in an individual's head. Although factors such as heat, testosterone and frustration all have a part to play, it is how that comes together in the cognitive appraisal of the situation that determines whether violence will occur or not.

Thus, exposure to violence and other problematic situations is a factor of concern but is insufficient as a sole explanation. In this regard, it is interesting to look at the effect of video games on aggression. There are theories that intense exposure to violent video games enables real-life aggression. The social modelling theory would certainly apply to that effect, whereas excitation transfer might also explain the occurrence of certain aggressive behaviours soon after exposure to a violent video game. Extensive play of such games might also serve to normalise aggression and therefore alter the way in which social information is processed. On the other hand, though, there is the Freudian concept of 'catharsis'. That, simply put, is letting off steam, so that, rather than inducing aggression, playing such games might actually be a way of getting rid of negative affect in a relatively harmless manner (Bensley and Van Eenwyk 2001).

Bensley and Van Eenwyk conducted an analysis of 28 research studies. They found that among young children (4–8 years old), play with an aggressive video game was often followed by a brief episode of aggressive play straight afterward. This was not found for other age groups, but the design of the studies involved did not consistently allow for this to be established. The inconclusive nature of the research findings led Bensley and Van Eenwyk (2001) to argue that 'current research evidence is not supportive of a major concern that violent video games lead to real-life violence'. But they also warn that as video games become more realistic and sophisticated this situation may well change in the future.

Alcohol

No one will dispute the notion that drink and violence go together. From there, we might assume that the relation between alcohol and violence is straightforward, but that is not the case. Drink-driving is one obvious offence for which alcohol consumption is an explicit constituent of the offence. It is also of interest that in military law, being drunk on duty, certainly in the case of senior officers, is an imprisonable offence.

It is obvious that alcohol has an influence on the mind. Alcohol as found in drinks (ethanol) is a mind-altering substance and works as a depressant with addictive properties. In this respect, we distinguish between dependence and addiction. Dependence is listed in the DSM-IV classification manual. We can say that someone suffers from alcohol dependence when they fulfil three or more of the following criteria:

- tolerance;
- withdrawal;
- substance taken for a longer period of time or greater amount than intended;
- desire or efforts to reduce or control use;
- much time spent in activities to obtain the substance;
- social, recreational or occupational activities given up or reduced;

- continued usage despite knowing that physical or psychological problems are worsened by it.

People who are alcohol dependent may need to drink daily and are unable to stop or cut down despite repeated efforts to abstain completely or to restrict drinking to certain periods of the day. They may go on occasional binges, remaining intoxicated for two, three or more days. They may suffer blackouts for the events that took place during a bout of intoxication. [...] Such drinking, of course, often causes social and occupational difficulties, quarrels with family or friends, sometimes violence when intoxicated, frequent absences from work, possibly loss of job, and arrests of intoxication and traffic accidents. (Davison *et al.* 2004: 360)

The extent to which alcohol affects a person depends on three types of factors. The first is the drink itself: its type, quantity, and speed and duration of the drinking session. The second is the consumer, whose age, gender, drinking habits, motivation for drinking, cultural knowledge and expectations are also significant factors. Thirdly, we need to take into account the setting in which the drinking (and the violence) occurs. That setting can be, for example, the societal context (such as a country's drinking culture), or the context of the drinking occasion: in the home, at a party, at a sports event, or in a public place.

Murdoch *et al.* (1990) estimate that half of all serious offences (murder, rape, assault and family violence) are committed under the influence of alcohol. Analysis of 1,575 custody records in Britain showed that a third of all arrests involved an arrestee who had been drinking (Man *et al.* 2002). Rossow (2001) set out to examine levels of alcohol use and homicide at country level, basing her analysis on alcohol sales and homicide rates in 14 countries. She found that the two did indeed correlate. However, this is more the case for the Nordic countries, Denmark, Finland, Norway and Sweden with a culture of binge drinking, and less the case for countries in southern Europe. Beer consumption related more strongly to homicide rates than other beverages, and finally, the correlation was much stronger for male offending than for female offending. Other research suggests that the effect possibly is even stronger in Russia: during an intensive alcohol campaign between 1985 and 1988, alcohol consumption dropped by 25 per cent. The murder rate was allegedly reduced by 40 per cent (Shkolnikov and Nemtsov 1997).

Thus, the relation between alcohol and crimes involving aggression does not need to be questioned. The key is the extent to which there is a causal relationship, and how that works. In this regard, three hypotheses are often put forward. One is the so-called common-cause hypothesis, which posits that people are driven to alcohol and to aggression by the same set of underlying problems. For instance, teenagers who experience violence and chaos in the home, bullying at school, and fear of crime elsewhere might be inclined to turn to drink and to be more aggressive than other youngsters. Alcohol abuse does not cause violence, according to this scenario, but both are caused by something else.

The second is the coincidence hypothesis. Certainly, drinking in public and semi-public spaces is often done by young males. Young males are frequently both victims and perpetrators of violent offences. The co-occurrence of both alcohol and violence might therefore be one of the lifestyle preference and risk-taking behaviours engaged in by young men. Thus, in this perspective, drinking and fighting go together without any sort of underlying causation.

The third hypothesis is the obvious one that alcohol is instrumental in producing aggression. There is a wealth of evidence for this (see Bushman and Cooper 1990; Berkowitz 1993) but there is, in fact, evidence for all three hypotheses. On top of that, the role of social and cultural expectations cannot be disregarded either, as Källmén and Gustafson (1998) argue: 'An alternative hypothesis that seems to explain many behaviors in an inebriated individual is the "time out" hypothesis, which states that drunken behavior is influenced more by norms about what it should be than by the pharmacological effect of alcohol' (Källmén and Gustafson 1998: 150).

We conclude this section with a number of assertions, derived from Plant *et al.* (2002: 211) of the University of Bristol:

1 Alcohol consumption may (and probably does) increase the propensity for aggression and violence in men, and to a lesser extent, in women.

2 The effects of alcohol consumption depend upon the interplay of the kind of alcoholic beverage, the characteristics of the drinking, and the setting in which consumption occurs.

3 The vast majority of drinking occasions do not result in aggressive or violent behaviour.

4 Alcohol consumption may contribute to aggression and violent behaviour. Even so, drinking is neither necessary nor sufficient to produce either of these.

5 Heavy drinking and intoxication are associated with both violent and non-violent crimes. Evidence suggests that heavy/problem drinkers are at risk of being violent or of being subjected to violence.

6 Experience of violence (including sexual abuse) in childhood or later in life is associated with the development of heavy or problem drinking.

7 The risk of exposure to alcohol-related violence is influenced by a constellation of demographic, lifestyle and contextual factors. The latter include a 'wet' or uncontrolled drinking environment, poverty, deprived area of residence, age (young adulthood is associated with high risk) and personal drinking habits.

The general aggression model

This chapter has shown that we know a great deal about the factors that influence aggression and violence. However, it is equally clear that the impact of any of these factors, be it television violence or levels of testosterone, is dependent upon other factors. All these factors interrelate, and that complicates the disentangling of these relationships. Anderson and Bushman (2002) compare this state of affairs to the building of a house: we have a heap of stones, that is, a number of findings, but that does not mean that we have a house, that is, a comprehensive theory. They have therefore formulated a so-called general aggression model. Its aim is not to dismiss or surpass previous findings but to mould them into a coherent whole. That should help our understanding of the multifaceted nature of aggression. It should also inform interventions for offenders. A general model, even if it is rather complex, might be required to do justice to the inherent complexity of aggression and violence in today's society.

The general aggression model distinguishes inputs from routes and outcomes. Inputs are factors that impinge on the person or the potentially violent situation. Routes are ways in which the internal state of the person is affected, and outcomes relate to decision processes and actions.

Much of the research we have described relates to inputs. These are either person factors or situation factors. Person factors include gender (the well-known difference in aggression and violence between men and women; e.g., Geary 1998) but also certain beliefs and attitudes. People who believe that they are adept at violence, for instance, because of skills in certain martial arts are likely be more aggressive, as will individuals who feel that violence will get them what they want. Similarly, certain attitudes toward women work to facilitate domestic violence. Elsewhere in this book, we discuss rape myths, beliefs that correlate with the likelihood that an individual will commit date rape or other forms of violence in a dating context.

In addition to person factors, we need to take situational factors into account. These include provocation, which is emerging as a potent factor in predicting violence, and frustration. The factors that tend to cause negative affect also fit this category, such as heat, pain and discomfort.

Routes are to do with how these inputs, personal or situational, change a person's internal state, cognition, affect or arousal. Cognition includes the acquisition and activation of aggressive scripts – for instance, via violence in the media or via observational learning. Hostile thoughts will trigger such scripts, and increase the likelihood that violence becomes an action to be considered. We have already established the importance of negative affect. No doubt, much aggression occurs when the perpetrator is in what is colloquially called a 'foul mood'. Finally, arousal can influence aggression in three ways. The first is when excitation energises aggressive tendencies. The second is via excitation transfer: arousal from an irrelevant source can be mislabelled as anger when situational aggressive inputs occur. This is reminiscent of the famous study by Schachter and Singer that also emphasises that how people label the way they are physically feeling determines to a large extent the actual emotions that they experience (Schachter and Singer 1962). Thirdly, it is possible that states of extremely high or low arousal are unpleasant states, and therefore produce negative affect by themselves.

Cognition, arousal and affect interrelate in many ways and that makes the situation even more complicated. The internal state, a combination of cognition, arousal and affect, can produce a variety of responses. Certain responses are almost like reflexes: they occur immediately before calm reflection can take place. These certainly account for some forms of aggression. However, it is more common for immediate appraisals to lead to further processing. These may be action oriented or reflective. Reflective appraisals often steer individuals away from impulsive aggressive. This reminds us of the advice sometimes given to count to 10 before hitting someone. That strategy gives reflection at least a chance. An added benefit of a short pause is that the level of anger arousal might drop. Thus, initial impressions might lead to action or to further thinking. Both might lead to aggressive behaviour, but in a different way, and that will account for different forms of aggression.

Conclusion

In short, predicting violence remains hazardous. We know a great deal about its causes and the various contexts in which it is most likely to occur. We know that information processing is key and that various physical responses and social events can combine to bring a person into a state of readiness for violence. We are aware of the role of provocation and negative affect upon anger. But all that knowledge does not make exact predictions easy. That is why the ability to predict effectively and prevent violence remains elusive. It is therefore possibly unsurprising that a frequently applied piece of information in criminology is that past violence is the best predictor of future violence (Blumstein *et al.* 1986; Gutheil and Appelbaum 2000; Monahan *et al.* 2001; also Rosenfeld 2004). People who have done it before are among the most likely to do it again.

Chapter 5

Sexual violence: from theory into practice

Introduction

What constitutes a sex offence or normal and abnormal sexual behaviour varies over time and place. With certain legal conditions attached, homosexual acts were decriminalised in England and Wales in the 1950s and 1960s, but in Afghanistan, male–male sex remains a criminal offence, and in Kuwait, Liberia, Lebanon, Morocco, Nigeria and Oman, any sexual activity other than that between males and females is outlawed. Even within a country such as the USA, the laws across the American states regarding male–male sex or female–female sex have variously been invalidated, or repealed, and even the age of consent to a sexual act is a social and culturally based construction.

The age of consent in Andorra is 13; in Tunisia 20; in the Dominican Republic, 18; and in most European countries, 16, but in countries such as Fiji and North Korea the age of consent to sexual activity remains unspecified (World Wide Ages of Consent 2006). This means that in some countries an activity is illegal, but in others it is not. These social and cultural differences affect the legal definition of what constitutes, for example, child sexual abuse, and the inclusive policing and citizenship of sexual activity as it relates to sexual minorities such as the lesbian, gay, bisexual and transgender communities.

This chapter does not aim to answer the question of what the appropriate age of consent is for sexual activity or whether some or all sexual activities should be legalised, because the law may tell us in detail what a sexual offence is, but an abstract definition remains nebulous and fails to capture the physical and emotional impact upon the victim. This chapter will explore sex offenders in terms of the types of violence that are associated with sexual offending and programmes of intervention that aim to minimise the risk that these individuals pose. The common theme that will be adopted is that nearly all sexual offending is the lack of real consent, whether by age or coercion (Abel *et al.* 1984). Sexual offending will be understood as the inducement or coercion of adults and children into sexual activities to which they have not given true consent, and sexual violence as physical and emotional violation to attain sexual gratification from a person unwilling or unable to consent to the activity.

Settings, scenarios and issues of consent

Sex offending is too often characterised as either adult rape or child molestation by strangers. However, to understand the breadth of sex-offending behaviour, it is useful to explore the types of settings and scenarios that are associated with a lack of consent.

Adults may be coerced into sexual activity against their will by threats of violence, and this includes coercion by poverty and economic imperatives that drive women and men to engage in pornographic acts or prostitution; for while the adult is of an age and mental capacity to give informed consent, the circumstances surrounding the coercion mean that it is not true consent. The UK is a major destination for trafficked women, and the police believe that about 4,000 have been brought into the country and forced to work as prostitutes (BBC 2006). Offences may be committed against men and women with mental impairments who are unable to give true, informed consent. For example, the Healthcare Commission and Commission for Social Care Inspection (CSCI) (2007) catalogued widespread, institutional physical and sexual abuse of learning disabled patients in centres in the Cornwall Partnership NHS Trust. Violent attacks on women in which there is no sexual element can still be interpreted as sexual assaults, because the victim is targeted as a female, and although this is most commonly linked to assaults on females, it is also associated with assaults on males, as in the homophobic murder of gay barman Jody Dobrowski in 2005. Some offences may be committed even where there is consent by the adult parties concerned; most notably, this includes adults who enter 'prohibited' (e.g., incestuous) relationships, and sexual activities that take place between consenting adults in a public rather than a private place when they are deemed to offend concepts of public decency.

The concept of child sexual abuse as a social problem is relatively new and did not emerge in the academic literature until the 1980s (Quayle and Taylor 2003). Issues of consent in the UK have posed problematic legal issues, especially where young people who are both under the age of 16 engage in sexual activity. Securing convictions is also made more difficult by the impact of the processes of the adversarial system upon a child witness, and also by the child's fear to testify against the perpetrator, especially when this is a family member and coercion and fear have been used to secure the silence of the victim (Vizard *et al.* 1995; Paine and Hansen 2002). This is especially significant, as 'within-family' (intrafamilial) sex offences (either incestuous or by significant family others) are far more common than extrafamilial sex offences (Grubin 1998). The latter is known as 'stranger danger', but about 80 per cent of offences take place in the home of either the offender or the victim. The majority of perpetrators sexually assault children known to them, and some may find their victims outside the family, as in nurseries, schools, or youth clubs, or through involvement in substitute care. With the rise of the Internet and worldwide electronic communication, the sexual exploitation of children is also increasingly taking place by involving them in the production of pornography, which is then disseminated in either paper or electronic format. In The Netherlands, the police have been examining the nature of pornography on the Internet, and it is estimated that about 10 per cent of this relates to children (Grubin 1998; Michael *et al.* 2002; Quayle and Taylor 2003). In 2004, the police in the UK reported that they were blocking up to 20,000 pornographic images of children per day on the Internet.

In short, what we know about sex offending is that adult and child sexual abuse cuts across economic and class boundaries (Finkelhor and Baron 1986), and that the behaviour is so complex that, even now, we lack an adequate theoretical psychological, biological, sociological or other explanation (Quayle and Taylor 2003).

Profile of sex offending in England and Wales

It is well known that official statistics of convictions underestimate greatly the annual incidence of sex offences committed against adults and children (Grubin 1998). This can be for a number of reasons, but under-reporting and failure to achieve a conviction are the most prominent. At present, fewer than 6 per cent of allegations result in a conviction. Despite this, Table 5.1 demonstrates that overall convictions for sexual offences have doubled over the past decade.

What can be seen from Table 5.1 is that there are some offences that were not recorded at all 10 years ago, and there have also been changes in how crime is recorded. This is mainly due to changes

Table 5.1 Criminal convictions in England and Wales for sex offences recorded for 1996 and 2005/6

Offence	Recorded crime	
	1996	2005/6
Buggery	278	39
Indecent assault on a male	3,330	345
Sexual assault on males aged 13 and over	–	1,427
Sexual assault on a male child under 13	–	1,394
Rape of a female	5,759	61
Rape of females aged 16 and over	–	8,729
Rape of a female child under 16	–	3,152
Rape of a female child under 13	–	1,389
Rape of a female (total recorded)	**5,759**	**13,331**
Rape of a male	231	23
Rape of males aged 16 and over	–	440
Rape of a male child under 13	–	290
Rape of a male (total recorded)	**231**	**1,118**
Indecent assault on a female	17,643	1,120
Sexual assault on females aged 13 and over	–	17,171
Sexual assault on a female child under 13	–	4,645
Sexual activity with child under 13	–	1,942
Sexual activity with child under 16	–	3,281
Causing sexual activity without consent	–	742
Familial sexual offences	157	971
Sexual activity with a person with a mental disorder	–	139
Abuse of children through prostitution and pornography	–	125
Trafficking for sexual exploitation	–	33
Abuse of trust	–	463
Gross indecency with a child	1,215	127
Sexual grooming	–	238
Total sexual offences	**31,391**	**62,081**

(Source: Walker *et al.* 2006).

in legislation that introduced no less than 600 new offences through various criminal justice legislative initiatives, and this figure includes revisions as to what can be prosecuted as a sex offence, such as rape in marriage. There are also examples in which the sexual activity was ahead of the legislation, such as sexual grooming, which was being widely debated in the academic literature (see, for example, Finkelhor 1986; Salter 1998) but had not as yet become fully legally recognised as part of the premeditation and escalation associated with the sexual offence cycle (see Wolf 1985; Finkelhor 1986), especially as it is linked to Internet activity. However, it is also clear that in terms of frequency, the most serious and violent of offences are committed against females, including rape of females and sexual assault on females over 13, which together represent just under half of the total of sexual offences recorded over the period 2005/6.

Recent legislation

Until 1991, the law on sex offences was archaic. Much of it was contained in the Sexual Offences Act 1956. However, since 1991, attempts have been made to bring the legislation more in line with political initiatives on public protection and to reflect public attitudes more accurately with regard to sexual violence.

The Criminal Justice Act 1991 (Section 25) provides for sex offenders to serve 'terms of imprisonment longer than would be justified by the seriousness of the offence if it is considered necessary in the interests of the protection of the public', and this has, of course, stimulated a long-running debate on human rights. Perhaps less contentiously, Section 44 of the same Act extended post-release supervision of sex offenders to the end of their sentence.

The Sex Offenders Act 1997 focused upon the management of risk by identification and monitoring, including the introduction of the Sex Offender Register for a minimum period of 5 years. However, there are a number of problems with the Sex Offender Register. Offenders who committed sexual offences before 1997 do not have to register, it does not distinguish between predatory paedophiles and those who pose a minimal risk to the public – such as in the case in 2006 of a 23-year-old schoolteacher who engaged in sexual activity with a 15-year-old pupil who later became his wife – and there is no national sex offender register. While the compliance rate with notification is high (97 per cent), this still leaves around 300 sexual offenders at large and untracked by the authorities at any time, and the effectiveness of merely registering in terms of its deterrence value has been questioned, resulting in a number of highly publicised media campaigns demanding the introduction of Sarah's Law. Sarah's Law, proposed following the murder of Sarah Payne in 2001, would bring the Sex Offender Register into the public domain, so that convicted sex offenders living in the community could be identified. However, this move has so far been resisted, both because of the risk of scapegoating leading to public disorder, such as that seen in Portsmouth in 2000, when anti-paedophile protestors mistook paediatricians for paedophiles and because research evidence from the USA (Prentky 1996; Zevitz and Farkas 2000; Tewksbury 2005) suggests that allowing the names of convicted sex offenders living in the community to be released has negative consequences, simply driving their activities under the radar of the official monitoring activities.

The Crime and Disorder Act 1998 (Section 58), focusing upon the public protection agenda, gave powers to extend post-release supervision of sex offenders to a maximum of 10 years for a prison sentence of any length, and Section 2 introduced the Sex Offender Order. This order can be requested by the police for any sex offender in the community whose behaviour gives the police reasonable cause for concern.

The Sexual Offences Act 2003 was an attempt to write a cohesive body of law that reflects current knowledge about the settings and scenarios in which sex offending occurs, and to address the concerns of the public. The notification requirements for the register were strengthened and made easier to enforce, and new offences were created that widened the scope of existing ones, with an emphasis on the protection of vulnerable individuals from abuse and exploitation. Most significantly, rape was redefined to include penetration of the mouth as well as penetration of the vagina or anus by the penis, and consent was legally defined, as well as lack of consent, such that people were considered most unlikely to have agreed to sexual activity if they were subject to threats or fear of serious harm; were unconscious, drugged, or abducted; or were unable to communicate because of physical disability. In terms of child abuse, the Act closed a loophole that had allowed those accused of child rape to argue that the child had consented, and individuals who cause or encourage a child to engage in a sexual activity could also be prosecuted. Familial child sex offences would now cover assaults by not only blood relatives but also foster and adoptive parents and live-in partners.

The offence of abuse of a position of trust was amended to prohibit sexual contact between adults and children under 18 in schools, colleges and residential care, in order to protect vulnerable 16- and 17-year-olds. Defined as 'grooming', it became an offence for an adult to befriend children over the Internet with the intent to set up a meeting to abuse them, and a new civil, preventative order, the Risk of Sexual Harm Order, may be imposed that prohibits adults from engaging in, for example, sexual conversation with children online. The offence of voyeurism has been introduced, and behaviour that can be demonstrated to be preparatory to an offence has also been addressed, including administering drugs to people with the intent of sexually exploiting them. There are also new offences against trafficking people for the purposes of sexual exploitation.

In summary, therefore, a range of behaviours, involving both physical and non-physical contact, are now identified and proscribed, and a distinction has been made between children under 13 and those of 13 years and over. However, as children and young persons commit sexual crimes against other children, these offences apply not only to adults but also to persons under 18.

The context, range and legislative responses to sex offending in the UK having now been briefly established, there are two further important areas to explore, that of the causes of sex offending and that of the treatment of sex offenders.

Sexual violence and typology

While child and female perpetrators of sex offences make up a small proportion of offenders, the majority of sex offenders are adult males, and it is upon this group that much of research has been conducted.

There is no single cause of sex offending that has been identified, but psychologists have focused upon developing typologies for clinical applications, such as police profiles of the type of person who may have perpetrated an offence, or prison and probation programmes that target the characteristics underpinning and sustaining offending behaviour, and interventions striving to stop the behaviour and ensure that it does not escalate in frequency and seriousness.

While sexual offenders are a heterogeneous group, it has been shown to be useful to categorise them by the nature of the act. In terms of aggression, not all uses of violence are expressions of loss of control or inappropriate response, and this especially applies to sex offenders, in whom issues of 'power' and 'control need' are significant contributory factors to sexual assaults (Groth *et al.* 1977; Groth 1979).

Although much of this research was conducted in the 1970s, the premise that power needs drives much sexual offending is now widely accepted. Groth originally identified four categories of power and control needs that sex offenders display. Power-reassurance is classified as non-aggressive behaviour that serves the purpose of normalising an attack for offenders where the need is to restore their doubts about their desirability. Power-assertive behaviour is identified as aggressive but rarely lethal, showing no outward doubt of masculinity but serving the need to restore inner doubts and fears. Anger-retaliatory types display high levels of physical and sexual aggression that act as an outlet for feelings of pervasive and cumulative rage. In anger-excitation behaviour, pain and suffering inflicted on the victim heighten the offender's sexual pleasure.

Recognition of the differentiation of the types of power and control need that underpin sexual aggression has been adopted in the development of the Massachusetts Treatment Center Rapist Typology, Version 3 (MTC:R3), which is arguably the most empirically validated rapist typology in use today. Using this, Knight and Prentky (1987; 1990) demonstrated the following types of motivation underpinning rape offences.

Opportunistic and assertive

These rapes are impulsive, motivated by opportunity that may arise in the context of some other antisocial act, such as robbery or burglary. The desire is for immediate gratification, and deviant sexual arousal is uncommon, as is the use of gratuitous force or aggression. However, impulse control is a feature of all aspects of the lifestyle of the opportunistic/assertive rapist, as is a callous disregard for others generally and for the victim specifically. Non-assertive types generally exhibit the same offence profile but will be less socially competent, with a longer history of impulsiveness from adolescence.

Pervasively angry

These rapists are motivated by pervasive, non-sexualised anger, which may be linked to antisocial personality or psychopathic disorder. The offence is usually associated with extreme violence toward the victim. Sexual assault is only part of a pattern of generalised aggression in such an individual's lifestyle, and deviant sexual fantasies are unlikely to feature in the profile of this type of perpetrator.

Vindictive

Vindictive rapists appear to focus their anger exclusively on women. Non-assertive types use rape to humiliate and degrade women, selecting victims who appear assertive, independent or professional, and victim resistance is likely to escalate the violence. Assertive types will usually be in a relationship, and their aggression may be part of a profile of domestic violence, and the specific attack of rape may be associated with biting, cutting or tearing the body. Both non-assertive and assertive vindictive types show a lower level of impulsivity than opportunistic or angry types, and aggression is not eroticised.

Sexually motivated

This type of rapist, whether non-sadistic or sadistic, has sexual preoccupations which motivate the offending, and sex may be fused with aggression, dominance, coercion or feelings of inadequacy. Sadistic types do not always have fantasies but enjoy abusing victims and interpret victim resistance as a game. Those who have fantasies have well-rehearsed scenarios and play these out with the victim during the assault. Those who demonstrate sexual non-sadistic and non-assertive characteristics are most likely to have a power reassurance need to 'prove' their sexual prowess and adequacy to the victim, and they may fantasise that the victim will fall in love with them afterward. While being highly sexualised, they are most likely to flee in the face of resistance and have multiple cognitive-perceptual distortions of reality. Sexual non-sadistic assertive offenders are more socially assured and demonstrate fewer cognitive-perceptual distortions, but they are also predatory and most likely to stalk their victims before attack.

Overt sadists

Overt sadists have similar motivations to pervasively angry rapists, but their profile demonstrates that planning and premeditation are evident.

Muted sadistic types

Muted sadistic types mainly express sadism symbolically or in fantasy, and this type of motivation is linked to voyeuristic behaviour that may escalate to actual victim contact.

(Categories of the MTC:R3 have been adapted from the following sources: Briggs 1998; Holmes and Holmes 2002; Bartol and Bartol 2004).

Typology of child molesters

In addition to their work on the typology of rapists, Knight and Prentky (1990) proposed what is regarded as the most comprehensive, theory-driven typology of child molesters (Bickley and Beech 2001), known as the MTC:CM3 (Massachusetts Treatment Center Child Molester Typology, Version 3).

Knight and Prentky base their system on stable traits that have identifiable roots in childhood and in organising offenders into types on the basis of these characteristics. The MTC:CM3 has two main axes classified as degree of fixation and amount of contact with the victim. Fixated offenders never attain normalcy in relationships and always remain attracted to children, whereas non-fixated or regressed offenders are people who show the capacity to form appropriate peer relationships and sexual attachments but tend to regress after stresses of various kinds. Fixation is thought to become established at an earlier developmental stage, and the attraction of the perpetrator may most likely be toward prepubescent and/or pubescent children. The degree of fixation is classified as high or low and then differentiated as to high or low social competence. The amount of contact is classified as high or low, with high contact grouped into motivation as either interpersonal (the desire to be part of a relationship) or narcissistic (to service inner doubts and uncertainties), and low contact grouped into low- or high-physical injury and non-sadistic or sadistic behaviour. This theoretically yields 24 different types of child molesters, and from this Knight and Prentky claim that it is possible to identify developmental pathways for different types of abusers.

Bickley and Beech (2001), while acknowledging the significance of the contribution of Knight and Prentky, cite Hall (1996) and Fisher and Mair (1998) in suggesting that the level of complexity that their typology introduces may mean that its practical applications are somewhat limited, because the subtypes may not be clinically meaningful and the detailed information to assign an offender accurately to one of the subtypes may not be available to the clinician or practitioner. Despite that, the information that an offence may yield, as in high contact or low contact, and the degree of fixation may give relevant indications as to the type of offender that is being sought or the intensity of intervention that is appropriate.

A more accessible typology has been developed by Hudson and Ward (Ward and Hudson 1998; Ward *et al.* 1998) who, using grounded theory, have developed what is called a self-regulation model, which classifies offenders into one of four groups identified by 'individual goal toward deviant sex' (Bickley and Beech 2001: 63). These translate into four pathways with distinct clusters of cognitive, affective and behaviour offence variables.

Bickley and Beech (2001) claim to have provided independent support for the Hudson and Ward framework by demonstrating that

> when compared with avoidant-goal offenders, the approach-goal offenders reported significantly higher levels of cognitive distortions regarding children, demonstrated higher levels of emotional congruence with children, and reported more distortions about the impact of the abuse on their victim. (Bickley and Beech 2001: 64)

If it is assumed that pathways indicate how, through treatment, the behaviour could be disrupted, such a typology has important applications in developing cognitive behavioural programmes of intervention.

However, in terms of validity, both the Prentky and Knight and the Hudson and Ward typologies have methodological weaknesses and cannot fully explain why motivations and behaviours transcend different offender categories. It is therefore not possible to state confidently their wider applications to the offence group (Fisher and Mair 1998), and, overall, the agreement is that there is no single causal explanation for sexual offending. However, a number of integrated theories based on studies of sex offenders in North America have influenced much of the work undertaken in the UK.

Integrated theory and the sexual cycle of offending

Integrated theory is based on the premise that sex offences appear to be best explained by previous learning linked to disturbed sexual and emotional life experience(s) that result in distorted self-perception and cognition, leading to an identifiable cycle of offending that Wolf (1985) linked to a form of addictive behaviour.

Marshall and Barbaree (1990) first proposed an integrated theory, which used developmental and learning theory to explain sexual offending. It is argued that an individual has failed to understand sexual norms, has not learnt to control natural impulses, and confuses sex and aggression. These factors plus 'opportunity' are likely to result in an offence. This is probably most useful in explaining sex offending among people who also have learning difficulties, and it generally led the way to further work on developmental pathways to sex offending.

Another integrated theory of influence was presented by Wolf (1985). He claimed that an individual's early history leads to the development of a type of personality that predisposes to development of deviant sexual interests whereby egocentricity and low self-esteem lead to a poor self-image, resulting in defensiveness and distorted thinking. Distorted cognitions then trigger obsessive thinking and behaviour, exacerbating social alienation and sexual preoccupation. Wolf's explanation of offending thus begins with poor self-image, rejection and withdrawal into pleasant sexual fantasies, and planning and commission of the offence, resulting in guilt, which reinforces low self-esteem, and so on, into a cycle that becomes addictive and compulsive. The typologies are useful here in assessing the degree of disturbance.

The cycle of sexual offending behaviour includes how the offender plans and fantasises, targets and grooms his victims, and what the triggers and thinking sequences are, and it enables the idea that the offence 'just happened' to be challenged (Spencer 1999: 95). Throughout the process of the cycle, distorted thinking allows the offender to justify or legitimise his acts, excuse himself, or transfer blame to someone else. The speed at which the cycle progresses varies enormously: For some, there may be lengthy gaps between offences acts (up to 20 years or more); for others, lengthy planning periods are followed very quickly by the offence, while others demonstrate an escalation in frequency and seriousness of crimes, the length of time reducing between each offence.

Hilary Eldridge (1992) argued that sex offenders of whatever type display one of two basic cycles, depending on their attitudes, beliefs and motivations. She has described them as continuous or inhibited. The continuous cycle runs through from fantasy rehearsal to fantasy reinforced by the act of abuse. These offenders have belief systems which legitimise their abuse and which may be interrupted only by the risk of getting caught, with few concerns about the effects upon the victim or their own self-image.

The inhibited cycle might run through the whole cycle. These offenders have concerns about the effects upon themselves and the harm to the victim, and they do have internal inhibitors that act as brakes some of the time. Thoughts which legitimise their offending and fantasy, however, only add to an excuse to offend. They often deny any planning to offend, having made a whole range of 'apparently irrelevant decisions' leading to the opportunity to abuse.

Eldridge also suggests that some offenders can operate both types of cycles at the same time. Thus, incest with their own child might demand the inhibited cycle, while sexual activity with an older stepdaughter may be seen as acceptable and thus continuous in process. 'Short-circuiting' can occur at any stage of the cycle. For example, as the need for planning, targeting and grooming becomes less of a requirement, as in incest abuse, and bribes and threats take less time to carry out, the victim is well rehearsed as to what a special look or a brief verbal threat actually means.

In 1984, Finkelhor and his colleagues, studying research related to child sexual abuse, identified four factors or preconditions which they claim must exist before sexual abuse can take place. Although related to the child abuser, it is also used as a model for rapists. The model of child sexual abuse describes the process of child sexual offending as well as the characteristics of the offenders, drawing on the literature which suggests that underlying attitudes and beliefs (which may be acquired in childhood) are significant contributory factors to sexual abuse occurring.

Finkelhor's four preconditions for sexual abuse (adapted from Finkelhor 1986)

1. Motivation to abuse: arising out of the attitudes and beliefs that stimulate the desire to abuse, including attitudes to women, power, male sexuality, sexual knowledge, and child–adult relationships linked to masturbation and fantasy.

2. Overcoming internal inhibitors against acting on that motivation: ways in which the offenders convince themselves that their behaviour is reasonable by rationalising cognitions and also substances, such as alcohol, that act as disinhibitors.

3. Overcoming external inhibitors to committing sexual abuse: the manipulation and grooming of environments (workplace, social situations, home) and others (partners, caretaker adults, employers) in order to gain access to the victim.

4. Undermining or overcoming the child's resistance to the sexual abuse: using a range of strategies from the very subtle (seduction, bribery) to aggression and force (abduction, threat) over periods of time.

Distinctive in the integrated theories and associated models of offending is the link between a sexual offender's own past and becoming a sexual offender. Given the emphasis on early developmental pathways in integrated theories, the experience of child sexual abuse could be expected to demonstrate disruption in the learning of social norms and the distorted thinking associated with becoming a perpetrator. Studying the prevalence of child sexual abuse among those who had themselves gone on to abuse sexually Dhawan and Marshall (1996), relying mainly on self-reports, found the prevalent rate of sexual abuse of their sample was high (46 per cent) when compared with the general population, and reports of sexual abuse were much higher among the sex offender prison population (58 per cent) than the non-sex offender inmates (20 per cent). Other studies (Cooper *et al.* 1996) indicate that offenders who were sexually abused as children began their offending at an earlier age, had more victims, were likely to abuse both males and females, and tended to show more psychopathology and personal problems.

However, the evidence is contradictory, and a meta-analysis (Hanson and Bussiere 1998) examining predictors of sexual recidivism concluded that being sexually abused as a child was not associated with an increased risk of becoming a perpetrator. Supporting this are studies using polygraph testing (Hindman and Peters 2001; Grubin and Madsen 2006) that demonstrate that sexual offenders' self-reports of their behaviour and previous sexual history are unreliable, as they tend to minimise the history of their own abusive behaviour and to overstate their own histories of victimisation. With this group of offenders, therefore, theory supported by studies which rely upon self-reports needs to be treated with caution, and this casts some doubt upon early developmental pathways as the sole explanation for the development of deviant sexual behaviour.

There are also several criticisms of the models that are generated from integrated theory. A critique (Ward and Hudson 2001) of Finkelhor's model states that it suffers from vagueness and contains overlapping constructs. This is not dissimilar to the methodological difficulties identified with typologies and confirms the complexity of attempting to theorise a group of offenders whose behaviour may be rooted in differential social, psychological and biological processes, and that just as there is no single cause of sex offending, there is no typical sex offender. This will inevitably mean that individual differences in this group will consistently highlight flaws in the explanatory theory and associated treatment approaches.

Biological and evolutionary explanations of sexual aggression

Biological perspectives focus on sexual aggression as a form of deviant behaviour based on underlying biological processes linked to hormonal secretions and the nervous system. Hormonally, sex and aggression are linked to male androgens (e.g. testosterone), which are the chemicals involved in sexual development and arousal. Early medical explanations suggested that because testosterone was a main factor in sexual aggression, it could be dealt with by physical castration.

Surgical castration requires the removal of a man's testosterone-producing testicles, but, as Taylor (2002) points out, sexual desire is not directly linked to reproductive ability, and testosterone is also excreted by the adrenal glands. Medication referred to as 'chemical castration' swiftly superseded surgical castration.

Chemical castration involves the injection of anti-androgen drugs into the body to reduce a man's testosterone levels, as practised in some parts of the world, including the USA. Harrison (2005) suggests, however, that this type of intervention only works with certain classes of sex offenders, and that

> Most of the research shows effectiveness only for those offenders who are classed as paedophiles and to be more specific, it is probably only useful for those who are preferential paedophiles – those who have sexual relationships with children and never adults. (Harrison 2005: 26)

Studies also suggest that if maximum effectiveness is to be achieved, even in this limited group, chemical castration must be used in combination with psychotherapy or some other form of counselling that addresses those aspects identified in the development of integrated theory as sustaining the behaviour, such as distorted perceptions, denial, minimisation and attitudes to children. Biological perspectives alone, therefore, do not appear to be able to explain comprehensively the sexual aggression linked to sex-offending behaviours, and castration, physical or chemical, is only a partial and limited response to managing the risks posed by sex offenders.

Interventions and effectiveness

The value base of working with sex offenders is the belief that sexual abuse involves the abuse of power in all cases and the abuse of trust in most cases. Sexually abusive behaviour is not an illness and therefore cannot be 'cured'. It is however behaviour over which abusers can learn to exercise control, and thus the work is approached with a belief in the capacity for people to change. (Briggs 1998: 15)

During the 1970s, surgical (castration and lobotomy) and psychoanalytic interventions were increasingly replaced by drug treatments. By the 1980s, most treatments were cognitive-behavioural and based on the developing integrated theories and multifactorial explanations discussed above. Psychologists have also made substantial advances in clearly identifying factors that increase an offender's risk of committing an offence after release. These factors include the number of offences, intimacy deficits, sexual preoccupations and age (Hanson 2000).

In 1992, the Home Office commissioned a three-stage Sex Offender Treatment Evaluation Project, the STEP Project (Beckett *et al.* 1994). This was the first major study of the effectiveness of community-based programmes in England and Wales, including six probation programmes and one private residential programme.

A 2-year follow-up published in October 1996 concluded that focused, systematic and properly evaluated interventions can reduce further victimisation. Beckett *et al.* (1994) noted that most programmes in the UK focused on four main elements, drawing their underpinning knowledge from integrated theory and sexual cycles of abuse. These four elements identified were as follows:

- altering patterns of deviant arousal;
- correcting distorted thinking;
- increasing social competence;
- educating offenders about the effects of abuse.

Two further key issues were also identified, these being amenability to treatment and the timing of the intervention. Research demonstrated that attempting to challenge sex offenders' beliefs about the impact of their offending on others before they are able to cope with the recognition of what they have done may push them further into denial and minimisation and actually reduce the development of victim empathy (Beckett *et al.* 1994).

New developments have also been made in the cognitive-behavioural approach focusing upon cognitive distortions, that is, the deep-rooted pro-offending attitudes, where positive correlations have been made between external attributions and offence-supporting attitudes (Blumentahl *et al.* 1999). Schema-based therapy has also been used to identify underlying cognitive schemes in order to address patterns in beliefs and attitudes and overcome dysfunctional self-talk associated with dysfunctional schemas (Mann and Shingler 1999). Relapse prevention is based upon a self-regulation model and uses self-regulatory deficits (see typology and self-regulation model) to account for the diversity in pathways to offending, such as approach-goal/avoidant-goal motivations (Bickley and Beech 2002).

On the basis of such research and the outcomes of the STEP evaluation of effectiveness, the development of national sex offender treatment programmes was authorised for England and Wales, to be overseen by the joint Correctional Services Accreditation Panel, whose brief it was to ensure that interventions delivered by the statutory sector were based upon agreed, evidence-based theoretical and delivery principles, demonstrated as being those most likely to affect recidivism.

A range of programmes are available, based on cognitive-behavioural approaches, to reduce offending by child and adult male sex offenders. These may also include provision of support to partners of perpetrators. These include:

- Community Sex Offender Group Programme (C-SOGP);
- Thames Valley Sex Offender Group Programme (TV-SOGP);
- Northumbria Sex Offender Group Programme (N-SOGP);
- Prison Services Sex Offender Treatment Programme (SOTP): family of programmes.

These programmes have in common that they address the different levels of risks and range of behaviours associated with sex offending and challenge the thinking patterns used by offenders to excuse and justify their actions, while developing victim empathy. They aim to teach new attitudes and behaviour related to positive offence-free living.

The SOTP (prison) programme has 86 sessions, which are run 2–5 times a week. The adapted programme of 85 sessions is designed for those with learning difficulties. There is also an extended programme (70 additional sessions) for high-risk sex offenders, a booster programme (32 sessions) for those who have previously completed the core programme and are preparing for release, and a rolling programme for low-risk sex offenders.

An evaluation of the attitudinal effectiveness of the SOTP (prison) (Beech *et al.* 1999; 2002) claimed success in increasing the level of disclosure of child abusers, reducing denial in pro-offending attitudes, enhancing victim awareness, and improving social competence, with 67 per cent (*n* = 77) of the sample judged to have shown a treatment effect in the main areas targeted. Longer treatment for highly deviant offenders showed an improved retention of attitudinal change after release.

An evaluation of reconviction effectiveness of the TC-SOGP (Bates *et al.* 2004) concludes that the structured cognitive-behavioural approach addressing known factors of behavioural cycles of sex offending resulted, over a 3.9-year follow-up, in a reduction in recidivism from an expected 9 per cent (over 2 years) to 5.5 per cent (*n* = 183).

Measuring effectiveness by recidivism rates is particularly problematic with sex offenders, as they have low reconviction rates when compared to other offenders. Some sex offenders are not reconvicted for the first time until over 20 years after completing a prison sentence (Barker and Morgan 1993), and recidivism rates for sex offenders have been found to have doubled from 11 per cent to 22 per cent when measured between 5 and 22 years rather than the conventional 2-year follow-up. There is also the issue that while reconviction may be low (as compared to non-sexual offending), the offences, when committed, can be of an extremely serious nature (Hood *et al.* 2002), and this factor makes release and parole decisions even more difficult.

Cognitive-behavioural work has also not been so successful in reducing recidivism in rapists and exhibitionists, and this may relate to the lack of amenability as well as to the level of entrenched behaviour. Harrison (2005) concludes that England and Wales do not currently appear to have an effective intervention to reduce the threat posed by high-risk, highly deviant sex offenders.

Programmes offered to and adapted for people with learning difficulties have also not worked well, possibly because they operate at a cognitive-behavioural level beyond the learning difficulty. For this group of offenders, monitoring and reducing the risk of opportunity appears to be the most effective strategy to date (Scottish Office 1997).

A review of Sex Offender Treatment Programmes undertaken at the Department of Psychology, Broadmoor Hospital (Perkins *et al.* 1998), concluded that evaluation of the effectiveness of sex offender programmes remains problematic methodologically in addressing the full range of criminogenic needs (those dynamic needs that can be affected by intervention, unlike static factors such as age) and risk factors relating to sex offending. It commends the SOTP (prison) for addressing important individual differences between sex offenders' risk factors and treatment needs, but it calls for further idiographic analyses to highlight the effect of treatment–offender interactions on treatment impact and outcome.

Risk prediction and management

> Psychologists are essentially being asked to determine what level of risk an individual poses to a community even though there is no definitive way to know for certain … They're being asked to balance that risk with the individual liberty concerns of an offender. Science has come up with tools to help them, but it's still a huge responsibility and a terrible burden. (Kersting 2004: 52).

There are a range of empirically driven actuarial assessment tools available for working with sex offenders that can be used for before and after intervention evaluation. These range from knowledge and attitudinal questionnaires, cognitive distortion scales, self-esteem inventories and actuarial risk calculators. The best known of these is Thornton's (1997) Structured Anchored Clinical Judgement Scale (SACJ), which uses a step-wise approach, and Risk Matrix 2000 (Thornton 2002; Thornton *et al.* 2003), developed as a revision of the SACJ, which has separate indicators for risk of sexual recidivism, non-sexual assault and overall violence.

However, while it is widely accepted that actuarial prediction outperforms clinical judgement, prediction in general, and of sexual aggression, in particular, is an extremely difficult task due to the complex and multifactorial nature of this type of crime (Borum 1996). It throws up the possibility of false positives or false negatives, and, as Craig *et al.* (2004) point out, using actuarial tools is also problematic, because 'To predict relatively rare (low base rate) events, such as sexual offences, increases the possibility of making false positive errors too high' (8).

A false outcome in actuarial risk assessment may also mean that the offender is not subjected to the intensity of treatment and intervention that may avert a future offence. There is also no such thing as static risk; it changes over time, place and circumstances, and actuarial risk tools are actually rather limited in the ways in which they can capture risk dynamic systems (Craig *et al.* 2004). As risk management depends on being able to identify the risk posed at any given point in time, the involvement of clinical interpretation of actuarial scores and changes in offender attitudes and behaviour is essential.

Risk-management planning requires an understanding of what motivates the offender, such as the meeting of emotional needs through the abuse of a child or, as with sadistic offenders, arousal through pain and suffering to the extent that the issue of 'consent' becomes irrelevant (a sadistic offender will probably not even bother to lie about the consent issue). The Finkelhor model is a useful tool in this respect because it distinguishes between motivational and maintenance factors, but because it is linear in design, it is limited in the ways in which the addictive nature of sexual offending can be explored with, and explained to, the offender. It is only after high-risk situations have been identified that interventions can be designed to train offenders to use ways to minimise lapses and keep them from evolving into full-blown relapses.

Managing the risk presented by sex offenders is usually undertaken through multiagency arrangements such as Multi-Agency Public Protection Panels (MAPPP) and the associated Multi-Agency Public Protection Arrangements (MAPPA), which, by actuarial and clinical assessment, categorise offenders into low-, medium- or high-risk groups, with associated intensity of intervention. It is recognised that there is no such thing as 'no risk', especially where sex offending is concerned.

There have of course been some spectacular failures in risk management because of the flaws in both assessment and organisational processes. After the murder of John Monckton in 2004 by Damien Hanson soon after he had been released early from a 12-year sentence, an investigation was ordered on what was perceived as a catalogue of failures by probation and police risk-management procedures. This concluded that nearly four out of ten serious sexual and violent offenders released from prison on licence were being freed without being screened for their risk to the public (HM Inspectorate of Probation 2006). Such failures put the spotlight on the Home Office and the statutory agencies, organisational arrangements, and decision-making skills required for the release for such offenders.

Notwithstanding the difficulties already noted in arriving at an accurate risk assessment, perhaps one of the most entrenched problems underpinning disastrous outcomes in risk management lies in the nature of multiagency working. This is notoriously problematic, and it is not uncommon for collaborative arrangements to become dysfunctional because of festering unresolved disputes due to clashes in philosophy, blurred roles, lack of clear management, and resource issues (RCP 2005). If the National Offender Management Service arrangements for end-to-end management of offenders are to be realised, this factor will need to be resolved with the enhanced training and clarity in resource streams that have been shown to improve practice and risk-management outcomes significantly in multiagency working (Offender Health Care Strategies 2005).

Conclusion

Psychologists consider individuals as a complex system of related facets based in cognition (thinking), affect (feeling) and behaviour operating in a social context. Psychological explanations and interventions developed around these core features of personality and functioning have made a significant contribution to the theory base upon which programmes to address sexual violence and sex offending are modelled. However, the most consistent finding is that this heterogeneous group require a multifaceted theoretical and intervention approach, and the literature continues to confirm that while approaches to the theorising and treatment of sex offenders have made enormous strides in the past two decades, the explanatory framework remains incomplete.

These gaps in the knowledge base inevitably have an impact on the effectiveness of treatment and risk management of sex offenders in all aspects of professional work, and, in this respect, criticism of hard-working and dedicated professionals serves only to exacerbate the problem rather than to resolve it. Further research using rigorous methodological approaches, and following up with a critical and constructive approach on the failures, as well as the successes, is more likely to generate new, and refine existing, resources.

Chapter 6

Insanity, mental health and the criminal justice system

Introduction

' "How dangerous is it that this man go loose?" was the question that Shakespeare asked in *Hamlet* and still today "remains the question to which the courts, lawyers, mental health professionals and the general public all want to know the answer" ' (Hucker 2005).

When a person with mental health problems (such as schizophrenia or a personality disorder) commits an offence that comes to the attention of the criminal justice system, a number of related concerns come to the fore. The first is the question of culpability. Are the mentally ill culpable for their actions? If not, is treatment the only proper response to a possibly horrific event? If so, what type of punishment is suitable? Or should we combine punishment with treatment? Are they antisocial by choice or by virtue of a clinically diagnosable mental health problem? A second issue is that of risk: do mentally disordered offenders pose higher risks to themselves or others as a result of their mental health problem?

The constitutional justification for punishment is that an individual is blameworthy, but an individual's insanity means that he or she is legally blameless, for he or she cannot possess '*mens rea*', a guilty mind. Furthermore, since punishment cannot have any of its intended individual or societal effects of rehabilitation, deterrence or retribution on a mentally disturbed person, it is irrelevant and arguably a miscarriage of justice to punish them: if they are sick or need help.

However, there are crimes that are so heinous, such as paedophilia, that the behaviour is often assumed to be underpinned by some mental deficit: 'they must be mad'. Moreover, mentally disordered offending and violent or sex offending are often placed side by side. This conflates mental illness with risk and dangerousness and therefore implies that people who commit appalling acts must almost by definition be insane.

This chapter aims to explore these assumptions by looking at types of mental illness and asking whether these predispose individuals to undesirable behaviours that may be perceived as antisocial but are only in relatively rare instances a clinical indicator and/or predictor of risk to others. However, it cannot be ruled out that people with mental illness may be in dire need of sustained and intensive medical support and may be far more likely to pose a risk to themselves than others by, for example, being unable to manage their treatment regime independently.

The strength of using a psychological perspective lies in the attempt to cut through stereotyping, bias and shared assumptions in order to lay bare the case for what is known and can be objectively demonstrated in mental health research. This will be used to inform the debate on the tired and yet ever-popular theme of whether disordered behaviour stems from being 'mad', 'bad' or 'dangerous', the three well-known paradigms in which this group is so often represented in the public domain.

Types of mental disorder

Psychiatrists have developed systems to classify mental disorders that describe the kinds of symptoms and behaviour commonly seen among those considered to be mentally disordered. These fall into three main groups: personality disorders, psychoses and neuroses. While some forms of personality disorder, such as sociopathy and psychopathy, and some forms of psychosis, such as schizophrenia, may make a small, independent contribution to the risk of offending, it is much more likely that other forms will be concomitant with, but not necessarily contributory to, offending behaviour (Badger *et al*. 1999).

In debating the classifications of mental disorder under three main groups, a word of caution is in order. Mental disorders can vary greatly in their symptoms, severity, course, outcome and amenability to treatment. Each of these disorders has subcategories, and the presenting features can vary in their severity. They can adversely and to differing degrees affect any and every aspect of a person's life, including enjoyment, mood, attitudes, occupation, career, sexual functioning, family and marital life, other interpersonal relations, and the management of financial affairs (Davison *et al.* 2004). To complicate matters further, there remains tension in the medical disciplines not only with regard to the exact diagnosis in individual cases but also as to whether some disorders actually exist as independent categories. We will discuss these in three broad categories in order to weave a path through a complex maze and draw out key attributes.

Personality disorder

Personality disorders are demonstrated in many forms, and the symptoms tend to exhibit themselves slowly over a number of years and have been attributed in part to distorted environmental influences in the socialisation process. They are the most problematic to diagnose, as in milder examples the individual may simply appear to have slightly exaggerated or eccentric behaviour. However, this is the most common type of mental disorder to be addressed by the court during the sentencing process (Badger *et al.* 1999) and the one most likely to be present in remand and sentenced prisoners (Singleton *et al.* 1998). In severe cases, it affects the person's ability to lead a normal life and is associated with antisocial behaviour and problems in all aspects of life. The fixed and rigid nature of these personality traits and the behaviour and attitudes associated with them may cause considerable distress to others if not to the individuals themselves.

Personality disorder is most easily understood when grouped into three types by symptoms; the first group comprises symptoms associated with odd and eccentric behaviour; the second group, those of dramatic, emotional or erratic behaviour; and the third group, those of anxious and fearful behaviour.

Odd and eccentric behaviour – schizoid, paranoid and schizotypal

In the first group of odd and eccentric behaviour is schizoid, paranoid and schizotypal personality disorder. According to the DSM-IV (1994: 638), the essential feature of the schizoid personality disorder 'is a pervasive pattern of detachment from social relationships and a restricted range of expression of emotions in interpersonal settings.' These individuals appear to lack a desire for intimacy, and are introverted, withdrawn and emotionally cold. They spend most of their time alone by choice and select activities that do not include interaction with others. Kalus (1995: 58) argues that the schizoid personality disorder is distinguished by the predominance of negative symptoms associated with the schizophrenia spectrum disorders, that is, social, interpersonal, and affective deficits without psychotic-like cognitive/perceptual distortions.

The paranoid personality is typified by undue suspicion and mistrust, considering others to be disloyal, deceitful and untrustworthy, and this may result in outbursts of anger. The rigidity of belief found in individuals with paranoid personality disorder makes them particularly resistant to corrective feedback, such as social cues or targeted intervention, meaning that they are prone to increasing distortions of reality. Paranoid personality disorder may first appear in childhood and adolescence associated with solitariness, poor peer relationships, hypersensitivity, peculiar thoughts and idiosyncratic fantasies. There is some evidence (DSM-IV 1994: 636–7) of increased prevalence of paranoid personality disorder in individuals with relatives who have a delusional disorder. The prevalence of paranoid personality disorder is estimated to be 2–10 per cent in outpatient mental health clinics and in clinical samples, it appears to be more common in males (DSM-IV 1994: 636–7).

Schizotypal disorders show a 'pervasive pattern of social and interpersonal deficits marked by acute discomfort with, and reduced capacity for, close relationships as well as by cognitive or perceptual distortions and eccentricities of behaviour' (DSM-IV 1994: 641). In general, the symptoms are marked by disconnected thought, speech, perception and behaviour. Individuals with schizotypal disorders may react inappropriately or not react at all, leading to consistently confusing social cues. Kantor (1992) notes that the inappropriateness of affect may result from missing a primary idea and reacting to a secondary or peripheral matter. Thus, the more irrelevant or peripheral the focus, the more unusual (and interpersonally disconcerting) the affective and cognitive responses will be (Kantor 1992: 78–84).

Dramatic, emotional or erratic behaviour – sociopaths, psychopaths and others

In the second group are antisocial personality disorder, borderline personality disorder and narcissistic disorder.

Antisocial personality disorder is associated with people who act out their conflicts and fail to observe socially accepted norms. A popular term for this type of individual is 'sociopath'. These individuals may be impulsive, irresponsible and callous, and the behaviour is frequently linked to infringements of the law, although not necessarily violence. It is said, for example (perhaps in jest), that, for sociopaths, the ability to commit fraud is a job skill, a core competency – this does not mean that sociopaths are responsible for all fraud, but that their particular mindset means they are exceptionally good at it.

Although the diagnosis of antisocial personality disorder is limited to those over 18 years of age, it usually involves a history of antisocial behaviour before the age of 15 with a pattern of lying, truancy, delinquency, substance abuse and running away from home (DSM-IV 1994: 301). The psychoanalytic explanation of sociopathy is that these individuals remain fixed in earlier levels of development, as often associated with this diagnosis is a history of parental rejection and/or indifference where needs for satisfaction and security have not been met. As a result of this, psychoanalytic theory holds that the ego, which controls urges between conscience and impulses, is underdeveloped. Behaviour is usually id directed due to this lack of ego strength, with a resulting need for immediate gratification of desires. An immature superego allows the individual to pursue gratification regardless of the means and without experiencing any feelings of guilt. Functioning has also been implicated as an important doctrine in determining whether an individual develops this disorder (DSM-IV 1994: 301).

Psychopathy is a concept subject to much debate, but is usually defined, at its most extreme, as a constellation of affective, interpersonal, and behavioural characteristics, including egocentricity, impulsivity, irresponsibility, shallow emotions, lack of empathy, guilt or remorse, pathological lying, manipulativeness, and the persistent violation of social norms and expectations (Hare 1999). Most psychopaths are antisocial personalities but not all antisocial personalities are psychopaths (Hare 1999). Connor (n.d.) suggests that psychopaths are the most dangerous to others, being 'natural-born intraspecies predators who satisfy their lust for power and control by charm, manipulation, intimidation, and violence'. Buchanan (2006), looking at 425 discharged patients over a 10-year period, found that those more likely to reoffend were classed as suffering from psychopathic disorder (see also Moran and Hagell 2001; Hare 2002). It would appear, therefore, that it is from within this small group, comprising individuals functioning at the extreme edge of what is possible, that we can identify the source of some of the fear arising from the danger thought to be posed generally by mentally disordered offenders.

Borderline personality disorder should not be confused with doubt as to whether a personality disorder exists or not. The symptoms observable are linked to instability in interpersonal relationships, behaviour, mood, and self-image. This may be exhibited as abrupt and extreme mood changes, stormy interpersonal relationships, an unstable and fluctuating self-image, and unpredictable and self-destructive actions. Linehan (1993), who developed a cognitive-behavioural intervention for this group, theorises that those with borderline personality are born with an innate biological tendency to react more intensely to lower levels of stress than others and to take longer to recover. They also peak 'higher' emotionally on less provocation and take longer to recover. In addition, there is some evidence to suggest that during early developmental stages they are more likely to have been reared in environments in which their beliefs about themselves were continually devalued and invalidated. These factors are hypothesised to combine to create adults who are uncertain of the truth of their own feelings and are in a continual state of internal psychological conflict.

In contrast, those with narcissistic personality disorder have an exaggerated sense of their own self-importance, with fantasies of unlimited success, which may be associated with attention seeking, mood swings, numerous somatic illnesses and exploitative personal relationships. The essential feature of the narcissistic personality disorder is a 'pervasive pattern of grandiosity, need for admiration, and lack of empathy' (DSM-I 1994: 658). Individuals with narcissistic personality disorder may show little real ability outside their fantasies. They can become self-destructive because their grandiosity and self-preoccupation impair their judgement and perspective, and in the most severe cases they can experience such inappropriate rage in response to someone diminishing their sense of superiority that they attack and attempt to destroy the source of criticism (Oldham 1990: 93–5). However, Kantor (1992: 207) argues that these individuals can sustain good judgement if they demand a performance of themselves that vindicates their self-esteem and that competent individuals are often in positions of authority themselves.

Anxious and fearful behaviour

In the third group, linked to anxious and fearful behaviour, is avoidant, dependent, and obsessive-compulsive personality disorder. The essential feature of avoidant personality disorder is a pervasive pattern of social inhibition, feelings of inadequacy and hypersensitivity to negative evaluation (DSM-IV 1994: 662). Such individuals believe that they are personally unappealing and interpersonally inadequate. They describe themselves as ill at ease, anxious and sad. They are lonely, and they feel unwanted and isolated. Individuals with avoidant personality disorder are introspective and self-conscious and they typically refer to themselves with contempt (Millon and Davis 1996: 263). The essential feature of the dependent personality disorder is an all-encompassing and excessive need to be taken care of that results in submissive and clinging behaviour. They fear separation and they engage in dependent behaviour to elicit care-giving (DSM-IV 1994: 665).

Both normal and personality-disordered individuals can exhibit strong dependency-related needs; it is the way these needs are expressed that distinguishes the two. Personality-disordered individuals tend to express dependency needs in a more uncontrolled and maladaptive manner. The pathological manifestations of dependency needs include 'intense fears of abandonment, passive, helpless behaviours in intimate relationships and phobic symptoms aimed at minimizing separation' (Bornstein and Costello, 1996: 123–32). Bornstein and Costello (1996: 124–5) suggest that genetic factors account for a relatively small proportion of the variability in dependency levels, and that the parent/child relationship appears to be the major causal factor in the development of dependent personality traits. They argue that two parenting styles can be identified as leading to high levels of dependency: authoritarian parenting and overprotective parenting. The consequences of these two types of parenting are the development of belief that the dependent individuals cannot function without the guidance and protection of others, and that the way to maintain relationships is to acquiesce to requests, expectations and demands.

Obsessive-compulsive personality disorder is a preoccupation with orderliness, perfectionism and control at the expense of flexibility, openness and efficiency. Individuals with obsessive-compulsive personality disorder are conscientious, self-critical, scrupulous, and inflexible about morality, ethics and values. They may force both themselves and others to follow rigid moral principles and very high standards of performance. They are deferential to authority and rules; they insist on literal compliance, regardless of circumstances (DSM-IV 1994: 669–70); and, apart from, perhaps, being very difficult to live with, they are very unlikely to come to the attention of the law.

It is clear that while 'personality disorder' has become a catch-all phrase, the different ways in which it is manifested demonstrate that it is highly unlikely that the majority of the behaviours will be associated with offending. Many a true word being spoken in jest, it is often claimed that highly successful entrepreneurs and politicians can be observed to share the traits of the sociopath, and eccentricity is tolerated when linked with high achievement; take, for example, Howard Hughes or Greta Garbo. Psychopaths, on the other hand, are likely to lead apparently normal lives and present a normal self-image; it is the fact that some within this group are those rare individuals who can lie and kill without remorse that constitutes the exception to the rule that most people with mental disorder are not dangerous to others. When children develop the ability to deceive, normally around the age of 3–4 they also develop the ability to empathise. In psychopaths, it is argued, this does not happen, and therefore they have no moral compass.

For example, in 1999, Alan Grimson, who had had a successful naval career serving on the *Hermes, Invincible, Ark Royal* and *Illustrious*, was convicted of the torture, mutilation and subsequent murder of Nicholas Wright in 1997 and Sion Jenkins in 1998. He was diagnosed as a psychopath because of not only the horrific and violent nature of his crimes but also his ability to continue to perform in his job and to make friends. He was able to describe coldly to the police the precise emotions of thrill and power he had experienced during the first murder and his disappointment that the second murder had not replicated those feelings. He was described in court as evil beyond belief, but friends and colleagues had thought him to be a good guy. The legal term 'dangerous and severe personality disorder' (DSPD) has no medical equivalent, but is currently part of a sentencing package, and it is presumably at these few that the label is targeted.

Psychosis – a break with reality

Psychosis describes mental disturbance that involves an actual break with reality, with distorted perceptions and irrational behaviour, often accompanied by hallucinations and delusions. These are the defining features of schizophrenia, schizophreniform disorder, schizoaffective disorder, delusional disorder, and the psychotic disorders.

Schizophrenia is a disease of the brain that is linked to thought disorder, delusions, hallucinations, and problems with feelings, behaviour, motivation and speech. The diagnostic criteria distinguish between paranoid, hebephrenic, catatonic, undifferentiated, post-schizophrenic depression, residual schizophrenia and simple schizophrenia.

Approximately one in 100 individuals develops schizophrenia. Most of these individuals present as young adults between the ages of 15 and 25; however, schizophrenia may develop at any age. Men and women from all cultures are equally likely to develop schizophrenia, although there is a tendency for men to develop the disorder slightly earlier in their lives than women. It presents in three stages, the prodormal state, the active state and the residual state (NHS n.d.).

During the prodromal state, it is not uncommon for a number of non-specific symptoms to be present in the weeks or months preceding the first onset of typical symptoms of schizophrenia, particularly in young people. These symptoms are incapacitating and include loss of interest, isolation, including avoidance of work or study, irritability, odd beliefs, and odd behaviour, such as talking to oneself in public and hearing voices. The length of the prodromal phase is extremely variable, and the prognosis is less favourable when the prodromal phase has had a lengthy course (NHS n.d.).

During the active phase of the illness, psychotic symptoms such as delusions and hallucinations are prominent and are often accompanied by odd behaviour and strong affect such as distress, anxiety, depression and fear. If untreated, the active phase can resolve independently or it may continue indefinitely. Treatment, usually in the form of medication, can bring the active phase under control.

The active phase of the illness is usually followed by a residual phase, and while psychotic symptoms may persist into the residual phase, they are less likely to be accompanied by such strong affect as experienced during the active phase. There is great variation in the severity of the symptoms during the residual phase, and some individuals will function extremely well while others may be significantly more impaired (NHS n.d.). Schizophrenia makes a small, independent contribution to the risk of acquiring a criminal record. More substantial influences are gender, substance abuse, ethnicity and age of onset (Badger *et al.* 1999). In other words, it is much more likely that a criminal offence will be committed by a young male person than by an individual suffering from schizophrenia.

Schizophreniform disorder appears to be related to abnormalities in the structure and chemistry of the brain and has strong genetic links. However, its course and severity can be altered by social factors such as stress or a lack of support within the family. It is characterised by the symptoms of schizophrenia, including delusions, hallucinations, disorganised speech, and disorganised or catatonic behaviour. The disorder throughout the three phases lasts longer than one month but less than 6 months. The cause of schizoaffective disorder is less clear cut than for schizophreniform, but biological factors are also suspected. It is also known as bipolar disorder and was previously called manic depression. It is a disorder characterised by the presence of affective bipolar (depressive or manic) symptoms and schizophrenic symptoms within the same episode of illness. Schizoaffective disorder (depressive type) is accompanied by depressive symptoms such as psychomotor retardation; insomnia; loss of energy, appetite, or weight; reduction of normal interests; impairment of concentration; guilt; feelings of hopelessness; and suicidal thoughts (NHS n.d.). In schizoaffective disorder (manic type), the disturbance of mood usually takes the form of elation, with increased self-esteem and grandiosity characterised by racing thoughts, insomnia, hyperactivity and impairment of social inhibition. The manic type of schizoaffective disorder is usually very pronounced with a swift onset and significantly disturbed behaviour. The relationship between schizophrenia and schizoaffective disorder is uncertain (NHS n.d.); however, the latter carries a separate diagnostic category because the symptoms are commonly observed.

The cause of delusional disorder is not known, and it appears to be distinct from schizophrenia and mood disorders (see below). Some studies suggest a biological component due to its increased prevalence in families. There is, however, no strong unifying theory in biological studies, while psychodynamic theory tends to focus on the use of the defence mechanisms of reaction formation, denial and projection to account for the paranoia. The symptoms include non-bizarre delusions such as feelings of being followed, poisoned, infected, deceived or conspired against, or loved at a distance (see Chapter 7 on stalking). Non-bizarre therefore refers to real-life situations that could be true, but are not, or are greatly exaggerated. By contrast, bizarre delusions, which would rule out this disorder, are those such as believing that your stomach is missing or that aliens are seeking you out to be their leader (PsychNet-UK n.d.). While antipsychotic drugs are the treatment of choice for delusional disorders, their efficacy is yet to be established.

Psychotic disorders are characterised by their brevity – the patient usually has symptoms from 1 to 30 days and eventually recovers completely. It is unexpected in onset and may be accompanied by delusions, hallucination, speech disorder, and disorganised or catatonic behaviour. The condition has been linked to important life stress, that is, an exogenous trigger, and in this respect it should be distinguished from mood disorders (PsychNet-UK n.d.).

In terms of posing a risk to self and others, there is evidence that a dual diagnosis of psychosis and substance abuse disorder is associated with an increased risk of violence (Swanson *et al.* 1997).

However, Berkson's fallacy (Mueser *et al.* 1998) suggests that sampling bias may be introduced in the research and that estimates of dual diagnosis are inflated when researched in treatment settings as opposed to the general population, because either disorder increases the likelihood that individuals will receive treatment. Coupled with such methodological issues are problems with weak assessment tools and clinical bias. Badger *et al.* (1999) produced empirical evidence that unintended bias in clinical assessment and professional judgement leads to an unrepresentative profile of mentally disordered offenders in the sentenced population. It was demonstrated that psychotic remand prisoners are more likely to be black and older than other mentally disordered prisoners, and these figures are particularly significant for women. Further findings were that non-white groups are over-represented in special hospitals, making up almost 20 per cent of the population. This would suggest that the symptoms of mental illness are (unintentionally) perceived as more risky when coupled with issues of ethnicity (Winstone and Pakes 2005).

Neurosis disorders

This is the most common mental illness in the UK, with around 16 per cent of the adult population experiencing some form at any one time. It is a 'catch-all' term that refers to any mental imbalance that causes distress. The diagnosis embraces everything from depression to panic attacks to post-traumatic stress disorder. Feelings of fear are usually accompanied by physical symptoms (such as heart racing, sweating, tense muscles and so on) and changes in behaviour, often called avoidance behaviours. These disorders are very unlikely to lead to an increased of risk of harm to others, and the usual treatment predominantly focuses upon some form of counselling.

Mood disorders

A very brief word concerning mood disorders – brief, because mood changes accompany many of the disturbances described, as in schizoaffective disorders, and yet, as in depression, they may have a severe impact on the individual, in terms of a diminished ability to cope with the demands of life, without necessarily being accompanied by distortions of reality or odd or bizarre behaviour. If there is a risk, it is posed mainly to self rather than others.

In conclusion to this section, we acknowledge that reading through all these symptoms and variations of mental disorder is not exactly gripping; the similarities in clinical presentation can be confusing, and the differences may sometimes appear negligible between different diagnoses. But for the mental health practitioner attempting to advise clinically on intervention, and for criminal justice professionals trying to make a judgement on motivation and to decide regarding the balance between risk to the public and human rights, such differences are crucial. Not only must professionals ensure that they do no harm and do not exacerbate any risks, but they must also ensure that their action is based on the principle of being able to identify effectively and ameliorate symptoms. It is the level of understanding that the professional has of mental illness, including any hidden bias in clinical assessment (Badger *et al.* 1999), that determines whether an individual is presented as mad, bad or simply dangerous. From this assessment, many subsequent decisions may follow, and the impact of getting it even a little wrong can be catastrophic for the public or for the individual.

Exploding the myth of mad, bad and dangerous

Crimes committed by mentally disordered offenders regularly grab the headlines, and as a means of mass communication there can be few more effective ways of creating and sustaining public and political views, opinions and fears.

Morrall (2002) published the quantitative results of a 5-year study (1994–9) of media representations of homicides and non-fatal violence attributed to people described as mentally disturbed. Taking one day, 3 June 2000, as an example, Morrall reports that the *Guardian* newspaper ran three separate stories about violence committed by this group. The first story referred to a Greek female 'axe murderer' who was being released from a prison psychiatric ward. The second was an account of a British male 'sword attacker', reported as suffering from paranoid schizophrenia, who had injured 11 people attending a church service. The third was coverage of a Tunisian man, described as a 'violent loner with a long history of mental illness' (*Guardian* 3 June 2000, cited in Morrall 2002). This could not fail to send the clear message that to be 'mad' is synonymous with being dangerous and violent. The study demonstrates that this 'snapshot' is far from an isolated example. Such stories entrench negative public attitudes to people with mental health problems; they instil fear and result in public demands for action to reduce the risk that this group is assumed to pose. As Bean and Mounser state:

> Patients with mental health problems are not a group whose cause is easy to espouse. They are not given the sympathy often granted to victims of crime, far too often they are the perpetrators of discord; frequently they are perceived as dangerous whether to the social order, to others or to themselves. (1993: 113)

As is evident from the outline of types of mental disorder, across the range very few individuals with a mental illness are likely to pose a risk to others. The greater risk is of self-harm and the risk posed by the public perception of the dangerousness of people with mental health problems and what this means for those with a diagnosis of mental disorder. The failed attempts (2002 and 2006) to get reforms of the outdated Mental Health Act 1983 passed into statute demonstrate that even the lawmakers have fallen into the trap of assuming that stringent policies are required to contain people who, by virtue of a diagnosis of mental disorder, may *in the future* pose a risk to the public. It was only the sustained resistance by professionals, on the basis that the proposals were objectionable and unworkable, that some, not all, of the more draconian powers contained in the bill were abandoned.

The basis for the belief that people with mental health problems generally pose a significant risk to society is consistently without any evidence base. The British reconviction data clearly show that reconvictions in this group are much lower than might be expected (Ly and Howard 2004). Home Office data show that of the 2,039 patients discharged for the first time between 1986 and 2001, 8 per cent were reconvicted of a standard list offence within 2 years of discharge, and 1 per cent were convicted for a grave offence. For those released between 1986 and 1998, the 5-year reconviction rates were 16 per cent for standard list and 3 per cent for grave offences. For people without a mental health problem, reconviction was about 50 per cent for a standard list offence and 9 per cent for grave offences during the comparable period (Prime 2002). Year in, year out, therefore, the percentage reconvictions rates for those with a mental disorder are significantly lower than would be expected of discharged prisoners without mental health problems. This leads McGuire (2002), among others, to argue that psychiatric patients do not, in general, pose an increased risk of violence in the community.

To develop the point further, the number of homicides carried out by people without a mental disorder is growing, while the homicide rate among the mentally disordered is relative static (Appleby 1999; Taylor and Gunn 1999). Around a third of all perpetrators of homicide over a 5-year period had a diagnosis of mental disorder. These mentally ill perpetrators had a lower rate of previous convictions for violence than those who were not mentally ill at the time of the offence, and 7 per cent of them were subsequently committed to psychiatric hospital (Monahan *et al.* 2001). The most common diagnoses among this group convicted of homicide were alcohol dependence, drug dependence and personality disorder. However, only 9 per cent of people convicted of homicide had a diagnosis of personality disorder, and only 5 per cent of all perpetrators of homicide in England and Wales had a diagnosis of schizophrenia. Notably, while being less likely to kill in general than their counterparts without a mental health illness, mentally ill perpetrators were also less likely to kill a stranger (Safety First 2001). It would therefore appear that people are far more likely to be killed by someone they live or associate with and that even stranger attacks are more likely to be committed by someone without a mental disorder – not a comforting fact but nonetheless one that police investigators have been well aware of for decades.

Apart from homicide, other offences could be thought to be more likely attributable to those with a diagnosis of mental illness. Among restricted patients detained in hospital under the Mental Health Act 1983 at the end of 2003, 50 per cent (1,554) had been convicted of, or charged with, acts of violence against the person; 13 per cent with, sexual offences; and 13 per cent with arson. Among the sentenced population, violent offences were the most common offences linked to patients suffering from mental illness and among patients with a diagnosis of psychopathic disorder, while sexual offences accounted for the highest proportion of offences among those with mental impairment and severe mental impairment (Ly and Howard 2004). However, those detained under normal sentencing processes under all categories of criminal activity currently number nearly 80,000, so, by comparison, the proportion of offenders considered sufficiently mentally ill to pose such a risk to self and others that they must be detained in restricted conditions is extremely low.

The observable link between mental disorder and offending should therefore not be confused with the notion that mental health problems per se predispose to criminal behaviour, or that having a mental health problem automatically means that the patient is pervasively mad and therefore dangerous. But what about notions of 'bad' and 'evil'? Here we enter the realm of philosophy in asking whether it is possible to engage in individual acts of atrocity without also being mentally disturbed. Psychopaths are a clear example of when an individual is both insane and not culpable; however, very few atrocities are committed by psychopaths, suggesting that cognitive distortions may well exist within the parameter of being judged sane – but not necessarily rational. Whether this is 'bad' or 'evil' will be a question of individual beliefs, morals and ethics, but it certainly is not a debate that is relevant to those who are clinically assessed as incapable of taking blame.

Treatment or punishment?

When considering the question of treatment or punishment, the most sensible response is to ask which is the most effective in determining positive clinical outcomes and deterring further offending.

However, in identifying effective strategies, there is a difficulty. The literature and evidence do not yet permit empirically based generalisation about treatment and rehabilitation efficacy (Hodgins 2000; Hodgins and Muller-Isberner 2000; McGuire 2000; Blackburn 2004). This is partly due to a lack of research linked to resource limitations, but also to ethical difficulties in researching this vulnerable group, particularly that of setting up and sustaining a comparison group when symptoms must be treated as and when they present. Evidence is also lacking in all aspects of psychological treatment and intervention and other non-clinical interventions for much the same reasons (Hodgins 2000; Hodgins and Muller-Isberner 2000; McGuire 2000; Blackburn 2004). A further limitation is that neither the technology of risk prediction nor the evidence from treatment research is yet sufficiently refined to allow precise guidance to be given in terms of the clinical or recidivism effectiveness of treatment outcomes (McGuire 2000). However, the research can indicate promising interventions to pursue.

In secure settings, pharmacological treatment for psychotic disorder is the most widely used intervention. However, this alone does not appear to address the issues, as patients exhibit a wide range of psychological problems, and a combined intervention delivery is therefore seen as the most promising and effective. This will include motivational and social skills training for problems of social withdrawal, psychodynamic and cognitive therapy for depression, anger management and training in problem-solving, and moral reasoning to deal with criminal thinking (Rice and Harris 1997, in Blackburn 2004).

Concerns about the treatability and risk of high-security patients centre particularly on psychopaths, which is often popularly used as an umbrella term for personality disorders. Although many clinicians believe that psychopaths are untreatable, the treatment literature provides no clear support for this view (Blackburn 2000). What evidence there is suggests that interventions can achieve short-term clinical goals, even though it is not possible to determine which specific procedures are responsible. Blackburn (2004) comments that, in this respect, the interventions are probably no less effective than comparable procedures employed in mental health services more widely.

Long-term follow-ups of mentally disordered offenders released from high security in Britain and North America have generally focused on recidivism as an indication of the effectiveness of intervention (Murray 1989; Quinsey *et al.* 1998, in Blackburn 2004). The most common findings have been that the overall rate of reoffending is lower than that usually reported for released prisoners (see also Ly and Howard 2004). Only a minority of patients go on to commit a further serious violent or sexual offence, psychotic patients reoffend at a lower rate than non-psychotic, personality-disordered patients, and there is some evidence that patients discharged with a condition of supervision are less likely to recidivate than those discharged directly to the community (see also Heilbrun and Peters 2000).

Therapeutic communities are an alternative setting for the management of those with an identified mental health problem linked to antisocial behaviour (see also Chapter 10). Lees *et al.* (1999) conducted a systematic international review of therapeutic community treatment for people with personality disorders and mentally disordered offenders. They concluded that there is meta-analytic and clinical evidence that therapeutic communities produce changes in people's mental health and functioning, and Blackburn (2004) suggests that, while a therapeutic community may not be a suitable environment for psychopaths, non-psychopathic offenders may benefit. However, these findings need to be replicated and further evidenced through qualitative and quantitative research.

Prison, as a form of punishment, is frequently used to manage the sentenced population who also have mental health problems. It is important to realise that mental health problems in prison are rife. This raises a chicken-and-egg question: it is conceivable that mental health problems were present before entering prison, but it is highly likely that the prison environment brings about or exacerbates any mental health problems present. The truth is that some eight or nine out of ten inmates report mental health problems (Singleton *et al.* 1998). The profile of the outcome of Singleton's study is set out in Table 6.1.

Despite these figures, which indicate that about 80 per cent of those sentenced have a mental health problem requiring care in the prison setting, the Department of Health (DOH 2005) acknowledges that there are severe shortcomings in all aspects of service delivery, provision and accessing resources for these detainees, clinically falling far short of what might be expected under NHS provision in the community.

In terms of a programmatic approach, the guidance offered by the Offending Behaviour Programme Board (2004) suggests that it is inappropriate ethically and possibly counterproductive in terms of outcomes to expose offenders with mental health problems to accredited programmes under the banner of the 'what works' initiative as run by the probation and prison service, even where the mental health problem is of a low-order status, such as, depression or anxiety.

There is, however, evidence from a range of sources that for all but the most seriously mentally disturbed the community is the environment in which patients are most likely to benefit from a regime that leads to improved mental health. Intervention in these settings mainly involves the effectiveness of different statutory or professional arrangements in minimising harmful behaviour and promoting autonomous living, although, as in the secure services, there is a paucity of evaluation studies (Heilbrun and Peters 2000;

Table 6.1 Prevalence of mental illness in prisoners and in the population (in percentages)

	Remand males	Remand females	Prison females	Prison males	Male popula-tion*	Female popula-tion*
Personality disorders	78	50 (combined)		64	5.4	3.4
Psychosis	10	14 (combined)		7	0.5	0.6
Neurosis	59	76	63	40	14.4	20.2

*Adults living in private households. *Source:* Singleton *et al.* (1998; 2000).

Hodgins and Muller-Isberner 2000; McGuire 2000; Blackburn 2004). Many studies are pragmatic rather than theory driven, and for the most part they have been developed in the USA and Canada.

What is notable is that over a quarter of perpetrators with schizophrenia had no contact with mental health services prior to committing homicide, suggesting that accurate diagnosis and consistent mental health support, rather than draconian laws leading to incarceration, are the key to managing the symptoms of mental disorder and protecting the public from risk of harm.

Again, while 15 per cent of people convicted of homicide in England and Wales had symptoms of mental illness at the time of the offence, only 9 per cent were in contact with mental health services at the time, suggesting that improved contact between mental health services and those in need could reduce this figure further.

Stone (2003) notes that a multiagency approach for treatment and intervention, such as Multi-Agency Public Protection Arrangements (MAPPA), is one of the most effective strategies in supporting offenders with mental health problems – when it works well. However, these arrangements continue to rely too heavily on good professional relationships, and too often they fail to deliver their full potential when, for example, resources and staffing are limited, professional philosophies clash, and there are frequent changes of personnel.

Reviewing the area of management in the community, Heilbrun and Peters (2000) concluded from the limited evidence available, that the most effective and cost-effective influences on minimising harmful (reoffending) behaviour in the community include:

- conditional release;
- intensive case management;
- skills-based training;
- delivery of a range of services that include housing support and vocational training;
- specialised treatment for substance abuse.

As you will see from the above, the last three points are dynamic risk factors, that is, factors in an offender's life that are linked to offending behaviour and can be changed through effective intervention with the aim of reducing recidivism. To explain this further, we cannot, for example, change the age of onset of criminal behaviour, which is a static risk factor, but we can meet identified employment or training needs to promote a pro-social lifestyle. Thus, the label dynamic risk factor or criminogenic (as opposed to social) need is used. Identifying and meeting criminogenic needs are the focus of evidence-based practice in the statutory agencies of prison and probation under the 'what works' banner of research.

There is little doubt that many of the static risk factors associated with reoffending generally apply to mentally disordered offenders – for example, age, gender, race, social class and prior criminality (McGuire 2005). The MacArthur project (Monahan *et al.* 2001) looked at, among other issues, criminological risk factors. They concluded that gender differences in propensity for violence are smaller in the mentally disordered offender population, but the type of violence differs. Unsurprisingly, prior violence was strongly associated with post-discharge violence. The study also identified similar dynamic risk factors in the wider offending population, such as, an effect of neighbourhood; that is, those discharged into areas that suffer more social deprivation are more likely to be violent (Monahan *et al.* 2001). Overall, this suggests that correctly identifying an offender's needs and managing these needs through multiagency intervention in an appropriate community environment is most likely to reduce the possibility of a further offence and promote the stability of mental well-being and coping skills.

In respect of the delivery of accredited 'what works' programmes to this group of offenders, McGuire (2002) states that given consistent linkages found with adjacent fields of treatment in which there are sizeable volumes of positive evidence (for example, cognitive-behavioural intervention and evidence-based practice as part of the 'what works' initiative), there is no reason why those interventions that have proved beneficial with other groups should not be *appropriately adapted* and offered to this group also. As community-based delivery, multiagency and multimodel approaches, skills-based training, and targeting criminogenic need are part of the evidence base of what constitutes effective practice of the 'what works' initiative, there would appear to be considerable merit in McGuire's recommendation if the findings of Heilbrun and Peters (2000) and Monahan *et al.* (2001) are accepted.

In answer to the question of punishment or treatment, it would therefore appear that the positive research evidence points most promisingly to community-based interventions within a multiagency approach to meet the dynamic risk factors identified for each individual and to include appropriate psychological and clinical treatment. Punishment in the main has always been ineffective (see Chapter 9), but especially for this group.

Conclusion

To have a mental disorder does not, in the vast majority of individuals, as the discussion exposed, increase the risk of a violent offence, or the risk of recidivism or the likely escalation of antisocial behaviour to harmful behaviour. Those most at risk are the mentally disordered themselves – at risk from the prejudice that leads to draconian laws, lack of resources and access to services, and paucity of appropriate provision after sentencing. In addition, there is an elevated risk of self-harm and suicide, both within and outside penal institutions. The climate of fear associated with mental disorder, typified by the label of 'mad', which has become synonymous with 'bad and dangerous', exacerbates the problem. There is much talk about the high rates of reoffending on release from prison, but many of those in prison are in an unsuitable environment to reduce the likelihood of recidivism on release because there is a restricted resource base and pool of trained staff to meet the clinical and psychological requirements of the 80 per cent of prisoners with a mental health problem.

As a starting point, two practical and achievable measures could be taken. First, we should revise the current legal use of the term 'mentally disordered offender' so that it embraces and recognises the needs of those sentenced with a mental health problem. Secondly, we should promote empirical research to identify effective assessment tools, interventions and treatment. Knowledge and understanding are the most certain route to reducing fear, and we need to know the ways in which these most vulnerable members of our society can be supported in order to identify the rare few who are truly dangerous to the public.

Chapter 7

Stalkers and their victims

Introduction

The pop singer Madonna is one of many celebrities who have suffered at the hands of a stalker. In June 1995, an obsessed fan managed to get access to her home in Los Angeles despite previous court orders forbidding him to do so. Robert Dewey Hoskins entered her house carrying a wooden heart that read, 'Love to my wife Madonna'. He stayed inside the property for several minutes as he ran around and had a swim in the pool. He eventually was shot by a guard, and he was charged with stalking the singer despite her absence from the house at the time of the incident. Eight months later, Hoskins was convicted and sentenced to 10 years' imprisonment. Madonna appeared in court in Los Angeles to testify, an experience that made her 'sick to her stomach' (MacFarlane 1997).

Many other celebrities have suffered similar types of victimisation. Tennis player Serena Williams was followed all over the world by a 34-year-old German, Albrecht Stromeyer, who tried to harass her at Wimbledon and also in Italy, France, and the USA. US talk show host David Letterman was stalked for years by a woman called Margaret Ray. She repeatedly broke into his house and was once stopped while driving his car and pretending to be Mrs Letterman. At the age of 46, after having spent time both in prison and in mental health institutions, Margaret Ray committed suicide. 'A sad end to a confused life,' said Letterman in a statement. Similarly, actor Michael J. Fox, footballer David Beckman, singer George Michael and violinist Vanessa May have all suffered from stalking.

There are two further examples that date from before celebrity stalking became, pardon the expression, fashionable. They concern former Beatle John Lennon and actress Jodie Foster. John Lennon was killed on 9 December 1980 by Mark Chapman, widely regarded as a stalker, even though that term did not have any legal status at that time. Jodie Foster's stalker, John Hinckley, went as far as attempting to assassinate US president Ronald Reagan, whom he shot and wounded in March 1981, in order to impress his target.

It is evident that there are celebrity stalkers who go to extreme lengths to impress or terrify their victim. Why do they do this? Are these people deluded or otherwise mentally ill? What about non-celebrities? Do other people suffer from stalkers, and what can be done to prevent victimisation or to bring stalkers to justice? From the start, it is important to realise what a terrifying ordeal being stalked can be: the fear of being watched, the recurrence of veiled or blatant threats, and the telephone ringing in the middle of the night. Victims worry about their own personal safety but also about that of their loved ones. It occupies their mind and drains energy away from other aspects of their life. In addition, apart from coming to terms with the situation in the here and now, victims also worry about the future: will it ever stop? Will it get worse?

The sad truth is that although stalking by strangers does regularly happen, most often the perpetrators are known to the victims. Quite frequently, they once were intimates. We shall see later in this chapter that despite the media portrayal of stalkers as deluded, lonely and obsessed with celebrity, most stalkers are embittered former lovers, vindictive neighbours or resentful ex-employees. Later in this chapter, we look at ways in which the criminal justice system seeks to bring the perpetrators to justice.

What is stalking?

Intuitively, it is easy to get a sense of what stalking is. It is persistent, unwanted attention that a victim receives from an offender, and it is assumed that there is a sinister motive underlying these actions. Stalking is not defined by individual actions but by patterns of behaviour: a number of seemingly innocent actions can constitute a behavioural pattern that we can call stalking (Tjaden and Thoenness 1998; Sheridan et al. 2000). Sometimes the classification of a course of conduct is straightforward, as in the case of countless harassing or threatening letters, emails or text messages. But unwanted and seemingly 'nice' actions can also constitute harassment, and hence stalking. This might raise an issue of definition, as some stalking behaviour might be well intended, but terrifying nevertheless. A stalker may send love letters, or follow a victim from home to work and back again, pleading for contact or attention. These behaviours can justifiably be perceived as threatening and can be classed as stalking behaviours.

It is difficult to put a lower limit on the intensity of behaviour required in order for a set of actions to be called a course of conduct. When there are dozens of telephone calls or when every day or every week there is an unpleasant letter in the post, the case is straightforward. But even when contact is sporadic, there still can be the 'continuity of purpose' required for the establishment of a course of conduct. Imagine a nasty letter only once a year, but always on the day that a loved one died: it can and does constitute stalking.

Sheridan and Davies define stalking as 'a set of actions which, taken as a whole, amount to harassment or intimidation directed at one individual by another' (2001: 134). There inevitably is a subjective element in this definition. As we shall see later in this chapter, this has had repercussions in the way antistalking legislation has been drafted. Further confusion comes from the fact that many victims might not realise that they are being stalked, because they do not realise that a set of behaviours to which they are subjected is more than an annoyance and is actually a crime. Connor *et al.* (2004) showed various scenarios that involved persistent unwanted attention to US college psychology students and asked them whether these scenarios constituted stalking or not. These participants were less likely to characterise a vignette as stalking when the actors were previously involved in an intimate relationship compared to vignettes that involved mere acquaintances or strangers. As we will see, this is in contrast with the fact that stalking is far more common among former intimates than acquaintances or strangers (e.g., Tjaden and Thoenness 1998; Budd and Mattinson 1998). Interestingly, Sheridan *et al.* (2003) also touch upon this subject and suggest that outsiders might feel as if ex-partners somehow commit less of a crime when they engage in stalking behaviours. Later, we will see that this form of stalking is often preceded by abuse within the relation prior to break-up, so that it is doubtful whether such views are valid.

Winkel *et al.* (2002) looked at data from four studies, and found a fair deal of communality regarding the behaviours that stalkers exhibit. Unwanted attention and communications, as well as threats and invasions of personal and private space, are common behaviours.

But actual physical assault does happen in a large number of cases as well, as does the destruction of property. It puts into perspective the naive idea that perhaps stalkers are simply inadequate in their expression of affection: many instances of stalking behaviour are criminal in their own right, so that the criminalisation of a pattern that underlies it all should not be controversial. Sheridan *et al.* (2001) provide a comprehensive list of specific stalking behaviours, obtained from a British sample of victims (Table 7.1).

The behaviours are varied, but obviously constitute a pattern of threats, violence and harassment. The intensity is equally varied. Data from Sheridan *et al.* (2001) are outlined in Table 7.2 below. They analysed the experience of 95 victims who contacted the Suzy Lamplugh Trust. This sample therefore concerns self-defined victims of stalking. Later in the section, we shall examine data from the

Table 7.1 Prevalence of specific stalking behaviours

Stalking behaviour	%
Watches victim	91
Follows victim	82
Tries to gain information from victim's family, friends, etc.	77
Trespasses on victim's property	68
Approaches and tries to speak to victim	66
Slanders victims/defames character	60
Stalks family members	59
Threatens physical assaults	53
Shouts abuse/obscenities at victim	51
Damages victim's car	40
Makes counter-allegations of stalking	39
Threatens family/friends/partner of victim	39
Damage outside victim's home/garden	36
Carries out physical assault	32
Breaks into/damages victim's home inside	32
Steals from victim	30
Attempts to kill victim	25
Tries to move into victim's social circle	22
Assaults family/friends/partner	17
Bugs victim's home	13
Carries out sexual assault	3
	(data from 22 victims only)

Source: Sheridan *et al.* 2001.

Table 7.2 Frequency of contact by stalker (based on a sample of 95 cases)

Frequency of contact	At worst/most intense	On average
More than once per day	74%	20%
Once per day	6%	17%
2–3 times per week	15%	31%
Several times per month	4%	23%
Less frequently	1%	10%

Source: Sheridan *et al.* 2001.

British Crime Survey, but as these data are rather comprehensive, they will feature in more detail in this section.

Before doing that, it is possibly helpful to highlight the work of the Suzy Lamplugh Trust (www.suzylamplugh.org). The trust was established in 1986, named after Suzy Lamplugh, an estate agent, who disappeared after meeting an unknown client. The trust's mission is to raise awareness of the importance of personal safety and to provide solutions that bring about change in order to help people to avoid violence and aggression and live safer, more confident lives.

Of the 95 cases of stalking Sheridan *et al.* investigated, 7 victims were male and 87 were female. Their age (when the stalking began) ranged from 2 to 70 years, with an average age of 33 years. The age of the stalkers (when known) varied from 11 to 73 years of age, with an average of 35 years of age. The duration of the victimisation varied widely, varying from less than 1 month, to as long as 38 years.

How common is stalking?

It is important to note that both the Sheridan and Boon (2002) and the Sheridan *et al.* (2001) data concern samples with certain characteristics. They involved either victims who had taken certain steps, such as to contact the Suzy Lamplugh Trust, or cases that have come to the attention of the police. It might therefore be argued that these cases are possibly relatively serious, at least in the eyes of the victims, and therefore fail to provide a complete picture of the prevalence of stalking in Britain today.

In order to get that picture, it is instructive to consider the results of the British Crime Survey. This is a questionnaire administered throughout the UK on people's experiences with crime. The survey is undertaken under the auspices of the Home Office (see www.homeoffice.gov.uk/rds/bcs1.html for further information). The report that details the 2004/5 results (which involved no less than 45,000 respondents) is written by Nicholas (2005). It is repeated every year.

Questions about stalking and harassment have featured in the British Crime Survey since 1998 (Budd *et al.* 2000; Walby and Allen 2004). Within the survey, stalking was defined as a course of conduct involving two or more events of harassment causing fear, alarm or distress, of three types: telephone calls or letters, loitering outside home or work, or damaged property. It includes incidents by any perpetrator, not just by intimates (Walby and Allen 2004: 4). Respondents were asked about stalking experienced ever (i.e., including incidents prior to the age of 16) and also, particularly, in the last year.

The 2001 survey found that 19 per cent of women and 12 per cent of men reported having been victimised this way. In the 1998 measurement sweep, these figures were 16.1 per cent, and 6.8 per cent respectively. The 2001 results therefore represent a substantial increase, but part of the reason for that might lie in how stalking was defined in 1998 as compared to 2001. The 1998 measure defined stalking as follows: 'persistent and unwanted attention' (excluding incidents in which the victim and perpetrator were living with each other throughout the period over which the incidents occurred) (Budd *et al.* 2000). The 2001 definition highlights that two occurrences are enough for the behaviour to be labelled as stalking, and that might have prompted more positive responses. However, when we compare these self-report data to the data from Sheridan *et al.* and Sheridan and Boon, it is clear that the latter seem to under-represent male victimisation. It raises the question of whether male victims are less likely to contact either the Suzy Lamplugh Trust or the police when they are being stalked than women.

Despite the substantial levels of male victimisation, Budd *et al.* (2000) found young women to be particularly at risk, as 16.8 per cent of women aged 16–19 and 7.8 per cent of those aged 20–24 recalled being subject to persistent and unwanted attention during the previous year. Risks were also high among women who were single; students; living in privately rented accommodation; living in a flat or maisonette; and living in a lower-income household.

Thus, whereas media reports tend to focus on stalking as a crime particularly haunting the rich and famous, the data from the British crime survey show that, in fact, the opposite is true. It is also worth emphasising that, although women are more than twice as likely to become victims as men, it certainly is not the case that the victims are overwhelmingly female, as a good deal of victimisation involves a male target.

Stalkers and victim characteristics

In their sample of 95 cases, Sheridan *et al.* (2001) found most stalkers to be men, with an average age of 35 years, varying from 11 years to as old as 73 years of age. As compared to 'the average' offender regarding all crimes, stalkers were more likely to be professional and in employment. In that respect, they more closely resembled the general population than the 'typical' offender.

Regarding the relation to their victim, a large majority of offenders knew their victim and often knew them rather well. Only 12 per cent were complete strangers but almost half (48 per cent) were ex-husband or ex-wife, or former boyfriend or girlfriend. Most others were acquaintances of various kinds, often neighbours but also regularly fellow students or clients in some kind of professional context. Pathé and Mullen emphasise the risk that certain professions run, of becoming a victim: 'Any profession that comes into contact with the lonely and the disordered and in whom sympathy and attention is easily reconstructed as romantic interest are particularly vulnerable' (Pathé and Mullen 2002: 6).

The British crime survey data, based on victims' answers about their stalkers also reveal that most stalkers are either former acquaintances or former intimates. Overall, eight in ten (81 per cent) incidents reported to the survey were perpetrated by men. Male offenders were involved in 90 per cent of incidents against women, and 57 per cent of incidents against men. In 29 per cent of incidents, the perpetrator had had an intimate relationship with the victim (current or former spouse, partner, girl/boyfriend or date) at the beginning of the incident. Strangers were responsible in 34 per cent of incidents, a rate that is somewhat higher than that reported by Blaauw *et al.* (2002). The remaining incidents involved close friends, relatives, household members or acquaintances. Women were significantly more likely to be stalked by a stranger than were male victims (Walby and Allen 2004).

Disturbingly, 71 per cent of those who had been the subject of persistent and unwanted attention said they had changed their behaviour in at least one of three ways. Fifty-nine per cent had started avoiding certain places or certain people, 35 per cent went out less than before and 42 per cent had taken extra personal security measures (Budd *et al.* 2000).

Furthermore, 31 per cent of victims were very or fairly afraid that violence would be used against them. A similar proportion (27 per cent) reported fear that violence would be used against a friend, relative or someone else they knew. Victims were less likely to fear a sexual offence, though 17 per cent said they were. The latter data are consistent with what was found by Sheridan and Boon (2001). Stalking victims not only endure persistent and unwanted attention, but they also live in fear of what will happen next. In fact, Blaauw *et al.* (2002) report rather dramatic impacts of victimisation. They found high levels of mental illness and distress among victims. To be precise, they found that

> 77% of the stalking victims [...] were suffering from a diagnosable psychiatric disorder. Thus, not only were the victims' symptom levels found to be more in accordance with those of psychiatric outpatients than those of general population samples, but also three quarters of the victims displayed a symptom level that indicated psychiatric disorder. It must be concluded from these findings that stalking is indeed associated with serious mental health problems among victims. (Blaauw *et al.* 2002: 25)

The mental health problems Blaauw and colleagues identified were mostly to do with depression and anxiety. This finding is in line with Sheridan *et al.* (2001), who found that stalking victims are much more likely to lose jobs and careers, something that happens much less often to their stalkers. This may be because the anxiety caused by their victimisation prevents them from performing as well as they can. Another reason may be that the workplace is one of the places where stalking occurs, or because the stalker is someone from the workplace. Sheridan *et al.* found that the majority of victims in professional positions had lost that position after a prolonged period of stalking. In contrast, it often requires a prison sentence for stalkers to lose their job.

Attachment, power and delusion

It is an obvious as well as a pertinent question: what is wrong with the people that make other people's lives a misery through stalking? We are simplifying a bit, but it is useful to think of stalkers as having one or more sets of issues. The first is to do with attachment. Attachment is essential for normal adjustment and happiness: it is essential to healthy people to feel safe to love their nearest and dearest: they will not betray that love, by turning violent, by suddenly leaving them or by some other injury. To some individuals that rather is a leap of faith (Hazan and Shaver 1987). For these individuals, intimate relationships are not characterised by what is called secure attachment. Instead, their attachment is anxious. Anxious attachment is related to physical as well as psychological abuse (Dutton 1998) and also to jealousy (Guerrero 1998), and it seems to be the precursor to an excessive need for control. After the break-up of a relationship, stalking behaviour might be a desperate attempt to gain or regain a sense of control (Dye and Davis 2003; Tonin 2004). Ex-intimate stalking can therefore be seen as a new manifestation of a desire to control the partner or ex-partner. It is also known that ex-intimate stalkers often were abusive prior to break-up as well (Brewster 2003).

Others, such as Brewster (2003), discuss these dynamics in terms of power. That perspective also facilitates the view that what ex-intimate stalkers seek to do is thematically the same as what they did during the relationship: subsequent to break-up, they resort to other means to gain or exercise control over their former partner. Domestic violence is frequently analysed in terms of the perpetrators' need for power and control, and when that is under threat, they might use violence in an attempt to regain it. As was the case for control, the objective of regaining power can be the underlying motivation for persistent harassment after the relationship has finished. In Brewster's sample of 187 female victims of stalking by former intimates, many reported actions of control, financial, social, psychological, physical and sexual. As Brewster concludes:

> An objective observer might not understand the rationale for stalking once the perpetrator is clear that reconciliation has been ruled out as a possibility. In trying to make sense of stalking behaviour, it is clear that the desire to control the former partner is a great, if not the most important, motivating factor. (Brewster 2003: 216)

Most stalkers do not suffer from any form of mental illness, although some do. The disorder most typically associated with delusional stalking is called 'erotomania', which can be described as 'obsessive, excessive, unwanted or delusional love' (Fitzgerald and Seeman 2002). It is also sometimes called de Clérambault syndrome, as he was the first to describe comprehensively the disorder (de Clérambault 1942). He refers to three stages of obsessive love. The first is that of hope. The sufferers hope and at a certain level believe that the unattainable figure (often a celebrity) will one day be theirs. The second phase is despair: the sufferers become frustrated with the lack of reciprocity, blame intermediaries, and increasingly feel the urge to confront the object of their obsessive love, demanding that they admit that there actually is a relationship or a 'secret bond' between them. The third stage is that of revenge. This is where the delusional stalker might become dangerous (Fitzgerald and Seeman 2002). DSM-IV recognises a so-called *erotomania delusional disorder*, one of a set of delusional disorders:

> Delusional disorder is the presence of one or more nonbizarre delusions that persist for at least a month. Apart from the direct impact of the delusion, the person's behavior appears normal and their psychosocial functioning is not markedly impaired. [...]

> The central theme of the delusion is that another person is in love with the individual. The delusion often concerns idealized romantic love and spiritual union rather than sexual attraction. The person about whom this conviction is held is usually of higher status, but can be a complete stranger. (DSM-IV 2000: 197)

Thus, it is only certain types of stalkers who suffer from delusions. Most stalkers have a firm grip on reality and are more vindictive than delusional. Sheridan and Boon (2002) provide a typology of stalker who might or might not exhibit certain behaviours. There are other typologies to be found in the literature, but they are not always empirically arrived at, so that they tend to be impressionistic and arbitrary in nature. The typology offered below is based on a database of 124 cases of stalking where there has been involvement by law enforcement officials (Sheridan and Boon 2002). Five types are identified.

The first type is 'ex-partner harassment/stalking'. This type comprises 50 per cent of all cases in their sample. As the name obviously suggests, this is stalking by a former intimate and involves a great deal of anger and bitterness toward the victim. There is a definite risk that this type of stalker will exhibit violence. This will often be impulsive 'with corresponding lack of concern about coming to police attention' (Sheridan and Boon 2002: 71). Sheridan and Boon also argue that these relationships prior to break-up are not unlikely to have experienced domestic violence as well, so that it seems as if one type of abusive behaviour is, when circumstances change, substituted for another.

Sheridan and Boon's second type, infatuation harassment, comprises 18.5 per cent of their sample. This type's stalking behaviour tends to be non-malicious in intent and is not characterised by threats or sinister intrusions. Instead, it is characterised by intensive yearning, with the victim the focus of romantic and positive fantasies. Two subtypes are identified, based on age. The 'young love' subtype tends to involve teenagers; the 'midlife love' involves, obviously, much older perpetrators. Sheridan and Boon's (2002) argue that while their behaviours and motivations might be highly similar, different strategies for dealing with both subgroups might be appropriate.

The third type is delusional fixation stalking – dangerous. Of their sample, 15.3 per cent corresponded to this type. Their victims tend to be high-status women or celebrities. These stalkers firmly believe that there is a 'hidden' relationship between them and their victims, even when there has never been any contact. These offenders regularly suffer from mental health problems, and are likely to have a history of sexual problems as well as of offending behaviour. Their approaches lack subtlety or coherence, but there is a high risk of violence and of sexual assault when they discover that the victim does not feel the same way, or, in their deluded frame of mind, refuses to admit that stalker and victim are actually 'meant for each other'. Robert Dewey Hoskins, who stalked Madonna in the 1990s, is likely to fit this category, whereas erotomania as a diagnosis might frequently fit members of this group as well.

The next type Sheridan and Boon discuss is 'delusional fixation stalking – less dangerous'. Stalkers of this type make up 15.3 per cent of their sample. As with the other delusional fixated type, the disorder involves the belief that there is a relationship and elaborate fantasies, such as that the relationship is there, and both victim and stalker know it and want it, but something (a partner, or other prohibitive factor) is in play so that the victim cannot express his or her true feelings. Threats and violence are not typically part of the behaviour associated with this type. It is conceivable that Margaret Ray, who persistently stalked David Letterman, would fit this category.

The final type is 'sadistic stalking'. Such stalkers, making up 12.9 per cent of the sample, might have a history of controlling and stalking behaviours, and tend to be cold and calculated, with evidence of psychopathy. Their stalking is aimed at controlling and unsettling their victim, via fear, loss of privacy and curtailment of their social world (Sheridan and Boon 2002: 77). The stalkers were often, at some point, casual acquaintances, and the stalking behaviour is likely to get progressively more serious and dangerous.

In Australia, Mullen *et al.* (1999) examined 145 stalkers that were referred to a psychiatric institution for treatment. As the police, the courts or the correctional services had referred these people, we would expect high levels of mental health problems. Mullen and colleagues did indeed identify 74 perpetrators with a personality disorder; 36 also suffered from substance abuse-related disorders, and 59 were diagnosed with psychosis (including delusional disorders, schizophrenia and bipolar disorder, also referred to as manic depression). Thus, where there is evidence of mental disorder, it tends to be personality disorder, with or without exacerbating problems of substance abuse, and psychotic disorders. The distinction is important, as the latter group is much more likely to be 'honestly' delusional, whereas the former would not be.

Antistalking legislation

Given how serious the victimisation of stalking can be, it is no wonder that increasingly there is legislation specifically aimed at combating stalking. The world's first antistalking law was passed in the US state of California in 1990. Article 646.9 of the California Penal Code defines a stalker as someone who 'wilfully, maliciously and repeatedly follows or harasses another (victim) and who makes a credible threat with the intent to place the victim or victim's immediate family in fear for their safety'. The prosecution does not have to prove that the stalker had the intent to carry out the threat. The maximum penalty is 1 year's imprisonment. All US states now have antistalking legislation, and there are federal laws in place as well. It has, however, been argued that having a law in place does not guarantee effective enforcement. Miller (2001) argues that specialist units are required with expertise in the prosecution of stalking cases but that are also well equipped to advise victims on personal safety and the collection of evidence, and that are sympathetic to victims' physical and mental well-being. After all, the offence of stalking is atypical for law enforcement purposes: most crimes when reported to the police are past events. Stalking crimes are often in progress. Evidence gathering therefore is not only about reconstructing the past but also about anticipating future acts. The police are often reliant on the victim to collect evidence. A further complicating factor is that while evidence from the victim is vital, it usually is not enough. Finally, the process of gathering evidence against the stalker has to be balanced against an assessment of the risk that the stalker poses to the victim (Miller 2001). For evidential purposes, it might be decided to have the stalker undertake further action, but that action might put the victim at risk. Risk assessment is therefore a focal point for both psychological research and criminal justice.

Rosenfeld (2004) reviewed the literature on stalking and highlighted a number of risk factors for violence. Violence is far from a dismissible worry for victims, as he found that 38 per cent of all stalkers did, at some point, use violence (recall that Sheridan *et al.*'s figure was 32 per cent). The strongest predictive factors for violence were identified as threats, a prior intimate relationship (as opposed to mere acquaintance, or no relationship), and a stalker with substance abuse. Interestingly, Rosenberg found that having a psychotic illness did not carry an extra risk of violence but rather the opposite: it therefore seems as if the stalker who is deluded might not always be particularly dangerous. There are, of course, exceptions to this rule, as the existence of the type 'delusional fixation stalking – dangerous', identified by Sheridan and Boon (2002), testifies. Based on his secondary analysis of 13 studies involving over 1,500 offenders, Rosenfeld also found that female stalkers were no less violent than male offenders, and that the gender of the victims did not make a difference either (Rosenfeld 2004). This is another example that shows that some of our intuitions about offenders and victims might be correct, while others, when we examine the psychological research closely, turn out to be erroneous. The puzzling thing in Rosenfeld's analysis was the finding that previous violent behaviour (not in the context of the stalking) did not relate to violence in relation to the stalking behaviour. That is surprising because it is well known, for 'regular' offenders as well as for mentally disordered offenders, that previous violence is a strong predictor of future violence. It seems as if stalkers constitute an exception to this rule, but Rosenfeld warns that further risk assessment research specific to stalkers might be required in order to examine this further (Rosenfeld 2004).

The legislative framework is different in England and Wales to the extent that there is no separate antistalking law. There is, however, a law that usually is applicable, the Protection from Harassment Act 1997 (Brown 2000). It is debatable to what extent harassment and stalking are the same thing. The California definition is relatively specific: a stalker must wilfully and repeatedly do things that bring about fear of safety in a victim. Other words in the definition are also defined in the law. 'Harasses', for instance, means 'engages in a knowing and wilful course of conduct directed at a specific person that seriously alarms, annoys, torments, or terrorizes the person, and that serves no legitimate purpose' (California Penal Code, 646.9(e)). This precision has an advantage but also a disadvantage. The advantage is clarity. We can more precisely say what stalking is and what it is not, so that, at least in theory, we can draw the line where 'regular' annoying or intrusive behaviour ends and the crime of stalking begins. But in that also lies its disadvantage: all these elements need to be proven, and as stalkers quite often do their business in circumspect ways, proof might be difficult. A wider and more encompassing definition of stalking might therefore be more useful, and that is what has been established in Britain. Section 1 of the Protection from Harassment Act reads as follows:

> A person must not pursue a course of conduct (a) which amounts to harassment of another, and (b) which he knows or ought to know amounts to harassment of the other. For the purposes of this section, the person whose course of conduct is in question ought to know that it amounts to harassment of another if a reasonable person in possession of the same information would think the course of conduct amounted to harassment of the other.

This refers to what is known in law as the 'reasonable person-test'. The law is based on the argument that if a reasonable person would consider a course of conduct to be harassment, then it *is* harassment. A further offence has been created by the Protection from Harassment Act 1997. This offence is called 'putting people in fear of violence', which is defined along similar lines. It requires at least two occasions of a course of conduct that causes victims to fear that violence will be used against them. The 'reasonable person test' applies here as well. The maximum penalty for this offence is 5 years' imprisonment, whereas harassment carries 6 months in prison. What exactly is required to prove such a 'course of conduct' is not specified in the law, apart from the stipulation that it must consist of at least two occasions (Harris 2000).

Harris (2000) looked at 146 cases that utilised the Protection from Harassment Act 1997. She found that in this sample only 2 per cent involved strangers. Overwhelmingly, the alleged offender was an ex-intimate (83 per cent). Harris found rather a high attrition rate: many cases were dropped by either the police or prosecution so that the case never actually came to court. That was often because there was judged to be insufficient evidence, but also, regularly, because the victim no longer wished to proceed with the prosecution. Both outcomes are not uncommon in cases involving former intimates, be it domestic violence or sexual assault. Of those stalkers convicted, the most common penalties were a conditional discharge, a fine, or a community sentence. Less than a handful of the 146 cases the research started with ended with the imposition of a prison sentence. Those cases disposed of with a conditional discharge often also involved a restraining order. The most common restrictions were not to contact the victim, to stay away from the victim's home, not to contact the victim's family, and to keep away from the victim's workplace. Many practitioners in the criminal justice system said that the restraining order was most effective, as long as any breaches of it are dealt with effectively (Harris 2000).

Conclusion

It is easy to get the wrong idea about stalking behaviour, the victims involved and their relation to the offender. Media coverage focuses on the sensational and the salacious. That might yield a picture that does not correspond to the everyday reality of ordinary people fearful, depressed and anxious because of stalking. Spitzberg and Cadiz (2002) have analysed how the media tend to portray stalking. That rather contrasts with how we described it in this chapter: in the media, stalking is predominantly related to celebrities, and in those scenarios the stalker is usually a stranger to the victim: there was no prior relationship. In most cases, we know that there was. The gender portrayal similarly fails to correspond to reality (it is not always males who exclusively stalk women), although Spitzberg and Cadiz argue that certain films, such as *Fatal Attraction* (in which a woman stalks a man), and *Single White Female* (in which both victim and offender are female), do violate such gendered stereotypes. Finally, media coverage overemphasises the role of mental illness, in particular psychotic delusion and psychopathy. Most stalkers suffer from neither affliction (Spitzberg and Cadiz 2002).

Stalking is increasingly recognised as a serious offence. Initially, it was celebrity stalking that placed the issues on the public agenda, but we now know that many other groups suffer from it as well.

That includes older people (defined by Jasinski and Dietz as over the age of 55), who are hardly less susceptible to victimisation than other age groups. Of increasing concern is so-called cyberstalking, harmful, harassing behaviour making use of the Internet. Spence-Diehl (2003) identifies three categories of cyberstalking. In the first, stalking exclusively occurs on line. In the second, the stalking begins online but then transitions into 'terrestrial' stalking as well. In the third, cyberstalking is one of many ways in which regular stalkers seek to achieve their objectives. It might well be particularly young people who are mostly victimised by this emerging form of offending behaviour. Finn (2004) found that 10–15 per cent of university students reported repeatedly receiving emails or instant messages that threatened, insulted or harassed. Online stalking behaviour might also involve identity theft with the intent to harass or frighten, or the posting of private information on the Web. Finn argues that colleges and universities need to educate students about these issues, and promote an infrastructure that promotes safety. Clearly, there is a pressing need, particularly for vulnerable users, to become 'web-savvy' and be responsible in using the Internet for whatever purpose.

Chapter 8

The psychology of addiction – are there more questions than answers?

Introduction

When considering drugs and addiction, we must remember a few things at the outset. First, the differential prohibition of drugs changes over time, depending upon the demands and views within society. Secondly, we must not forget that the most widely available drugs include alcohol, caffeine and nicotine. We must therefore realise that the use of psychoactive substances is the norm and not necessarily deviant. It is this common experience (irrespective of the substance used) that should inform policy, practice and ethical considerations in this difficult and challenging area of work.

There is a consensus that addiction is 'a behaviour over which an individual has impaired control with harmful consequences' (West 2002: 3). In practice, this means that people may find themselves unable to stop behaving in a particular way when they try to do so; because of this violation of individual choice, West (2001; 2006) argues that addiction should be seen as a psychiatric disorder within which an impaired motivational system plays a central part.

Substance use and misuse (legal and illegal) causes a great deal of both pleasure and suffering, and there is the potential here for some deep-seated ambivalence about future behaviour (have you ever had a really bad hangover from drinking alcohol, or a chest infection from smoking tobacco?). The use of drugs is as old as human society itself (see *New Scientist* (2006), for a timeline), and the observations of the pleasures and problems associated with that use has led to the formulation of a number of key questions (Lindstrom 1992; Bickel and Potenza 2006):

- Why do people begin to use drugs?
- How and why does drug use escalate to misuse?
- Why does this continue despite severe and negative consequences?
- Why and how do people stop or modify their drug taking?
- Why is addiction so difficult to treat?
- Why is it so common for people to relapse after a period of abstinence or controlled use?
- What is the relationship between addiction and multiple problem areas, particularly psychiatric disorders?

Psychology makes a fundamentally important contribution to answering these questions; however, any understanding of addiction which stems from a psychological perspective has to consider that addiction is also a biological and social phenomenon, and this is referred to in the literature as the 'biopsychosocial' paradigm (Lindstrom 1992). This perspective argues that in theorising, assessing and intervening to address issues related to addictive behaviour (a possible), equal weighting should be given to each of these areas.

The biopsychosocial paradigm hypothesises that addiction is about more than the sum of the individual parts of biology, psychology and the social dimension (Lende and Smith 2002). It has been pointed out by Orford (1990) that it has been difficult to gain an integration of the human sciences to address these issues. Separate disciplines tending to work within their own fields, and Chick (2002: 474) warns that 'addiction science that is isolated will die out'. The need for insights from a variety of disciplines is essential, as Orford (1990: 211) argues: 'Because of the existence of undisputed determinants of dependence in each of these three major areas of study, and because of its ubiquity and importance, dependence may be of particular significance in the study of human kind.'

There have been (and still are) extremely heated debates about the nature of addiction and the implications of various definitions for treatment (see Heather and Robertson 1997, for an historical overview), but, logically, we have to assert that there can be no psychology or social interaction without biology (the fact of being alive) (see Goldstein 2001), and that there are powerful biological reasons why the use of psychoactive substances (and other behaviours such as gambling, exercise, and sexual behaviour (see Orford 2001)) can become self-perpetuating. For a detailed review of these explanations, see Goldstein (2001), Edwards (2004), and Miller and Carroll (2006), but, in summary, they involve the following:

- gratification of human need;
- artificial stimulation, disregulation or undermining of the brain's natural reward system;
- creation of stress or aversive states likely to increase the need for the positive reinforcement that a drug can give.

It has really been advances in neurobiology and the increased understanding of human DNA within an evolutionary context that has opened up a whole new way of understanding human behaviour and the complex interactions which it comprises. The idea of complexity is a key theme of this chapter.

From the criminal justice perspective and society's need for law and order, some of these new understandings and the consequent questions being asked are challenging. For example, if we look at the issue of drug use from an evolutionary perspective, certain substances stimulate brain regions to release naturally occurring chemicals that reinforce and potentially escalate drug taking, so that drug taking is precisely what we should expect from human beings (Nesse 2001).

In essence, then, this is a big deal. Drugs matter, firstly, because most of us use them in some shape or form; secondly, because the state and society take a keen interest in them (or some of them) and the problems associated with them; thirdly because of the apparent intractability of some of those problems; and finally, and perhaps most importantly of all, if we agree with Orford (1990), because drug taking may tell us something about the nature of being human.

This in itself is a timely debate; the National Drug Strategy (Home Office 1998; 2002) has seen a huge investment in the funding of services for drug users through the establishment of the National Treatment Agency for Substance Misuse, and through the provision of accredited programmes by the National Probation Service (NPS). The government's approach is clearly predicated upon the perceived link between drug use and acquisitive crime, and the need to reduce crime by getting more people into treatment, by coercive means if necessary. However, if we take the consensual view of addiction, which sees the addicted individual as having an impaired freedom of choice, as well as the view that relapse is a defining feature of addiction (see below), then an important question is whether linking treatment with punishment is in any sense ethical or indeed the best use of scarce public resources?

The amount of investigation by psychologists of the problem of addiction is vast, and for the purposes of this chapter I want to pick out some key themes that I see as essential in working with people who are experiencing difficulties with substance use. My intention is to assist the practitioner in addressing some key issues, and to this end I will utilise the trans-theoretical model of change (TTM) (DiClemente and Prochaska 1998) to highlight three psychological constructs, namely, motivation, self-efficacy and self-esteem.

The TTM is ubiquitous within professional approaches to dealing with the smoking of tobacco, illicit drug use, alcohol use, weight control, exercise, eating disorders, mental health, child welfare, domestic violence, organisational change, psychotherapy, and offender rehabilitation. The TTM is a complex, three-dimensional model comprised of stages, processes and levels of change that has spawned a large literature particularly relating to the stages of change (the cycle of change). Although ubiquitous in practice, this model has been heavily critiqued (most recently by West (2005), and these debates nicely demonstrate some of the strengths and weaknesses of psychological approaches to working with addiction. An examination of the psychological contribution to the biopsychosocial paradigm will lead to an argument that addiction is best viewed as an example of a complex, self-organising system. This approach challenges the traditional linear approach to diagnosis, treatment and the evaluation of outcomes, and adds to the argument that we need to review our ethical approach to addiction, particularly from the criminal justice perspective.

The assumptions of treatment approaches

In the application of theory to practice, Lindstrom (1992) summarises the assumptions made by different approaches to intervening in substance misuse issues (Table 8.1).

The technique hypothesis (the traditional basis for research in psychotherapy and psychology) expects to find a specific technique or setting that is better than other treatment for all people with a given diagnosis (currently, within the NPS, this is cognitive-behavioural therapy (CBT), whereas the matching hypothesis assumes variability in approach-based reciprocal interaction effects. It is therefore important consistently to pair client characteristics with treatment approaches, and it is argued that the research agenda needs to focus on which people are likely to respond to which treatments. The non-specific hypothesis argues that all treatments may be equally effective in producing beneficial and equivalent results, and this stems from the

Table 8.1 The assumptions of treatment approaches

	Is treatment effective?	Do therapies vary in efficacy?	Is there a superior therapy?
Technique hypothesis	Yes	Yes	Yes
Matching hypothesis	Yes	Yes	No
Non-specific hypothesis	Yes	No	–
Natural healing hypothesis	No	–	–

Source: Lindstrom 1992.

active ingredients involved in a range of therapeutic interventions. The natural healing hypothesis argues that any improvements that occur during the process of treatment are no greater than those that would have happened anyway without the treatment.

All of these assumptions are limited and in reality can be found in combination. Project MATCH (see below) demonstrates the limitations of matching specific people to specific interventions, and the pathfinder evaluations (see below) demonstrate the limitations of one approach. The natural healing hypothesis has implications for public order and public health that give rise to serious ethical issues, although an understanding of the ways in which people change without outside help makes an important contribution to our understanding of problematic behaviour. Probably most interest has been taken in the non-specific aspects, and it is some of these components that we will discuss via the TTM and the motivational work of Miller and Rollnick (1991).

Is there a whiff of 'nothing works' in the air?

Even a cursory reading of the evidence base for purely psychological interventions in offending behaviour and substance misuse would appear to demonstrate little impact. The evaluation of the pathfinder programmes for the NPS (Hollin *et al.* 2004) shows that the Alcohol and Substance Related Offending (ASRO) programme and the PRISM programme (both cognitive-behavioural programmes) were no more effective than an ordinary probation order. For these programmes, offenders were assigned to either an experimental group (those with a condition to attend programme) or a comparison group (those with a standard probation order without a condition). Within the current context of the NPS, the findings are nothing short of startling; there was a higher reconviction rate in the experimental group, and only one-third of the experimental group completed the programme. However, when the experimental group was divided into completers and non- completers, those who completed were less likely to be reconvicted. If we take this evidence and then look at the findings from Project MATCH (1997), a highly detailed study that found no significant difference in outcome between people assigned to motivational enhancement therapy, 12-step facilitation, or cognitive-behavioural coping skills therapy (all structured and delivered from manuals), there are some serious questions to be asked of what works in dealing with addiction.

West (2006), who is a psychologist and editor of the leading journal *Addiction*, argues that in substance misuse, psychological interventions appear to have very little impact. In addition, he and others (Herzog 2005) have argued that the key psychological construct utilised in the professional substance misuse field, the TTM (DiClemente and Prochaska 1998), should be abandoned (see below). How should we respond to these views from the field of psychology itself, given the huge implications for service delivery and professional training, particularly within the NPS, and keeping in mind that these are core tools for probation officers? The danger is, of course, that despite the huge investment by central government in psychological interventions and the desire for positive outcomes, we return to the ideology of 'nothing works' (Crow 2001: x) and abandon the rehabilitative ideal. However, before we all hold our hands up in horror and decide to go home, it is worth at this point recapping the work of Martinson (1974) and his own reflections on the issues of what works in changing problematic behaviour. Firstly, he thought that some of the programmes of the time (the early 1970s) may well have been working, but that our research methodology may not have been sensitive or sophisticated enough to measure those successes. Secondly, he held that the treatment programmes then may not have been good enough. Thirdly, he thought that the theoretical basis of the programmes may have been flawed in so far as the social phenomenon of crime may have been treated as a disease rather than a social problem. It is evident from the outcome literature that people do change behaviour, that people do overcome addictions, or the tendency to commit crimes, but we are not always sure of why or how. If the history of scientific research in this area tells us anything, it is that we need to become more sophisticated in our theory, research and interventions.

The substance misuse field had engaged with the implications of evidence-based practice (particularly in the USA) after the criticisms of 'nothing works' from an early stage. Despite the pessimism found in the areas of criminal justice, evaluative work continued to find the most effective forms of rehabilitation for people with drug and alcohol problems. Practitioners and researchers working with substance misuse were perhaps more comfortable with the idea of complexity, paradox and even contradiction in dealing with these issues. Substance misuse has only really been a major concern of government over the last 35 years or so, with the escalation in illicit drug use, and the so-called heroin epidemics in the late 1970s and early 1980s, and the spread of HIV/AIDS. In the UK, this led to a public health response from an unsympathetic, but ultimately realistic, Conservative government. In addition, with emerging discussion on the nature of social exclusion, drugs both legal and illegal were seen to be a key factor in criminal behaviour, and personal and communal dereliction (Home Office 1998; 2001).

The trans-theoretical model of change (TTM)

It is not my intention to outline the TTM in full in this chapter, and I refer the reader to the original authors for a full description of the model (DiClemente and Prochaska 1998).

Thus far, we have identified the importance of placing psychology within the context of the biopsychosocial paradigm, not least because questions have been asked about the effectiveness of treatment programmes predicated entirely upon psychological methods, and because other approaches (such as disease concepts utilised by self-help groups such as Alcoholics Anonymous (AA) and Narcotics Anonymous) appear to have some favourable outcomes as well. All approaches appear to have strengths and weaknesses, which may revolve around the ways in which those models perceive the limitations of personal responsibility and the reality of relapsing behaviour.

The TTM is not a theory of addiction, but it is a model of intentional behavioural change; this is why it has been applied across so many different settings. Although the model comprises stages, levels and processes of change, it is the stages or cycle of change that has caught the professional imagination and received the most attention from researchers. The model is an attempt to identify the core components of behavioural change that can be identified by reviewing the outcome literature on a range of therapeutic interventions, including cognitive, behavioural, humanistic and existential approaches. Although DiClemente and Prochaska (1998) propose the three-part model in its entirety, my experience of providing lecturing and training even to experienced practitioners is that those practitioners are aware only of the stages of change. A search of databases such as Medline and PsychInfo reveals a large literature on the stages, a much lesser amount on the processes, and virtually nothing on the levels. This in itself is very interesting, as the levels of change are linked to the issue of multiple needs, which are seen as being one of the biggest challenges facing the provision of public services (see Pycroft 2005).

The strengths of the TTM

DiClemente and Prochaska (1998) argue that a truly comprehensive model of behavioural change must not only be applicable across a range of addictive behaviours, but also must address the spectrum of ways in which people change. This spectrum covers self-help, brief interventions, and intensive therapeutic interventions; different people may need different approaches at different times. This search for core processes from diverse approaches is consistent with the psychological argument proposed by Bandura (1997) that all behaviours stem from common causes. The TTM thus provides a psychological framework for interventions that involve the core constructs of motivation and self-efficacy. An important distinction is made by Bandura (1997) (see below) between the concepts of self-efficacy and self-esteem, and self-esteem is not a construct within the TTM. I will argue that, in fact, self-esteem could form an important part of the TTM if all three parts of the model were utilised, particularly with reference to multiple needs.

Motivation

Miller (2006: 134) argues that 'addiction is fundamentally a problem of motivation' but, importantly, that this is not the same as saying that it is simply the result of people being unmotivated to address problematic behaviour, and therefore it is worthy of moral blame. Along with West (2001; 2006) and Koob (2006), Miller links the psychology of motivation to the neurological understanding of the brain's reward systems. Within the biopsychosocial paradigm, it is important not to privilege biology over the other factors (Orford 2001), and there are obviously complex connections here between biology, context and the expectancies of individuals using drugs (see Edwards, 2004, for a readable introduction). The issue of motivation is at the heart of motivational interviewing (MI), which has been developed by Miller and Rollnick (1991) as a key adjunct to the cycle of change. Along with the TTM, MI has also become a key feature of professional services. In its adoption by the community justice sector, MI may also raise some questions and conflicts for practitioners, given that it is not just a set of techniques but also an important statement of values in working with people who have addictions (and other problematic behaviours). Given that one of Miller's robust principles (2006: 149) in working with addictions is that 'once ... dependence has been established, education, persuasion, punishment and attention typically yield little or no beneficial effect, and sometimes even exert a paradoxical effect', we have to question seriously the relationship between punishment and treatment in working with addiction. In developing the idea of motivational working as a value-driven approach, research continues to demonstrate that the empathic qualities of the worker are fundamentally important in delivering effective programmes, because the same programmes can be delivered in exactly the same way (from manuals) by different people and provide different outcomes depending upon who delivered the programme (Miller and Rollnick 1991; Dowden and Andrews 2004).

In their review of effective treatments for alcohol problems, Raistrick *et al.* (2006) argue that MI should be a prominent component of modern treatment services because it increases the effectiveness of more extensive psychosocial treatments. They also argue that MI can be effective as a preparation for more intensive treatments of different kinds, and that it is no more effective than other forms of psychosocial treatments but it is less intensive and therefore potentially more cost-effective. There is agreement, then, that MI is as effective as other approaches, that this partly stems from the value base that it provides, and that it is adjunctive to other interventions of medical and/or social orientation and thus needs to be part of our thinking in working with addictions. Even the severest critics of the TTM (West 2005; 2006; Herzog 2005) argue that motivation is a key component of addictive behaviour and should continue to be a focus for both research and intervention.

Working with relapse

Of great significance is the fact that relapse is identified within the TTM, DiClemente and Prochaska (1998) arguing that relapse is the norm rather than the exception in overcoming addictive behaviour. The initial research by Prochaska and DiClemente, which found that people would revolve around the cycle of change, on average, six to eight times before giving up smoking, has clear links with social learning theory. This has raised new possibilities for interventions that might consider not just relapse-prevention approaches but also relapse management. Relapse is part of the process. The importance of this cannot be overstated, because the notion of relapse management is in complete contradistinction to popular disease models utilised by AA and Narcotics Anonymous. While the 12-step disease model agrees with the idea of impaired control, it also argues that alcoholics or addicts have an abnormal craving for drugs which marks them out from other people.

The principles of social learning theory are that anybody can develop problematic behaviour or become addicted to drugs, whereas the 12-step view is that alcoholics and addicts are physically and mentally different from the rest of the population (for more information, see www.alcoholics-anonymous.org.uk/). The disease is irreversible unless addicts completely abstain from drug use, and if they resume that use, all the symptoms of the disease quickly reappear (see Heather and Robertson (1997) for a review of 'diseased' theories). You will have noted from the Project MATCH research (1986) that 12-step facilitation had the same outcomes as the other interventions; however, in terms of interventions, the psychological approach has highlighted a major problem with the goal of total abstinence, the abstinence violation effect (AVE) (Marlatt 1985).

From the psychological perspective, addiction is dimensional and not unitary in nature; people vary in the difficulties they experience with their drug use, and require differing interventions and outcome goals dependent upon their situation. In practice, this may mean either stopping completely or cutting down (the harm-minimisation or controlled-drinking approach). Whatever the goal aimed for, it is still a matter of control. However, if a person is trying for complete abstinence but engaging in the initial use of a drug (a slip or lapse), feelings of failure, guilt and anger may ensue, leading to continued drug use, so that a full relapse occurs. People who use AA say 'that one drink is too many and a thousand is not enough' (Hamilton n.d.: 6). Relapse management tries to teach control mechanisms so that drug use does not increase, thereby maintaining the viability of the original goal. Within this approach and as it is expressed within the TTM, a mature understanding of relapse would view lapse and relapse as opportunities to review what is and what is not working in achieving personal treatment goals.

Self-efficacy

Self-efficacy has been presented by Bandura (1977) as a unifying theory of behaviour that 'plays a unique role in the addictive behaviors field … [influencing] both the initial development of addictive habits and the behavior change process' (Marlatt *et al.* 1995: 289). Self-efficacy is a core construct within CBT approaches and is a key part of the TTM. Bandura (1977; 1986) defines self-efficacy as the belief by people that they can cope with a situation that is of high risk to them in terms of engaging in unwanted behaviour. This is particularly of relevance to addiction whereby certain situations may increase the risk of relapse, and there is a substantial body of literature linking the development of self-efficacy with positive treatment outcomes (see Marlatt *et al.* 1995). Marlatt and Gordon's (1985) seminal relapse prevention model posits the idea that an individual with coping skills, when faced with a high-risk situation, is more likely to be able to deal with that situation in a functional way that, in itself, leads to an increase in confidence. Self-efficacy can be seen as a positive feedback loop that is linked to notions of mastery over one's own personal environments (Dweck 2000). In dealing with addictions, it has been found that it is success and trying to be successful that eventually predict success (Westerberg 1998). Conversely, failure to succeed can lead to an increased risk of relapse, and an increased salience of the drug-taking behaviour.

In practice, Bandura's theory of self-efficacy is somewhat narrow in focus, partly because he makes a clear distinction between it and the other self-concept of self-esteem. Bandura (1997) argues that there is a difference between the two concepts, because it is quite possible to achieve personal goals, aims and objectives without having a sense of self-worth or feeling good about it. There is no doubt from the research that self-efficacy (based upon situational confidence) is important precisely because it varies from situation to situation for individuals. However, this narrow definition of self-efficacy feeds into the TTM, which does not therefore identify concepts related to self-esteem. A consequence of this may be that our ability to theorise about and work with individuals who have the most complex problems may be hampered because of important links between confidence, self-worth and identity that will be discussed below.

Weaknesses of the TTM

Self-esteem

Self-esteem and self-efficacy are both self-concepts in that they are related to the individual's sense of self. Ideas of self-esteem are common in everyday professional conversations as well as reflective accounts from probation students concerning the work that they undertake. However, there may be little understanding about what self-esteem actually is, and clarity on this is important for both the practitioner and the academic researcher.

There are a number of differing definitions of self-esteem, and a comprehensive account of these and their components is provided by Mruk (1999), while Emler (2001) provides a good overview of the causes and consequences of low self-esteem. Mruk (1999) shows that self esteem is linked to identity and behaviour, and that positive self-esteem correlates with positive mental health and psychological well-being, whereas low self-esteem is correlated with depression and a range of other mental health disorders, as well as a lack of adequate personal and social functioning. The key to Bandura's view of the differences between self-esteem and self-efficacy lies in the relationship between confidence and feelings of worthiness. However, as Mruk (1999) shows, there are a number of differing definitions of self-esteem that incorporate differing components.

For example, probably the most widely used research instrument in this field is the Rosenberg Self-Esteem Scale (Emler 2001), which emphasises feelings of worthiness and stability (self-esteem is seen as stabilising in late adolescence, and, while it may fluctuate, it will return to a general level, whereas self-efficacy is seen as being situational and relatively open to change). However, other theories include other dimensions of self-esteem, such as confidence (competence), cognition as well as feelings, and openness. A reading of Mruk indicates that a mature definition of self-esteem that incorporates these other components (in the context of this chapter, especially confidence) may provide us with opportunities to develop our work with individuals who engage in problematic behaviour. DiClemente and Prochaska (1998) find that people's problematic behaviour may affect different areas of their lives to the point that they may experience intrapsychic conflict so that their sense of self or identity is bound up with that behaviour. This process of social, professional or self-labelling that designates people as 'alcoholic', 'junkie', or 'piss head', indicates a strong link with 'self-esteem [which] is central to the dynamics of the identity process' (Breakwell and Rowett 1982: 41).

These issues of identity are often bound up with multiple problem areas, and since people are presenting to services with increasingly complex matrices of problems, including multidrug use, homelessness, mental and physical health problems, and offending behaviour (see Gossop *et al.* 2003), this is an important area for theory building to inform effective practice. The levels of change are an important but ultimately limited attempt to address the issues related to identity and multiple needs. Given that 'psychology is the study of the individual in context' (Gifford and Humphreys 2007: 352), these levels do not give sufficient attention to other factors, particularly social ones, that affect behaviour (Barber 1995).

Stage change models

The perceived weaknesses of the TTM are thoroughly reviewed by West (2005; 2006), and although some of the core constructs that we have discussed are seen as being important in addressing addictive behaviour, the way that they are incorporated into the TTM is not. West argues that the dividing lines between the stages are arbitrary in terms of deciding whether someone is in the contemplation or the action stage, for example.

This raises some interesting issues in relation to utilising the TTM in professional practice. There are clear criteria for which stage patients should be allocated to by their plans to quit and their recent past attempts at quitting. However, West (2005) criticises this approach because it assumes that all individuals make coherent and stable plans, whereas, usually, intentions about change are not well formulated. He goes on to argue that the stage definitions represent different types of psychological constructs that do not fit well together (time since quitting, intention and past quitting attempts).

But perhaps more importantly for practice and the research agenda is the fact that for most professionals the allocation of an individual to a stage of change (which may determine the types of interventions offered) is not carried out in any systematic way. I have already described how most practitioners are not familiar with all three components of the TTM. To highlight the point about misapplication at a recent student conference, I asked a group of trainee probation officers (about 50 in total) how they allocated an individual to a stage of change, and they all answered that this was done after a discussion with the offender, but that this was not linked to the criteria given by DiClemente and Prochaska. In fact, they were not aware of the criteria. It can only be concluded that, although the

TTM may have some clear strengths, these are being undermined by a flawed application of its key constructs.

Is it stating the obvious?

West (2005) says that the proponents of the TTM argue that it is important because it enables individuals to be moved in the direction of change, citing the argument that those who are closer to the maintenance of change at any one time are more likely to have changed their behaviour when followed up. However, West argues that this is no more than saying that those who are in the process of behaviour change are more likely to change than those who are only thinking about it, and that people who want or plan to do something are more likely to try to do it, and those who try are more likely to succeed than those who do not. This may in fact be just a statement of the obvious and not tell us very much about interventions required to overcome addiction.

The way forward

It is evident from the academic literature that the TTM incorporates some important psychological concepts in working with addictive behaviour. It marks an important attempt to transcend the boundaries and limitations of narrow approaches to behavioural change. The model is complex and, in practice, given the demands upon busy practitioners, may be too complex to utilise in its entirety.

This is an issue that needs to be addressed and would not be an argument put forward for addressing other major issues such as cancer or diabetes. Complexity is the nature of the beast, and if we want fully to address these issues, it is important to continue building testable models and hypotheses to try to provide solutions to apparently intractable problems. After having considered the strengths and weaknesses of purely psychological approaches, and bearing in mind the biopsychosocial paradigm, I want now to discuss the idea of addiction as an example of a complex, self-organising system.

Complex self-organising systems

The study of complex systems in a unified framework has become recognized ... as a new scientific discipline, the ultimate of interdisciplinary fields. It is strongly rooted in the advances that have been made in diverse fields ranging from physics to anthropology, from which it draws inspiration and to which it is relevant. (Bar-Yam 1997: 1)

Complexity is a move away from studying neat and logical linear relationships in favour of a focus on decentralised interactions and feedback loops. It is the study of the ways in which complex behaviours can emerge from interactions among simple components, and this is known as emergence (Bar-Yam 1997). West (2006) says that complexity theory is a metaphor, in the sense that it describes a set of complex mathematical relationships between component parts of systems that, in practice, may not seem useful or relevant to the practitioner. However, as a metaphor, complexity theory is extremely useful as a tool of analysis, and we should not be afraid of asking difficult questions even if, as yet, there would seem to be no immediate solutions. Human beings, communities, families, ecosystems and governments are all examples of complex systems. Complex systems have commonalities that distinguish them from simple systems, and Bar-Yam (1997: 5) identifies the following:

- elements (and their number);
- interactions (and their strength);
- formation/operation (and their timescales);
- diversity/variability;
- environment (and its demands);
- activities (and their objectives).

As an introduction to this area of study, we can see that addiction clearly contains interaction effects between biology, psychology and sociology, and these interactions may give rise to a whole host of differing effects, some positive but many negative and unintended. The *sine qua non* of complexity theory is modern non-linear dynamics, which, despite its label, is incredibly simple! Goerner (1995: 19) describes it thus: 'Technically, a non-linear system is any system in which input is not proportional to output, that is, an increase in x does not mean a proportional increase or decrease in y.' For example, a traditional linear approach might argue that a serious persistent offender needs more frequent and intense levels of input than a less persistent offender, to address offending behaviour. However, a non-linear approach would say that there may be an improvement in behaviour, or there may not; in fact, things may get worse. These are precisely the kinds of paradoxical effects that Miller talks about (2006).

Increasingly, the concept of addiction itself is being seen as a type of complex, self-organising system. It is argued that the answers to some of the questions posed at the beginning of the chapter may be found in a new view of addiction that sees it as 'a self-organizing complex disorder that emerges from the interaction of evolutionary old behavioural processes and their associated brain regions', (Bickel and Potenza 2006: 9).

Traditionally, approaches to addiction have sought for singular causes such as craving, drug reinforcement, and sensitisation, whereas the self-organising system approach argues that 'There is no centralised control by a singular process in addiction' (Bickel and Potenza 2006: 9). This is an approach from evolutionary psychology that argues that the brain should not be viewed as an all-purpose computer that can solve any problem, but rather is modular in nature. Modules are units of the brain that are physically or functionally insulated subsystems preserved by natural selection because they solve adaptive problems. Within a 'modular system, control is distributed over the whole of the system without being centralised' (Bickel and Potenza 2006: 10). The implication of this is that if we only work on one module of the system, we are overlooking other important modules and their interaction effects.

Holder (1998) argues that an understanding of complexity theory within a community context is essential to understanding, preventing and working with drug problems. He proposes a new 'paradigm for prevention' with the following propositions (8–9):

- Drug problems are the natural results or outputs of dynamic, complex and adaptive systems called 'communities'.
- Working only with high-risk groups produces at best only short-term reductions in problems because the system will replace individuals leaving high-risk status, and the system will adapt to the changes in the behaviour and composition of subgroups and populations.
- Interventions in complex adaptive systems will often produce counter-intuitive results.
- The most effective prevention strategies are those that seek to alter the system that produces drug problems.
- Historically, prevention (and, I would argue, treatment approaches) have been focused on a single solution (the technique hypothesis) rather than concurrent, mutually reinforcing approaches.

- Without an understanding of community as a dynamic system, it is unlikely that the long-term prevention of drug problems will occur.

Complexity theory and its applications are now to be found across all areas of the human and life sciences, really challenging traditional thinking in all of these areas. However, the theory does start to address some of the key questions that have been consistently asked in the field of addiction over the course of the twentieth century and into the twenty-first. It reaffirms the view that complex problems do not have simple solutions. We know that some interventions have beneficial outcomes for individuals and communities, and that because of the nature of complex adaptive systems, these interventions need to be at least as dynamic as the problems that they are addressing. One of the features of complex systems is that, because of their dynamism and adaptability, even after they are seriously perturbed (challenged, threatened), they will return to how they were before, or in a modified form. One of the messages from the 'what works' research in the NPS has been the need for multimodal treatment approaches (Chapman and Hough 1998), suggesting the need for 'wrap around' and dynamic services that get to grips with a whole system rather than just a part of it.

Conclusion

The concept of addiction is complex, and the more that we find out about the human condition generally and all of its aspects, biological, psychological and sociological, the more complex even the component parts seem to become, with few answers and more questions. However, asking the right questions, as any dissertation student knows, is crucial. In this chapter, I have tried to examine the strengths and weaknesses of some core psychological constructs through the lens of research and ultimately practical application. Professionals are under real pressure to produce results in working with complex problems, and people experiencing those problems are under pressure to change. These conflicts will not disappear, but the way that we view and work with them may. The instillation of hope is key to any therapeutic relationship (Yalom 1995), and the reason for continued research in the field of addiction is to alleviate the incredible amount of suffering that it causes. Practitioners have a responsibility to ensure that they are up to date with the latest research in their areas of work, and to seek to apply it no matter how challenging that research is to their organisations or their professional identity.

Chapter 9

Date rape and drugs

Introduction

Consider the following billing of a BBC television drama:

> Late one night a live radio talk-show host gets a call from a listener, Kate (Keeley Hawes), saying she needs someone to believe her story. She claims that she's been raped, but that nobody believes her.
>
> But there is more to this story than meets the eye. The man who Kate says raped her is her colleague at a slick London architect's office, and, what's more, they're good friends.
>
> Alex (Stuart Laing), the man in question, has a very different view of what happened on the fateful night – their relationship had always been flirtatious and, as far as he's concerned, they had consensual sex.
>
> Even Kate's friends at the office seem to doubt her version of events. As a result Kate craves validation and devises a plan to make Alex admit he did it. But for Alex there is nothing to admit – as far as he's concerned he did nothing wrong.
>
> There are two versions of the event – who will you believe? (BBC 2006)

This is how the BBC3 drama *Sex and Lies*, written by Jeremy Lovering, is introduced. It contains a number of key characteristics of what is commonly known as 'date rape': the alleged victim and perpetrator know each other. There has been sexual intercourse, but the exact nature of that episode is controversial, which is, actually not uncommon. It is quite possible for a sex offence not to be regarded as a crime by the perpetrator, or even by the victim. Finally, there is the victim's struggle to come to terms with what has happened. We should never assume that any trauma incurred by this form of victimisation is necessarily lessened by the fact that is perpetrated by a non-stranger. In fact, psychological research suggests that the level of trauma is highly similar (Sampson 2000).

Date rape, or to place it in a wider context, sexual offending between people who know each other, often causes confusion, resentment and trauma. This confusion is possibly enhanced by the fact that young people are subjected to contrary expectations about what it is to be young and how to go out and have a good time. In Britain, having a drink is regarded, as long as it is within reasonable limits, as fun, and, in addition, there is considerable cultural acceptance of getting drunk. Similarly, meeting and socialising can be rewarding, even exhilarating experiences. Flirting, 'snogging', and 'having a fling' are experiences that many youngsters have without experiencing coercion, threats or violence. However, it is exactly this social and cultural context in which many young people do suffer victimisation. This chapter will outline the level of victimisation and the social and cognitive processes involved within both offenders and victims.

Stranger rape, date rape and acquaintance rape

Date rape is often regarded a separate category of offence, although the Sexual Offences Act 2003 does not recognise it as such. It is in fact more meaningful to regard date rape or acquaintance rape, as it is also often referred to in the academic literature, as somewhere on a continuum of sexual offending. On one end of the scale, there is the predatory stranger's attack on an unsuspecting victim. These cases, the classic 'stranger rape', rare though they are, capture the public imagination and can induce a great deal of fear of crime. These, rather perversely, are sometimes referred to as 'real rapes', as if other forms of rape do not deserve that label (Kelly *et al.* 2005). On the other side of the spectrum is rape in marriage or between people in a long-term relationship who live together in the same household. Although such cases are less likely to make headlines, it is shocking in its own right that it is the ones we love who are seemingly most likely to commit a sex crime: sex crimes between intimates occur much more often than sexual attacks by strangers.

Ironically, rape in marriage was, until relatively recently, an oxymoron: in the criminal law in England and Wales (and many other countries), it did not exist as a crime, a lingering vestige of the days of yore when a married woman was her husband's property as much as his partner. Unfortunately, the exemption of husbands in rape legislation as well as the 'wife-as-property' attitude has certainly not died out, in a global perspective, as many countries today continue to refuse to define it as a crime.

Date rape sits somewhere between. It is committed by offenders who casually or more or less intimately know their victim. Acquaintance rape is a slightly wider category than date rape. As Bletzer and Koss (2004) describe, 'Notions of "date rape" belong to the category of acquaintance rape, and the perpetrator may include, among others, male kin, co-workers, neighbors, and merchants all of whom may be known and trusted by a woman, as well as someone whom she agreed to "date"' (116).

The term 'date rape' is furthermore problematic because the concept of a 'date' and the activity we refer to as 'dating' mean different things to different people. In the US, the word 'dating' is often used for an ongoing relationship where both individuals socialise with each other repeatedly over a period of time. This is what in the UK might be called 'going out': it assumes a relationship beyond the social occasion of a single date. A 'date' in the UK is more likely to be understood as a possible one-off, or a first occasion in which two people socialise with potential romantic or sexual overtones or undercurrents. This is one reason why it makes sense to refer to acquaintance rape as a specific type of sex offence rather than date rape. We can, of course, quibble over who is and who is not an acquaintance, but the term 'date' carries a much wider variety of social and cultural expectations. A result of these problems of definition is that the prevalence of date rape depends on what one regards as a date, and also what victims law enforcement officials and researchers call rape.

Prevalence of date rape

In the USA, date rape is considered a substantial social problem, and its prevalence indeed seems to be high. Schubot (2001) established the prevalence of date rape victimisation in the US state of South Dakota among high-school (secondary school) girls. To the question, 'Have you ever been forced to have sexual intercourse when you didn't want to on a date?' 14.9 per cent answered 'yes' in 1993. In

1995 and 1997, the same survey was repeated and the prevalence had fallen to 11.8 per cent in both 1995 and 1997. Schubot, however, argued that these data are limited: first the item does not define 'sexual intercourse'. It transpired that of the girls who indicated that they had been raped by a date, more than 1 in 10 did not report ever having had sexual intercourse, forced or otherwise. That makes it difficult to make sense of their answers. Moreover, the question posed did not distinguish between physical force and other forms of intimidation or coercion.

To be fair, Schubot also referred to the ambiguity of the word 'date', and argues that his data may well be an underestimation. Hanson similarly argues that so-called broad screening questions as utilised by Schubot are not effective ways of measuring prevalence, primarily due to the fact that the key terms are left undefined. Hanson (2002) therefore argues that more specific questions should be asked of victims which was earlier advocated by Acierno *et al.* (1997). When victims answer more precise questions, the reported prevalence of unpleasant behaviours on a date dramatically increases. Jackson *et al.* (2000) found that 82 per cent of girls and 76 per cent of boys reported experience of some form of psychological abuse in a dating context. They also found that 77 per cent of female and 67 per cent of male high-school students reported some form of sexual coercion, ranging from unwanted embraces and kissing to genital contact and sexual intercourse (Jackson *et al.* 2000). These are, as Hanson (2002) argues, staggering figures. That makes it all the more amazing that, until recently, these figures were unknown, and the risks associated with dating were underestimated. We are increasingly aware of its high prevalence, and this Fisher *et al.* call 'a remarkable transformation in social and legal consciousness' (Fisher *et al.* 2005: 494).

Neville *et al.* (2004) found that although only a small minority of victims contact the police, over 75 per cent do not stay silent: they confide in someone (usually between one and three people), and they report that the support they received from those individuals was good. A survey among US college students found that one in three said that a woman had disclosed to them that she had been raped by a date or an acquaintance (Dunn *et al.* 1999). However, while good social support is important it does not necessarily rebuild a victim's self-esteem (Nurius *et al.* 2004).

Who is at risk? Victims and offenders

The 1999 national school-based Youth Risk Behavior Surveillance (YRBS) survey carried out in the USA, sought to identify which girls would be particularly at risk of being on the receiving end of sexual violence in a dating environment. With over 15,000 pupils surveyed, the survey found that 9.0 per cent of young people had ever been forced to have sexual intercourse against their will on a date (YRBS 2004). It must once more be emphasised that this is a very high number. When extrapolated to the US population as a whole, this represents hundreds of thousands of victims.

As with all types of victimisation, people with certain characteristics are more at risk than others. Howard and Wang analysed the YRBS data to identify risk factors for dating violence. That is a broader category than sexual violence alone, but it is likely that their findings would generalise to sexual violence more specifically as well. A number of behavioural or lifestyle factors were identified. Binge drinking, having had more than one sexual partner, having had unsafe sex, and use of cocaine on the part of the victim all increased the likelihood of being subjected to violence in a dating context. There is also a statistical link between carrying a weapon and fighting, and dating victimisation.

Furthermore, respondents who reported 'feeling sad' were more likely to also report dating violence against them. These risk factors are interrelated, and from that a profile of at-risk women emerges:

> Girls who reported fighting and weapon carrying, the use of a variety of substances (such as tobacco, cocaine, and inhalants), and engaging in risky behaviors (e.g. not using condoms) were at greater risk for being a victim of dating violence. The co-occurrence of these factors supports the notion of an at-risk profile for adolescent girls, and reinforces the concept of problem behaviour, in that adolescents who engage in one risky behavior are likely to be involved in other risky behaviors as well. (Howard and Wang 2003: 10)

Just as there are certain women who are more susceptible to being victimised in a dating situation, there are also males who are more or less likely to offend. The factors that impinge on males' propensity to commit acquaintance rape can be characterised as either situational or attitudinal. Situational variables seek to predict whether certain events, happenings or characteristics on a date might make a date rape more likely to occur. Attitudinal variables have to do with the male's attitudes, to women, their attitudes about rape, and about where the boundaries of acceptable behaviour lie. Finally, we will look at the possibility that males' misperception of sexual intent by the female and misperceptions of consent can be regarded as explanatory factors.

A number of attitudes conducive to rape have been identified. These are discussed in terms of so-called rape myths. These are defined as 'attitudes and beliefs that are generally false but are widely and persistently held, and that serve to deny and justify male sexual aggression against women' (Lonsway and Fitzgerald 1994: 134). These ideas can take a number of forms: they can be that women who protest against sex in a dating situation only do so to put up token resistance; that women who go on a date should expect to 'deliver the goods' in terms of sex; that violence is part and parcel of romantic relationships; that men are entitled to 'get sex' from their dating partner regardless of her wishes; or that sexual relationships usually are characterised by exploitation. Such beliefs can be measured by the Burt Rape Myth Acceptance Scale (BRMAS) (Burt 1980). It is list of statements to which respondents can more or less strongly agree or disagree, on the Likert scale, such as 'Any healthy woman can successfully resist a rape if she really wants to'; 'When women go around braless or wearing short skirts and tight tops, they are just asking for trouble'; and 'If a girl engages in necking or petting and she lets things get out of hand, it is her own fault if her partner forces sex on her.'

It has been found that men who score higher on the BRMAS are more likely to commit acquaintance rape (Burt 1980). Since then, the scale has been widely used particularly in the USA, where it has been found that certain universities seem to contain settings in which women are particularly at risk. Interestingly, Sawyer *et al.* (2002) in a survey of US intercollegiate athletes in various sports from five universities, found that males who play in a team sport such as basketball score higher than those who pursue an individual sport, such as swimming or running. Higher levels of date rape acceptance were also found among fraternity (male student society) members (Boeringer 1999). Unsurprisingly, hostile attitudes to women, and so-called hostile masculinities whereby suppression of and violence against women are believed to be a trait that 'makes a man' are also related to date rape proclivity (Malamuth *et al.* 1995).

Thus, part of the explanation of date rape lies in the attitudes of the men who commit it. Situational variables add to this picture. These variables can include a misperception of sexual intent, that is, the male wrongly perceives the female to be consenting to sex leading to sexual situational frustration. In order to look at these variables, Willan and Pollard (2003) had 50 male and 50 female students at a British university read a scenario that depicted a hypothetical sexual encounter. The story was based on the so-called traditional sexual script (Sarler 2006). Although both men and women read the same scenarios, the men received a version that told the story from the man's perspective, whereas the women's version related the story from the woman's point of view. The scenario consisted of four stages. In the first stage, the couple, Sarah and Steve, met and socialised. In the second, they were back at Steve's room in a student hall of residence and engaged in kissing; in the third, there was bodily and genital touching; and in the final stage, the couple engaged in consensual mutual masturbation.

The experiment had two conditions: one group of students read only stages 1 and 2, after which Sarah says she has to leave but would love to see Steve again next week. The other group read stages 1–4, after which Sarah leaves, and agrees to see Steve again next week. Thus, both groups read a scenario that involves Sarah's non-consenting to further sexual activities, but the stage at which that occurs differs: either after kissing or after mutual masturbation. After each stage, the participants were asked to indicate whether (placing themselves in either Steve or Sarah's position) they would have desired 'go further'. They also indicated whether they felt that the 'other party' wanted to go further as well. At the end of the story, the men completed four other measures, one measuring the perceived level of frustration of the male protagonist; a 'hostility against women' rating scale; the rape myth scale, as originally devised by Burt (1980) and adapted by Lonsway and Fitzgerald (1994); and a brief but telling 'date rape proclivity' measure: 'How likely would you be to force the female to have sexual intercourse?'.

The findings were of interest. Regarding the perceived desire to 'go further', the male respondents perceived a greater desire in all sexual activity than the female respondents. In addition, the male students overestimated the desire of the female in the story to engage in later sexual activity. Thus, males might assume women to be more intent on sex than they actually are at the early stages of a romantic or sexual encounter. Interestingly, the difference between the male and female participants was greatest after stage 1, the meeting and socialising stage: here men overestimated the woman's desire to engage in sexual behaviours, including intercourse. How does this relate to self-professed date rape proclivity? Situational factors were found to be more predictive of date rape proclivity than attitudes. The strongest correlate was males' perception of female intent to sexual intercourse at stage 1, that is, the level of belief that 'she is up for it' at the stage of meeting and socialising. Secondly, the level of indicated disappointment when the female withdraws consent is the next strongest predictor. A high level of hostility toward women was the third factor to impinge on self-reported date rape propensity. Thus, in summary, male attitudes to rape and women are a factor of importance in explaining date rape, but it is characteristics of the situation (and the offender's interpretation of that situation) that provide stronger cues as to how this type of offending occurs.

A second study reported in the same publication sheds further light on sexual communication. It explores the issue of men possibly misunderstanding a woman's sexual communications (Willan and Pollard 2003). This is of importance, as it is a common criminal defence in rape and sexual assault cases. Defendants very regularly claim that there was consent, or at least that it was reasonable to assume that there was consent. It makes the communication of consent an issue of considerable psychological as well as legal significance. Generally, it seems that men and women understand consent to be communicated in the same way. Byers found that both male and female respondents found 'fondling male's genitals' to be the number one method of communicating consent; verbal consent 'only' came second, and 'no resistance to genital fondling' was third.

On the other hand, communicating non-consent was best achieved verbally. The second most important method of communicating non-consent was 'to be unresponsive and passive'. A key finding seems to be that consent is often given non-verbally, whereas non-consent often is communicated via a verbal message.

With that in mind, Willan and Pollard offered another group of male and female students a scenario not dissimilar to the one described above. They did not find that males over-perceive consent. 'These findings raise questions as to the validity of legal defences based on the male's "reasonable" misperception of sexual consent, due to the ambiguous nature of the female's sexual communication' (Willan and Pollard 2003: 658). Thus, if there is a mismatch between men and women's expectations in dating situations, it is the perceived likelihood of sex (later) at the stage of kissing. But men in this study have no problem understanding whether or not consent was given.

It is in this regard interesting that a current British government campaign is actually targeted at achieving clarity on consent in such situations. The Home Office has launched a £500,000 campaign with the slogan, 'If you don't get a yes, don't have sex.' Posters carrying this message, aimed at 18–24-year-old men, are on display in pubs and clubs. Of course, it is good advice to be sure about one's partner's wishes, particularly when there is alcohol involved, but Willan and Pollard's findings suggest that it is not the misperception of consent that is the issue. That makes us question the effectiveness – but, of course, not the righteousness – of the campaign.

In addition, Carol Sarler in the newspaper the *Guardian* criticised the campaign for its failing to appreciate the realities of casual, acquaintance sex: 'Real life says that two people out together, particularly those who have just met – which is when trouble seems most likely to occur – drink nervously and frequently until both are stumbling, both are fumbling, neither is capable of anything approaching rational consent' (*Guardian*, 16 March 2006). The anti-rape posters mean well, but making men entirely responsible for sex implies that women are incompetent.

Drug-facilitated sexual assault (DFSA)

The environment in which alcohol and recreational drugs are commonplace provides further risk to women. It is the context in which so-called drugs rape is most likely to occur. As it is seen to be a major factor about which considerable concern exists, we will discuss it in detail. In the typical scenario, a woman goes out in the evening to socialise, suffers acute and complete memory loss, and wakes up the next morning, to discover, in a state of shock, that she has had sex, but is unable to recollect with whom or any other circumstances of the event. This phenomenon is often referred as either drug rape or drugs-induced date rape. The official term is drug-facilitated sexual assault' (DFSA).

We do not know much about the prevalence of DFSA for various reasons. Firstly, we have to examine the situation in which the victims find themselves, and their loss of memory makes it difficult to establish exactly what happened and who the perpetrator was. That might make victims rather disinclined to take any official steps, as they are likely to be confused and may, as victims often erroneously seem to do, blame themselves. It is well known that there is a great deal of reluctance by victims in general, and victims of sex offences in particular, to come forward, and it is fair to say that their experience of the criminal justice system, at least in England and Wales, is too often not good (Kelly *et al.* 2004).

The presence of certain drugs such as cannabis can be detected in the human body for quite some time, but some of the drugs associated with DFSA disappear very quickly, so that a forensic examination of blood or urine, if it is not done very quickly after the alleged event, might not yield positive results. Needless to say, such crimes will often occur without anyone else witnessing both the administration of the substance and the sexual offence. All these factors make the establishment of exactly how often drug-facilitated date rape occurs very difficult indeed. Despite the paucity of data, drugs rape is a concern, and there have been campaigns to highlight the dangers of leaving drinks unattended and accepting drinks from strangers. The short film *Spiked!* with the slogan, 'Who is watching your drink?' (Jones 2003) was shown in British cinemas in 2003.

Date rape drugs

A number of substances can be utilised to facilitate a sexual offence, not least large quantities of alcohol, and this is an issue to which we return later. Many drugs prescribed for patients suffering from depression or anxiety, and anaesthetic drugs might be used, as they might render a victim incapacitated, comatose or otherwise incapable of preventing the offence from occurring. However, the two drugs most notably associated with date rape are GHB and Rohypnol.

GHB, short for gamma-hydroxybutyric acid, is a synthetic drug. In the USA, it is classified as a Schedule 1 drug, which is the most severe category in the Hillory J. Farias and Samantha Reid Date Rape Drug Prohibition Act 2000 (Hensley 2003). Farias and Reid were two young women who died of GHB overdose. GHB (also sometimes called 'liquid ecstasy') has a number of characteristics that make it dangerous (Rodgers *et al.* 2004). First of all, it is relatively easy to manufacture. In addition, it is colourless and odourless. The fluid has a slightly salty taste, but that is easily masked when mixed with alcoholic drinks. A teaspoonful is enough to produce substantial changes in a victim within 15 minutes. It can bring about a number of effects such as euphoria or drowsiness, and in higher dosages it relaxes the muscles, and can bring on vomiting and coma. An overdose can be fatal, and numerous deaths have been reported in the USA (Li *et al.* 1998). It is also noteworthy that those intoxicated by GHB might simply seem very drunk to their environment. Another effect is lasting anterograde amnesia; there will be no recollection of the events that occur while under the influence of the drug. GHB is eliminated from the body in 10–12 hours. That makes timing of the essence in forensic testing for the substance, which should be performed as soon after the event as possible.

The following advice is adapted from Hensley (2003):

1. Students should avoid any drink that they did not receive directly from the bar or that they did not open themselves.
2. If someone offers students a drink, they should walk with him or her to the bar, watch it being poured, and carry it themselves.
3. When at a bar or party, students should avoid trying new concoctions that they have never tasted. Shooters, shots, and drinks with multiple liquors may mask the slightly salty taste of GHB. Concoctions such as margaritas, Long Island iced teas, fruity daiquiris, Goldschlager (a cinnamon-flavored liquor), and 'fishbowl' drinks have all been used to drug women without their knowledge.
4. Students should not accept a drink poured from a punchbowl. They should also avoid sharing drinks that are passed from person to person.
5. Students should not leave their drinks unattended for any reason – they can carry drinks with them when going to the lavatory, dancing, talking to someone across the room, and using the telephone. If their drinks have been left unattended for any reason, they should discard them immediately.
6. Students should use the buddy system. They should watch friends for signs of sudden intoxication such as slurred speech or difficulty in walking. If a friend is disproportionately intoxicated in relation to the amount of alcohol he or she has consumed, students should assist him or her in leaving the situation immediately.
7. If friends have passed out (particularly if disproportionately intoxicated in relation to the amount of alcohol known to have been consumed), students should not allow them to 'sleep it off'. GHB-related deaths have occurred from deciding to put friends to bed rather than seeking immediate medical assistance. While waiting for medical intervention, students should make sure the victim is on his or her side to prevent aspiration. They should not leave the victim unattended for any reason.

8. If students suspect they have ingested GHB, they should go to the emergency room immediately. Students should request a urine sample to screen for the presence of GHB within 12 hours of ingestion. This screen is not routinely done, as many medical professionals are not familiar with GHB symptoms.

Unlike GHB, Rohypnol (a brand name; the drug is also known as flunitrazepam) is a pill that dissolves in water (Fitzgerald and Riley 2000). Like GHB, it is odourless and colourless; in addition, it is tasteless. The predominant clinical manifestations are drowsiness, impaired motor skills, and anterograde amnesia. Gable calls the effects of Rohypnol (and the similar benzodiazepines) complex and unpredictable, particularly when alcohol is being used at the same time. Exposure to Rohypnol can be detected by analysis of urine samples. For the best chance of detection, urine samples need to be collected within 72 hours after taking the substance. Very little Rohypnol is directly excreted into the urine. Instead, once in the body, Rohypnol is converted to other substances called metabolites, which are found in the user's urine. Gable reports that Rohypnol is being used as a date rape drug but, seemingly, not very frequently. He quotes US research by Mullins (1999) showing that in samples of victims of suspected date rape cases, the prevalence of Rohypnol was less than 1 per cent. Slaughter (2000) analysed over 2,000 urine samples obtained from sexual assault victims. Less than 3 per cent were positive for flunitrazepam.

One reason for a possible decline in the abuse of this drug in sexual offending might be that the producer (Rohypnol is used for medicinal purposes) had added 'colour' to the product so that it shows up blue when dissolved in water. However, it seems that unofficially manufactured flunitrazepam is still widely available (Hensley 2003).

Despite all the attention to specific date rape drugs, the drug most commonly used is, ironically, alcohol. We say ironically, as this is very often taken entirely voluntarily and not without knowledge of its effects. Recent forensic research from the UK proves that point. Scott-Ham and Burton forensically examined urine and blood samples, forwarded to the Forensic Science Service for analysis by the police over a 3-year period. Altogether, they examined over 1,000 samples of blood and/or urine of victims who reported to the police because they suspected that they were the victim of a DFSA.

We have seen that timing of the production of these samples is essential, and Scott-Ham and Burton report that 87 per cent of the urine samples and 84 per cent of the blood samples had been acquired within 24 hours after the alleged event. They subsequently examined the samples for the presence of alcohol and a range of prescription and recreational drugs. Unsurprisingly, the drug found most often was alcohol (46 per cent), followed by cannabis (26 per cent), and cocaine (11 per cent). Also frequently found were benzodiazepines (9 per cent) and antidepressants (8 per cent), reflecting prescription practice in the UK. In addition, ibuprofen and paracetamol were also frequently found, and it is likely that many of these drugs were not used to spike drink but were regularly taken by the victim, or were taken afterward to deal with the trauma of victimisation.

Scott-Ham and Burton argue that very few sedative or disinhibiting drugs were found that came as a total surprise to the victim; their estimate is that, of these 1,000 cases, in only 2 per cent was there good evidence of deliberate spiking of drinks. These data are in accord with US studies as well. Not a single instance of Rohypnol (detectable until up to 72 hours after the event) was obtained. Scott-Ham and Burton acknowledge that, whereas Rohypnol would have been detected, in 35 per cent of their sample the delay between alleged event and blood or urine sample was too long to be able to detect presence of GHB. Despite these methodological issues, Scott-Ham and Burton's conclusion is sobering: they warn of the dangers of alcohol and of illicit drugs not generally associated with date rape:

> The widespread media interest has generated a greater awareness of the issues surrounding DFSA, including good advice on how to avoid being spiked with a drug. However, attention could also be directed to giving advice regarding alcohol consumption e.g. drinking steadily, not drinking on an empty stomach and the dangers of illicit drug use. The results from this study suggest that if such advice were taken, there would almost certainly be a significant decrease in the number of cases of alleged DFSA as fewer persons would find themselves in a vulnerable position through heavy alcohol and/or drug intoxication (Scott-Ham and Burton 2005: 186).

Conclusion

Prevention of date rape can occur at a number of levels. A straightforward list of preventive measures against the spiking of drinks has already been provided. Other forms of prevention might involve the education of men who have committed sexual violence, in order to stop them from reoffending. In addition, at-risk women might be taught about risk appraisal. It must, however, be realised that that is far from straightforward. Many at-risk situations in life are straightforwardly 'risky': it is easy to advise against driving without wearing a seat belt, or wandering into dark alleys at night. Dating, on the other hand, can be both a risky business and potentially a most enjoyable experience. Simple avoidance is therefore nonsensical advice. Risk appraisal in such ambiguous social situations needs to be more refined.

Nurius *et al.* (2004) looked at the social information processing performed by 415 date or acquaintance rape victims. The model of risk appraisal has three phases. The first step is a so-called primary appraisal: a woman must determine whether a man's actions are beneficial, harmful or neutral, and this may not always be easily assessed. When a man on a date wants to 'go somewhere quiet', he might wish to enhance the level of privacy, and that might be a good thing. On the other hand, it might also serve to isolate his potential victim.

After a primary appraisal has suggested that the woman is at risk, secondary appraisals occur. Evaluating who is responsible for the 'risky' situation, possible courses of action to take, and their feasibility and likelihood of success are considered as part of the secondary appraisal. It must be noted that although the primary appraisal has resulted in an awareness of risk, that does not mean that an imminent attack is certain. The woman is likely to remain calculative of the social costs of overreacting or misinterpreting. Embarrassment and concerns of the negative impact of this episode on her relationship with the male are all factors that come into the equation. Thus, the essence of secondary assessment is a balancing act between concerns of personal safety and social relationship outcomes. Nurius *et al.* (2004) specify four elements of concern: relationship with the assailant, level of self-blame, sense of personal power in the situation, and level of resentment.

Thirdly, the researchers identify three behavioural response patterns (see also Nurius *et al.* 2000). The first is *assertive*, characterised by the victim speaking in a raised voice, using strong language, and leaving, or, if necessary, fleeing. The second is called *diplomatic* and involves behaviour such as explaining that she is not interested in sex, making excuses as to why she is not interested, or agreeing to kiss or hug, but not have sex. The third, *immobility*, is characterised by a sense of paralysis, and passively undergoing the man's advances.

On primary appraisal, the victimised women reported both manipulative and invasive behaviours as triggers. Manipulative behaviours were reflected in statements such 'he said really nice things about how much he needed me', whereas invasive behaviours were intrusion into personal space and touching against the victim's will. Both manipulative (more ambiguous) and intrusive behaviour can trigger a sense of risk. In selecting a response, the way in which secondary appraisal occurs is of importance. Women who are less inclined to blame themselves and who have a stronger sense of personal power are more inclined to respond assertively to a threatening dating situation. Those responses are advantageous in the sense that they tend to be more successful in preventing victimisation, and they are also more likely to leave the victim's self-worth intact. On the other hand, it was found that immobility is often the response chosen by women who score high on self-blame and who report a feeling of powerlessness in the situation. 'Immobilization is particularly worrisome in that it has been found not only to be relatively ineffective toward rape avoidance and injury prevention but is also associated with higher levels of subsequent guilt, self-denigration, self-blame and concern that others would blame or not believe one' (Nurius *et al.* 2004: 471). Neville *et al.* (2004) found that avoidance coping had a negative impact on self-esteem, which is directly linked to physical and psychological health. Nurius *et al.* argue that overcoming psychological barriers to resistance represents a formidable but crucial challenge in self-defence training.

Much of the work with victims revolves around awareness and empowerment. Much of the work with male assailants focuses on anger and rape myth acceptance. However, acquaintance rape prevention is probably most effective when it is multifaceted. Sampson (2000) therefore suggests a number of initiatives. They are particularly tailored to the US college context, but, as most of her suggestions would also apply elsewhere, we discuss a number of them here. Sampson argues that educational programmes work best. She advocates compulsory acquaintance rape programmes for first-year students that involve discussions on date rape prevalence, legal definitions of rape, issues of consent and of alcohol abuse, and dispelling rape myths. Female students should be offered programmes on risk appraisal, legal definitions of rape, and the counselling and crisis services available. In addition, victims should be counselled and educated about repeat victimisation.

Sampson further argues that the police need further education on acquaintance rape, that key university personnel need specific training, and that key at-risk groups (in the USA involving student fraternities and sororities) should be specifically targeted. However, Nurius *et al.* do emphasise that all the targeted programmes can have only limited success if the ultimate primary prevention, aimed at men targeting women for assault, fails to succeed. It reminds us starkly of what Kellie and Radford (1987) called 'the problem of men'. Without wanting to dismiss male victimisation or female offending as rare or ineffectual, it is there, in the minds of assailants, that prevention efforts should focus.

Chapter 10

Can prison ever work?

Introduction

What does society want from imprisoning people for their crimes? What do people think that prison is for? If it is to lock away sex offenders and violent offenders to ensure that there are no future victims for the duration of detention, then retributive theory can certainly provide the philosophical basis on which to base the sentencing process, and prison will work. If prison is to rehabilitate people whose persistent criminal behaviour is prolific (that is, they have a high frequency of offending) but non-violent, then the answer is much more complex. It is about this group, who have committed such crimes as burglary, robbery, fraud and theft, and who make up the majority of the prison population, that the question is posed as to whether prison can ever work.

Most of the standard arguments against the retributive view are not new, ranging from the criticism that it is merely a rationalisation of a primitive desire for revenge to debates on the moral authority to inflict punishment. But perhaps one of the most damning critiques is that when it is put into practice, it does not work. The modern prison, that is, the notion of imprisoning people to promote deterrence of offending behaviour through punishment and to prevent further criminal offences during the interim of the detention, was first introduced in France in the eighteenth century. In England, prison was rarely used as a punishment for felony before 1775, but, increasingly, the French ideas were adopted, and since that time it has proved to be the most popular, long-standing and failed response to reducing reoffending (McGuire 2005).

Critiques of the prison system emerged shortly after its implementation. Foucault (1977: 264) stated that after its introduction in France 'the prison in its reality and visible effects, was denounced at once as the great failure of penal justice'. For the past 180 years, the evidence has consistently demonstrated that a term of imprisonment fails to act as a deterrent and fails to rehabilitate or to reduce the rates of reoffending (Martinson 1974; 1979; Von Hirsch 1976). But this has not deterred society or politicians of all persuasions from continuing to uphold a criminal justice system that relies heavily upon prison as one of its main responses to offending behaviour. Even the introduction of electronic monitoring in the community, a form of prison without bars, has failed to make an impact upon the ever-increasing numbers of convicted offenders and those awaiting trial being held in custody.

The prison population

As Zimring and Hawkins (1993) point out, 'the jurisprudence of prison is rarely precise about the number of offenders who must be sent to prison or about the duration of their imprisonment' (xii). There may be mandatory schemes and guidance targeted at the most violent or prolific offenders, but, on the whole, the use of imprisonment versus community sanctions fluctuates with what Zimring and Hawkins call 'the political economy of imprisonment' (xii), which can be heavily influenced by populist agendas. Thus, there is no necessary correlation between judicial principles and the extent of the prison population. As Goldson (2006) points out, over time, there have been significant upward and downward trends in the prison population without any significant changes in the crime rates that might explain this.

In the UK, the 'get tough' political ethos has seen a steady rise in the prison population over the past decade. During the 1980s and early 1990s, the figures remained fairly stable at around 45,000. However, there was an increase of 77 per cent between 1993 and 2003, and the average prison population in 2007 stands at just over 80,000 inmates (Prison Reform Trust 2007). This figure suggests that the total capacity of 79,559 has been exceeded, although a further 900 additional places are under construction to bring the prison estate to a capacity of 80,400 by the end of 2007 (NOMS 2006). It is therefore not surprising that spending on prisons has increased by more that 25 per cent since 1997 (Reid 2006).

It is not anticipated that the prison population is likely to decrease in the near or distant future. In July 2006, the Home Secretary, John Reid, announced that a further 8,000 new prison places would be created as part of 'a package of measures to protect the public and rebalance the criminal justice system in favour of the law-abiding majority' (CJS 2006: 1). These plans are described as the 'backbone' (CJS 2006: 1) of a raft of measures to protect the public. A further aim of this initiative is to impose a 4-year maximum penalty for carrying a knife, and tougher sentences for violent and persistent offenders, offenders who will be subject to restrictions on release from prison. This latter measure hardly represents a vote of confidence in the likelihood that a prison sentence will result in a reformed character being released into the community.

These proposals to protect the 'law-abiding majority' may be well and good for offenders who pose a high risk of harm, but the question arises as to their effectiveness for those who are persistent/prolific offenders. Will this new raft of measures work for them and for the public, in terms of reducing reoffending upon release? The proposals claim that the Human Rights Act will be reviewed to promote a 'common-sense balance between the rights of the individuals and the rights of the public to be protected against harm' (CJS 2006: 1). However, human rights would surely include serving both the public and individual offender by imposing sanctions that actually deter reoffending and promote a pro-social lifestyle. Of the increase in the number of offenders receiving a custodial sentence since 1996, over half had no previous convictions (Prison Reform Trust 2007), and yet the record high prison population is accompanied by a record high reoffending rate. Current statistics on reconviction therefore suggest that the 'backbone' of the proposals, which when simplified seem merely to mean that there will be more people sent to prison, is deeply flawed. Imprisonment simply does not stop people from reoffending.

To examine this more closely, it is useful to consider a profile of the sentenced population in Prison in England and Wales (Table 10.1). The number of prisoners as a rate per 100,000 population in England and Wales in 2001 was 127, the second highest in Western Europe, after Portugal at 128 (Home Office 2003). From Table 10.1, it can be concluded that in 2001 34,236 (67.86 per cent) of male prisoners and 2,372 (83.63 per cent) of female prisoners were prolific offenders rather than violent or sexual offenders. Given the time-lag in the production of official statistics, it can also be assumed that the rising prison population has seen a proportionate expansion across all the categories of offending and reoffending and across male and female

Table 10.1 Sentenced population in Prison Service establishments by offence group (30 June 2001)

Offence type	Males*	Females*	Reconviction (%)
Violence against the person	11,198	464**	46
Sexual offences	5,039	–	18
Burglary	8,361	154	75
Robbery	6,561	252	51
Theft and handling	4,150	434	74
Fraud and forgery	893	127	37
Drug offences	7,963	1,132	38
Motoring offences	2,630	–	–
Other offences	3,678	273***	–
Total (2001†)	50,446	2,836	

*Total excludes those held for offence not recorded and in default of payment of a fine; **includes sexual offences; ***includes motoring offences;
†percentage of prisoners (all) reconvicted of an offence within 2 years of release.
Source: Home Office (2003).

groups, and the Prison Reform Trust (2007) reports that 67.4 per cent are reconvicted within 2 years; for young men aged 18–21 years, the figure is 78.4 per cent.

In a civilised society the numbers in prison are justifiable, perhaps, if prison worked to reduce offending, but it is clear from the reconviction data that this is far from the case. On 14 June 2005, a question put in Parliament to the Secretary of State for the Home Department confirmed that, based on a sample in 2002, it was estimated that 53 per cent of serving prisoners had also served a previous term of imprisonment (House of Commons 2005). From the reconviction statistics of 2001, it can therefore be assumed that approximately 17,200 prolific male offenders and 1,180 prolific female offenders would continue to commit offences upon release from a term of imprisonment. This is presumably what is meant by a great failure in penal justice – both for the population and for the offender.

The psychology of prison

In 1971, a study of prisons was funded by the US Navy to try to solve problems in Marine Corps' prisons (Haney *et al.* 1973). The study was led by psychologist Philip G. Zimbardo and a group of researchers at Stanford University. The experiment was set up to create a controlled environment in a university building to simulate a prison with mock-up cells. Participants would be recruited to play both the prisoners and the guards, and the experiment would last for 2 weeks.

It was not anticipated that the study would pose significant problems. The tasks were based on role-playing, and the careful recruitment of subjects excluded the possibility that any of the individuals were psychologically unsuitable to participate. However, within a week, the 'prisoners' were demonstrating symptoms of becoming psychologically disturbed, and the 'guards' were demonstrating brutal and sadistic behaviours. In that short period of time, there were riots, hunger strikes, and abusive treatment.

The study had to be terminated early and subsequently raised a number of critical questions about the morality and ethics of research experiments. It also raised significant questions about the psychology and organisational culture of the prison environment, most importantly, what is it about the prison environment that affects individual behaviour in such negative ways, and why does control break down and things go wrong? The overall conclusion of the Stanford researchers was that people fit their roles to institutions surprisingly well, despite their individual differences. That is, the situation and the role they played dictated how the participants acted, rather than their own dispositions. Well-adjusted individuals assumed the role of prisoner or guard to such an extent that their behaviour became wholly divorced from their everyday conduct. In this way, studying what happens when things go wrong can give some insight on the dynamics of the individual with the environment, culture and organisation.

When things go wrong – the prison officer role

It would be wrong to assume that all prisons are run by cruel or sadistic people attracted to such a job. In fact, much of the prison officer's day is taken up with routine tasks (Liebling and Price 2001), and, as Crawley (2004: 158) points out, control in this environment is achieved in the main by positive staff–prisoner relations and underpinned by guidelines regarding policy and procedures. But the Stanford experiment does point to a change in behavioural norms when people are placed in institutions of incarceration. Instances of abuse of authority by guards or prison officers are documented both nationally and internationally. The most recent examples being linked to the detention of US prisoners at Guantánamo Bay, Cuba; Abu Ghraib Prison, Iraq; Feltham Young Offenders Institution in 2000, resulting in the Zahid Mubarek Inquiry (HOC 2006); and HMP Wormwood Scrubs, where it is claimed that 160 prison officers were involved in inflicting and covering up an abusive regime of savage beatings, death threats and sexual assaults inflicted on inmates over a 9-year period between 1992 and 2001 (Dodd 2006).

There is no one theory that can unequivocally explain behaviour of this type, but there are theories which can shed some light upon the phenomena and tell us something about the impact of prisons upon the psychology of the individual in the prison environment.

It could be argued that the institutional roles in prison provide a framework that underpins a 'them' and 'us' mentality. Crawley (2004) also refers to this when debating the complex process of becoming a prison officer and negotiating the relationship to the prisoner. First of all, the individual admitted to the institution is given a label – this does not just apply to the offender, for those who work in institutions, such as a prison, also have labels, such as, 'prison officer', 'governor', etc. Labels signify the attribution of role/task-appropriate behaviour – quite simply, the role of the prison officer is to oversee the detention of the prisoner, who has been confined by the state for purposes of punishment. Becker (1963) set out the theoretical principles of the ways in which labelling influences the personal perception of self, claiming that labels work favourably for those who make and sustain social rules, but tend to work unfavourably for those who are deemed to have broken social rules. In this sense, the label of prison officer could be perceived as giving permission to those who have an enforcement role to behave in ways that would not be seen as appropriate outside that role. As Milgram (1963) demonstrated, in a series of experiments, obedience to authority and to the completion of a task can overrule personal objections to the morality of the task required.

But labelling theory is only a partial explanation. It does not tell us why some individuals in roles of authority would interpret their tasks as legitimising draconian and abusive behaviour. In addition to labelling theory, we need to consider schema theory. Schema theory, unlike some other learning theories, such as behaviourism or cognitive dissonance, does not seek to explain the acquisition of certain types of knowledge, such as behaviours or attitudes; rather, it seeks to explain how human beings possess categorical rules or scripts that they use to interpret the world. New information is processed according to how it fits these scripts. According to Driscoll (1994: 152), what this means is that 'people bring to tasks imprecise, partial, and idiosyncratic understandings that evolve with experience'.

In the cognitive consistency theoretical tradition, it can be understood that idiosyncratic and partial understanding contributes to the development of bias and stereotypical attitudes that, in turn, allow individuals to engage in seemingly contradictory behaviour to sustain a coherent interpretation of self to themselves and to the world (Greenwald *et al.* 2002) – thus avoiding the ambivalence and self-doubt that might arise through the cognitive dissonance of behaviours that are seemingly incompatible. Commonly held simplistic beliefs, therefore, that prisoners are 'bad' and 'dangerous', reinforced by their incarceration, could contribute to the manifestation of abuse of power wrapped up in the label of the prison officer role.

The roles that people take in institutions should therefore not be divorced from the social function and moral authority that is claimed for the institution and that it represents to society. From an organisational analysis perspective, control and coordination of inmates is ultimately the only effectively attainable goal of prisons and jails (Scharf 1983). Inmate resistance can be met with such responses as lockdowns, reclassification, loss of association time, or withdrawal of other privileges (Hamm *et al.*, 1994). However, as Patrick *et al.* (1999: 2) observe, this can result in the legitimate escalation of draconian actions when initial measures fail to achieve the desired outcome; 'the greater the separation of inmates' actual compliance from that level of compliance desired by the prison, the greater or more extreme the efforts taken by officials to restore compliance'. It also appears that the dysfunctional organisational dynamics, especially when things go wrong, may be disseminated by the highest political authority. For example, David Blunkett, Home Secretary in 2002, is said to have responded to a prison riot by telling Martin Narey that he did not care about lives: he wanted to call in the Army, machine-gun the prisoners and take the prison back immediately (BBC News, 17 October 2006). When we remember that most inmates are non-violent, non-sexual offenders, that is quite a stance to take. It demonstrates the type of attitude that condones abuse of power by authority figures.

Whereas Foucault (1977: 308) saw prisons as 'institutions of repression, rejection, exclusion, marginalization', the other side of the coin is that prisons become a place where the psychology of a regime is manifested and perpetuated on a socially approved set of norms and values as to what constitutes appropriate punishment for wrong-doers. Individuals given a role of authority over others in such an institution are (in some cases, misguidedly and based on imperfect understanding and biases) doing what they believe they are supposed to be doing (Milgram 1963), that is, following a code or moral imperative that applies in this context that would not apply or be acceptable under normal social interaction.

When things go wrong – the detainee role

Thus far, the debate has focused on the ways in which the psychology of prison can become that of an abusive setting as a feature of role and label dysfunction. Still to be explored is how individuals may come to be repressed, rejected, excluded and marginalised, and how they may react when experiencing such a regime.

Labels and the roles assigned to labels are acquired through a process of external and internal reinforcement and internalisation. The specific role attached to the label of 'offender' linked to being a prisoner starts at the moment of entering the prison. Goffman (1968: 24) comments that the inmate finds that certain roles are immediately lost by virtue of the barrier that separates the detainee from the outside world. After all, by going to prison, any inmate almost entirely loses the role of partner, parent or child. The change in status is reinforced by the prison process, which Crawley (2004: 95) details as bringing with it 'other kinds of loss and mortification' such as fingerprinting, removal of home clothes and issuing of prison clothes, removal of personal effects, and assigning of number and cell. There is subsequently assignment of tasks, set times for meals and the ordering of daily activity by an institutional timetable. The label and role of prisoner is therefore one that depends upon the individual's behaving as a part of the collective in order for the prison officer 'control' function to be sustained. However, the positive relationship between prison officer and prisoner needs to be built upon the prison officer seeing the prisoner as an individual (Crawley 2004: 95). This is one area where there appears to be a potential for role dysfunction to emerge.

The prison environment severely restricts the individual from maintaining contact with family and friends, leading to family breakdown and difficulty in sustaining external links to employment and accommodation. This is a process of marginalisation that means that prisoners increasingly become defined by their experiences within the prison and the culture of the prison, which is marked by the daily reality of a managed detention regime imposed on them. In a 'them and us' analogy, it is therefore least likely that prisoners will form friendships with prison officers, and most likely that they will form friendships or alliances with other offenders/prisoners.

Tajfel (1982) explored the processes underpinning social categorisation, social identity, social comparisons and positive group distinctiveness. In a series of experiments conducted in the 1970s, he showed that when people are linked to a group of individuals by a unifying factor (relating it to our present debate, that would be the role and label of prisoner or prison officer), given the choice between maximising the profit for all and maximising the profit for their own group, they chose the latter. Even more interestingly, though, the experiments demonstrated that individuals are more concerned with creating as large a difference as possible between the unifying factors allocated to each group (in favour of their own group) than in gaining a greater amount for everybody across the two groups. Tajfel points out that this last finding was caused by categorising the subjects into *meaningless* groups, and therefore it can be posited how much more powerful this process could be when categorising people into *meaningful* groups, such as prisoner and prison officer. It is arguable that this is another area where there is potential for group dysfunction to occur.

Although Tajfel's theory is not as popular as it was some decades ago, it could provide some understanding of what occurs when conflict arises in prisons. The reasons why the Stanford experiment broke down appear to be associated with the collective and antagonistic actions of two groups: officers and prisoners.

The first prison riot ever recorded took place in New England in 1774 at Newgate jail in Simsbury, Connecticut. The national and international literature on prisons records numerous subsequent riots, the most recent examples in the USA being at Attica, New York (1971); Santa Fe, New Mexico (1980); Atlanta, Georgia; Oakdale, Louisiana (1989); and Lucasville, Ohio (1993). The worst prison riot in the UK took place at Strangeways between 1 and 25 April 1990 and virtually destroyed some of the original buildings and some prison records. A total of 147 staff and 47 prisoners were injured, and one prisoner was killed. These riots led to the Woolf Report (1991), with a brief to review conditions under which prisoners were held, and to new policies being implemented, along with a programme for modernising prison establishments in the UK. However, as disturbances at Doncaster, Dorset and Nottinghamshire prisons in 2002; the riot at Harmondsworth Immigration Prison in 2006; and the two riots in one week in February 2007 at County Durham Young Offenders Institution demonstrate, conditions alone may not be the sole cause of unrest in prisons; the actual status, role and group identification of prisoners can trigger conflict between detainee and enforcer.

As Patrick *et al.* (1999) point out, inmate group behaviour is a complex phenomenon, and most of the individual theories applied to this issue have had limited success. While the control processes used by prisons generally produce compliance by inmates, these same control processes can result in episodic periods of negative inmate and prison officer group behaviour, and this may tell us a great deal about the stressors in the environment that cause the coping strategies of both the prisoner and the prison officer to break down.

Rehabilitation and the prison experience

Rehabilitation is often equated with reform. However, reform is much more closely associated with the late-nineteenth-century philosophy of salvation, whereas rehabilitation is about the reintegration of the individual into society and the adoption of pro-social attitudes and lifestyle. While reform refers to a spiritual transformation that brings about behaviour change, and could in effect take place virtually anywhere and in any context, rehabilitation implies that the pro-offending attitudes and the values underpinning undesirable behaviour will be supplanted and replaced. While there are many instances of those who have found spiritual awareness in prison and who claim that their lives have been changed by this, for the majority it is the deterrence of the punishment, coupled with participation in rehabilitation programmes, upon which the prison service pin their hopes of bringing about sustained behaviour change.

Currently, rehabilitation interventions are delivered through structured, research-led, evidenced-based, group work programmes, first developed in North America, which have been demonstrated to have a greater impact on recidivism than other models of intervention. The body of evidence underpinning the programmes is based upon cognitive-behavioural theory, and the evidence-based practice associated with this has come to be known as 'what works', and it has been adopted across both secure and community punishment provisions, and is supported by the Home Office. These focused learning programmes also target life skills such as education and training, and are supported by the pro-social modelling of those given the responsibility for managing the offender (McGuire 2002).

However, while the initial evaluation studies of groups exposed to 'what works' programmes were very promising in terms of reconviction rates, there has been some difficulty in replicating that success in a national UK context. Two Home Office publications (Falshaw *et al.* 2003; Friendship *et al.* 2003) acknowledge that subsequent evaluations found no differences in the 2-year reconviction rates for prisoners who had participated in a cognitive skills programme between 1996 and 1998 and a matched comparison group, concluding that the evidence from rigorously conducted reconviction studies suggests that the major impact promised by the 'what works' literature was unlikely to materialise and that any short-term impact decayed into no difference in reconviction over 2 years.

The methodological difficulties of rolling out a national programme of evidence-led practice have been the subject of extensive academic and practitioner debate, and some of these difficulties may well have contributed to the lack of apparent success in replicating the initial studies. However, some of the problems can surely be attributed to the environment in which such programmes are delivered. It seems a supremely difficult task to try to rehabilitate a person in society while at the same time preventing that person from interacting with society; it amounts to the marriage of two potentially competing philosophies (punishment and rehabilitation) delivered within one of the most socially excluding environments (Goldson 2002; Nellis 2005; Muncie 2006). Furthermore, people who receive repeated prison sentences are frequently those who already come from socially deprived backgrounds and have spent so much of their lives in formal care environments of one type or another that they have become institutionalised (Goffman 1963) – that is, they are either insufficiently skilled or too deskilled by the regime of an institutional care setting to implement or sustain an independent lifestyle.

In support of this claim, Lader *et al.* (1999), analysing data from the Office of National Statistics, demonstrated that the proportion of young offenders in each sample group who had been taken into local authority care as a child was 29 per cent of the male sentenced group, 35 per cent of the female and 42 per cent of the male remand group. Three-fifths of the sample reported leaving school before their sixteenth birthday, and about 1 in 10 respondents had left school aged 13 or younger – thus suggesting that a significant proportion of the youth prison population lack the education, experience or social networks to stand a reasonable chance of making an independent pro-social lifestyle on release from custody into the community. Whatever programme of rehabilitation they are exposed to, its relatively short-term nature could not possibly make good the multiple deprivations and their consequences experienced by these young people.

There is strong evidence that long-term criminal lifestyles are established within this group of young offenders. It is therefore significant that 1-year reconviction rates for young offenders released from custody stand at somewhere between 41.3 per cent (Whiting and Cuppleditch 2006) and 90 per cent for those sent to prison for a first offence (Prison Reform Trust 2006) in 2004. It appears therefore that the rehabilitation aims of both youth and adult secure estate provision are very difficult to achieve in the prison environment – and that a prison sentence is counterproductive in reducing the numbers of those going on to see offending behaviour as a lifestyle.

To make the point that prison as a rehabilitation experience may be incompatible with the current organisational structure of containment, the words of a prisoner may do it better than any academic analysis. The following is an extract of the response by Erwin James (2006) to Prime Minister Blair's comment in 1993 that prison was 'an opportunity for people with dysfunctional lives to try to get their lives back on track'.

> When Tony Blair said that it in 1993 I had been in prison for nine years. I wanted him to shout it from the roof tops. For most of that time I'd had a bed, a chair and a small table in my cell, and my toilet had been a bucket that I emptied each morning along with 50 other men in the communal sluice. I didn't mind. I didn't complain. Life inside was robust, undignified and often dangerous … [Under Blair] prisons became overcrowded warehouses. The odds against anyone having a successful outcome from their sentence were already high. Under Blair they increased. This week the prime minister boasted that more than a thousand people had been sentenced to 'indeterminate sentences'. He gave no indication of what rehabilitative measures might be in store for those men and women. (James 2006: 1)

James (2006) highlights what appears to be a fundamental misconstruction of the research evidence in government thinking: at one and the same time making claims for prison as a punishment regime and a rehabilitative environment. This message appears to have resulted in an increase in prison sentences almost beyond the capacity of current provision. As a result of such sentencing practices, the Prison Reform Trust (2006) has demonstrated that overcrowding in prisons is now commonplace, and this, in itself, undermines rehabilitative initiatives. Overcrowding is shown to increase the problems of control and enforcement, decrease the amount of time individuals can spend in rehabilitative programmes or in association, and increase the likelihood of being shunted at frequent intervals between prisons. This last factor disrupts any educational or other constructive activity and often ends with individuals being located further and further away from their families so that the problem of maintaining social networks is made even harder.

The Prison Reform Trust (2006) calls for some basic reforms to be made in recognition of the real-world issues of the prison regime and to improve the chances that the impact of social neglect, which has been a contributory factor in so many inmates' offending lifestyles, and which undermines rehabilitative initiatives, will not be exacerbated by the prison environment.

At the top of the list of suggestions of the Prison Reform Trust is to stop using prisons as asylums and to resource community settings to manage offenders with mental health problems. Most of these are not dangerous offenders, and their problems cannot be adequately dealt with in prison at any level (for a full discussion, see Chapter 6; also see Winstone and Pakes 2005); they are people who require multiagency support in the community. The second suggestion is to tackle addictions. Most acquisitive crime is fuelled by drugs or alcohol, and this is a habit that does not appear to be dealt with in prisons and may even be acquired in prisons. The Prison Reform Trust suggests that residential drug treatment places at £35,000 a year will save millions compared to over £40,000 a year for a revolving-door prison place for prolific offenders. The third suggestion is to stop sending women to prison for petty offences. The Prison Reform Trust states that it is time for government to deliver on its promise to develop women-only bail hostels:

> The vast majority of these women are also mothers with dependent children. Their households are broken up and scattered. There are better alternatives in the community that

focus on support and supervision with drugs, drinking, mental healthcare and debt recovery that can break the pattern of offending without destroying families. (Prison Reform Trust 2006: no page number).

The trust condemns the practice of child imprisonment, pointing to the success of specialist fostering care, mentoring, and intensive supervision as rehabilitative alternatives for young people whose crimes pose no risk of harm to the public (Audit Commission 2004), and the trust points to the early positive indications that community-based Prolific Offender Programmes run by the police and probation and community payback schemes are working well, but are underused and suffer from patchy provision. The trust calls for strong political leadership to recognise the deleterious impact of prison upon rehabilitation and reconviction rates, to demonstrate commitment to making prison work to cut serious and violent crime, and to promote community-based sentences for all others.

However, the continued political defiance of the research evidence with regard to rehabilitative outcomes is mirrored in both adult and youth provision. Bateman (2005) states that while the Youth Justice Board (YJB) and the Home Office appear to share the consensus that the current number of children within penal institutions should be reduced, the YJB seeking a 10 per cent reduction in the number of child prisoners by 2007 (Youth Justice Board 2004), there is an apparent tension between government rhetoric and government policy that suggests a less optimistic outcome. Young people continue to be sent into detention under current legislation and sentencing guidelines – in defiance of the research evidence that most youthful misdemeanours should not be dealt with by criminal sanctions, and that of those that should, very few children are so dangerous – while alternative strategies are so numerous – that they need to be locked away. This type of strategy simply acts to swell the numbers of those who will go on to be prolific adult offenders for whom criminal activity is their social and economic mainstay (for a fuller discussion, see Chapter 3).

Rehabilitation and prison – the alternatives

The current organisational structure that brings so many problems for the rehabilitative aim does have alternatives to a traditional secure setting; these are the so-called therapeutic communities.

The origins of the therapeutic community can be traced to the Belmont Centre in Surrey, which was established for the medical treatment and psychiatric supervision of the post-traumatic shock/stress symptoms of soldiers returning from World War II. Currently, secure therapeutic communities are located mainly within prison and correctional services, of which only Her Majesty's Prison (HMP) Grendon, with about 200 residents, is an entirely therapeutic community prison. Other therapeutic communities comprise small units inside larger mainstream prisons, such as the provision at HMP Send, for women. While HMP Grendon aims at a holistic approach based on an entire setting, in the main, the concept-based/hierarchical therapeutic community is usually a unit developed within a prison or secure hospital setting. The aim is to promote intrapsychic forms of behaviour change intervention requiring a long-term commitment from both staff and inmate group, and treatment is usually voluntary.

In secure therapeutic communities, inmates are generally selected by staff. All units offer a regime of group activities, daily or community meetings, and democratic or patient participation in decision-making and running the therapeutic community (Association of Therapeutic Communities 1999). HMP Grendon also takes high-risk offenders, such as violent and sex offenders and those with personality disorder. A 7-year reconviction study (Taylor 2000) demonstrated that a stay of 18 months in Grendon produced a reduction in reconviction rates of about one-fifth to one-quarter, and reimprisonment was also reduced by the same amount when compared to those prisoners who had been referred to HMP Grendon but did not go there. There was also evidence of an effect on reconviction rates for HMP Grendon life-sentence prisoners, which was thought to be due to the longer time in treatment.

The experience at HMP Grendon suggests that there is every possibility that prison could provide a rehabilitative environment that would reduce reoffending for even the most violent and dangerous offenders, but not as conditions are at present for the majority of detainees. This is not to say that there is not also a tremendous effort in other types of prisons put into creating schemes to support offenders as they show progression in pro-social behaviour, such as organising work outside prison. But there is evidence that many initiatives, including the 'what works' accredited programmes in prisons, appear to be overwhelmed by the organisational requirement to maintain the status quo of control and enforcement, and this is exacerbated by the demands of managing overcrowding. The problems appear to require an organisational response if rehabilitative efforts are to be realised in a consistent and measurable outcome.

Coyle (2002) observes that there is no inevitability for the model used in prisons today, and that much of the structure and regime have developed in an ad hoc style that has been reactive rather than planned. As Coyle (2005: 9) observes, 'It may be that the time has come for a radical review of the use of imprisonment ... and re-thinking whether locking up large numbers of men, women and children in a very confined space – is appropriate in the twenty-first century.'

The UK prison population can be demonstrated to be representative of the most deprived sections of our society, and the prison environment appears to impede this group from learning the life skills required to sustain a pro-social lifestyle, as they are being detained in a setting that is, as James (2006) described, undignified and often dangerous. When it comes down to it, it is unrealistic to expect people to learn to behave well when their environment is so difficult to cope with that the suicide rate for prisoners is often four times that of the general population (Liebling 1992).

Conclusion

To respond to the question of whether prison can ever work, the historical and current research evidence is consistent in its message that it never has, and, if things carry on in the same way, never will reduce recidivism. If punishment is the intent, it is certainly a very punishing environment, but that does not appear to have the required effect of releasing a pro-social individual back into the community. On the whole, the evidence shows that it is rehabilitation that reduces reoffending. For the most prolific offenders and those whose offences pose no risk of violence to the public, there seems little point in continuing to invest in the present organisational structures that appear to perpetuate offending behaviour when there are community-based alternatives shown to have greater success in reintegrating individuals into society.

The SmartJustice and Victim Support Survey showed that almost two-thirds of victims of crime do not believe that prison works to reduce non-violent crime and offences such as shoplifting, stealing cars and vandalism (Prison Reform Trust 2007: 11), but it is a message that politicians do not appear to be taking on board.

As a final note, society discriminates against people with a history of imprisonment. On release, it is more difficult for them to find employers willing to give work and stable accommodation. Yet, it is these very factors (accommodation, employment, and family) that have been demonstrated as being the key to reducing recidivism (McGuire 2002; SEU 2006b). The 'catch-22' is that it is difficult to break the impact of this negative spiral of marginalisation before relapse into offending behaviour takes place.

The exclusion from society that prison represents, which is intended to protect victims from crime for the duration of the sentence, becomes the tool of social exclusion. This requires the development of coping strategies, that are, in themselves, the architect of criminal behaviour. While this remains the case, it is unlikely that prison can ever work. At present, it most often achieves the opposite of rehabilitation.

Chapter 11

Victims and fear of crime

Introduction

The victim, political rhetoric claims, has been placed at the heart of the criminal justice system, and a stated aim is to rebalance the criminal justice system in favour of victims. But who are victims, and what do we know about their experiences? First of all, it is perhaps a truism to say that few things in life are scarier than to be the victim of a serious crime. Even crimes that might seem relatively minor can have devastating effects. Burglary is a property crime, but is perceived by many victims as much more than that. It is an intrusion into personal space, and a violation of something that is held very dearly, the sense of ownership of and safety in one's own home. Many burglary victims find the feeling that someone has been in their house, looking through their drawers, sitting on their bed, throwing personal items on the floor, very difficult to overcome.

Victimisation begets fear. Many victims of crime are fearful that it might happen again. Certainly, in burglary, 'repeat victimisation' is a serious concern. Equally, those who are victimised on the street might find it difficult to go out, and the post-traumatic stress often suffered by victims of serious violent or sexual crime can make living a normal life almost impossible. There is no doubt that, while, of course, 'crime hurts', the fear of it hurts in a different and separate way as well.

However, just because being the victim of a crime makes us fearful, should 'fear of crime' be made a separate area of study? Rather than thinking about tackling fear of crime, is it not more important to reduce crime itself? When we reduce levels of crime, are we not at the same time reducing levels of the fear of crime? After all, it is often said that the only thing we have to fear is fear itself, a saying often attributed to former US President Franklin Roosevelt in 1933, although he did not mean it in relation to crime. But the point is, if we deal with crime itself, will the fear factor disappear with it?

Before addressing that question, it is important to realise that fear of crime is a significant factor in crime and justice policymaking. Fear of crime matters to voters, and therefore it is of importance to the government. People often base their judgements on government performance on law and order, not on a careful analysis of policies and statistics, but on how worried they and their loved ones are about crime, incivilities, terrorism or antisocial behaviour. And it is widely acknowledged that fear of crime does not simply equate to probability of becoming a victim. The Home Office, when discussing fear of crime, emphasises exactly that in discussing fear of crime on public transport:

Scared to travel on public transport?

Lots of people find the crowds on trains, tubes and buses overwhelming, but crime levels are actually very low. If you find travelling on public transport makes you nervous, you're not alone. Plenty of people find the idea a bit intimidating. But the simple fact is, you're just as safe on a bus or train as you are walking down a street in any average British city, since crime levels on public transport are much the same as those for Britain in general. In fact, in recent years, crime on public transport has been falling at about the same rate as overall crime throughout the country [...] Over the last few years the British Transport Police have been expanding their staffing to include more officers. There are now 2,494 police officers, and 248 special constables working with British Transport to make travel safer for everyone. Overall, the number of crimes in 2004/05 fell by two per cent compared to the previous year. These figures included an almost 20 per cent reduction in the number of robberies. (Home Office 2006)

In this fashion, the government attempts to do two things. The first is to acknowledge that fear of crime is an issue that affects people; that is, it wants to demonstrate that it takes fear of crime seriously. On

183

the other hand, however, it wants to make sure that people realise that many situations are actually not all that dangerous.

Is our fear of crime an overreaction? Or, alternatively, should we be worried about other types of crime in other contexts than we normally do? This chapter will discuss such issues and analyse, from a psychological perspective, the emotion of fear and how that can help us understand, and possibly reduce, the levels of fear in society.

We must not forget that fear of crime is a political thing. A government that fails to control crime, but is able to ease people's feelings about it, might still be in business after the next general election. Conversely, the current British New Labour government frequently emphasises that crime rates are falling, but is well aware that that alone will not satisfy the voting public. Not only do people need to be told that their streets and neighbourhoods are experiencing less crime, but they must also feel safe. That is why fear of crime as a research object has become an active subdiscipline within criminology and criminal psychology alike (Hale 1996; Lee 2001).

Who is afraid?

Establishing who is afraid is a very different matter from deciding who *should* be afraid. There is consistent evidence that young males who are already in contact with the criminal justice system are significantly more likely to become victims of crime themselves than any other group of people. But this does not generally fit ideal notions of the victims of crime. Ironically, those who are statistically very unlikely to become victims of crime may feel themselves to be most at risk.

The International Crime Victimisation Survey contains questions on fear of crime. A key question put to respondents from 17 industrialised countries, including the UK, is as follows: 'How safe do you feel walking alone in your area after dark?' As their answer, respondents could pick either 'very safe' 'fairly safe', 'a bit unsafe', or 'very unsafe'. On the whole, people in England and Wales feel 'fairly safe', and the same is true for Scotland, and most other industrialised countries. People in Eastern European countries, such as the Czech Republic, Bulgaria and Lithuania, report somewhat higher levels of fear.

Generally, people do feel safer in their homes, and men somewhat more so than women. This finding is also repeated in other European countries and the USA, Canada and New Zealand. Thus, across the board in many countries, there is a widespread wariness regarding crime. But does this assume the level of paralysing fear? Does it interfere with how people live their life? At a certain level, the answer must be 'yes'. We are careful after dark, and we are mindful not to provide strangers with unnecessary personal details. We keep our PIN codes safe, and lock our doors, cars and bicycles. But it is probably fair to say that many people are mindful of the chance of becoming a victim, rather than being actually fearful.

Fear of crime is one of those commodities that is unevenly distributed in society. Certain groups of people feel it much more than others, and the first group to be mentioned is those who have been previously victimised. It has been reported that previous experience of burglary, for instance, does increase people's worry about that type of crime (Hough 1995; Skogan 1995; Clancy et al. 2001). In addition, older people, and older women more so than men, tend to report increased fear of crime (Tulloch 2000). This is, seemingly, in contrast to the fact that old people are less often victims than young people, but it might reflect their increased physical vulnerability. Indeed, British Crime Survey data established that older people who judge themselves to be in good health are less fearful than those who do not. Another explanation is that social isolation can enhance fear of crime, as is possibly a reliance on the media as a source of information on local safety issues.

Women have been frequently found to be more fearful than men (Stanko 1992; 1996). Indeed, the 2001 British Crime Survey found that women are more worried than men about being burgled, mugged, and physically attacked. The area where women are at higher risk than men is, of course, sexual offending, where they have been estimated to be 11 times more likely to become a victim (Tjaden and Thoenness 1998). It has therefore been suggested that their vulnerability to sex offending makes it no more than realistic for women to be more fearful and to adjust their daily behaviour to a degree in light of that. However, the relation between gender and fear of crime is not always straightforward. Older women, as we said before, tend to be more fearful than older men, but younger women are also particularly worried. Thus, it is younger and older women who are most anxious, whereas the middle-aged group is less affected. Ferraro (1995) suggests that women of different ages are afraid of different things. Increased fear of crime among young women has a lot to do with sexual offences. Elderly women instead are more concerned about any sort of contact crime, such as robbery or mugging, due to increased physical vulnerability.

Women who are most fearful do restrict their behaviour substantially. This sometimes occurs to a degree that some, such as Jock Young, speak of as a self-imposed curfew (Young, n.d.). Women who avoid walking by boys and men, do not walk alone at night, do not use public transport in the evening, and do not use parking garages after dark are the women who are most fearful of crime (Scott 2003). This highlights the fact the fear of crime is not an abstract concept: it directly affects people's lives.

People who live in urban areas report more fear than those in rural areas (British Crime Survey 2001). But it must be noted that crime is also a relatively urban phenomenon. Related perhaps is the finding that type of neighbourhood affects people's levels of fear. Graffiti, drugs, disorder, and noise enhance feelings of insecurity and fear, whereas good informal relationships with neighbours serve to reduce such sentiments. Also possibly related is the finding that those with lower incomes are more fearful. Those who are unemployed are twice as likely to be afraid than those in employment (Van Dijk en Toornvliet 1996).

Salisbury and Upson (2004) found ethnic minorities to be quite fearful of crime. Similar findings from the USA have suggested that blacks worry more about crime than white people. However, Skogan (1995) argued that that fear is in a way rational, as blacks are victims more often. Salisbury and Upson looked at both actual rates of victimisation and fear of crime. Disturbingly, they found that ethnic minorities are more often the victim of a personal crime than white people. People of mixed race are particularly at risk of such crimes. Fear of crime among ethnic minorities is substantially higher than among the white population (Table 11.1), but one striking finding is that those most at risk, those of mixed race, are actually somewhat less worried and rank between white people and the other groups.

In summary, certain groups are more fearful of crime and antisocial behaviour than others. But to what extent is that justified? We have seen that the elderly tend to be more fearful, but their victimisation rates tend to be lower. Does that mean that their fear is exaggerated? This is a matter of debate. Their risk of becoming a victim is not as high, but any minor assault might result in serious injury. Their fear is possibly more informed by the potential consequences than the likelihood of victimisation. It is also noteworthy that the women who mostly adjust their everyday behaviours are most afraid, whereas we would hope that their adjustments would have made them

Table 11.1 Percentage feeling worried about violence by ethnic group

	Mugging/burglary	Physical attack by stranger	Racially motivated assault
	%	%	%
White	13	14	14
Mixed	21	22	21
Asian or Asian British	31	29	29
Black or black British	25	28	27
Chinese or other	30	27	29

Source: Salisbury and Upson 2004

less fearful. At the same time, we know that female fear of crime is often related to 'stranger danger', although it is well known that they (as is everybody else) are more likely to be hurt by intimates or acquaintances than by strangers.

Conversely, as stated in the introduction, those who are least worried are outgoing young men. They are most likely to be offenders, but also most likely to be victims. This is sometimes referred to as the fear of crime paradox. Those who are most afraid (seem to) have least to worry about, and those who are most likely to become victims do not seem to be bothered by that. One thing this does show is that fear of crime and the likelihood of becoming a victim do not easily map onto each other. There are other factors at work that we need to examine.

Fear of crime and the media

It is not long ago that people who worried about rising levels of crime were told to calm down, and told that they were 'watching too much TV' (Young 1997: 478). The doctrine was that crime is not a big social problem and that those who worry about it are listening to the wrong people, or allowing themselves to be scared by sensationalist television or newspaper coverage. In that light, the relation between the media and fear of crime has been subject to considerable scrutiny.

In a piece in the *Guardian*, Cozens wrote, on the basis of British Crime Survey data:

Attitudes to crime are hugely influenced by newspaper reports, with tabloid readers almost twice as likely to be worried about crime as those who favour broadsheets, according to government figures. The latest Home Office survey on crime showed the tabloids' penchant for human interest stories involving violence and law-breaking have had a marked effect as 43% of tabloid readers believe crime has increased 'a lot' compared with just 26% of broadsheet readers. Tabloid readers were more than twice as likely to fear being mugged, with 16% admitting they were 'very worried' about a possible assault compared with just 7% of broadsheet readers. When it came to the threat of physical attacks, the difference was even more marked with 17% of tabloid readers claiming to be 'very worried' compared with just 6% of broadsheet readers. (Cozens 2003: 11)

Thus, it seems to matter which newspaper one reads. However, the direction of the relationship is unclear: do people become more scared because their newspaper carries more crime stories? Or is it the other way round: people select their preferred paper because it features a lot about crime, a subject that concerns them? There may well be merit in both sides of the argument.

Apart from newspapers, television is a potent shaper of views on crime and pretty much everything else in life. In the area of fear of crime, local rather than national television seems most influential, at least in the USA. As Romer *et al.* (2003) argue:

One news source that has the potential to cultivate stable expectations in the public is local television news. Not only has it become the most widely used news source for Americans […], but it also has unique conventions that make its content especially relevant for the public's views of crime […]. Although this news source presumes to give viewers factual stories about their media region, it relies heavily on sensational coverage of crime and other mayhem with particular emphasis on homicide and violence […]. This coverage could well increase crime by cultivating expectations that victimization is both likely and beyond our control. (Romer *et al.* 2003: 89)

Their research from the USA indeed bears out the assumption that local news is linked to increased fear of crime. In their study, the extent to which people watch national news did not have an impact, nor did the type of newspaper that people usually read. This shows that local news has a unique potency in influencing the way in which we perceive our immediate environment (Pew Center 1998). However, perceptions are also skewed because crime is over-represented, and violent crime in particular is more likely to get coverage in local news media: if it bleeds, it leads (Gross and Aday 2003). Romer *et al.* (2003) also note that while local news might skew our perceptions on the likelihood of becoming a victim, an added effect is that it might lead to erroneous perceptions about the places where crimes occur and the people that commit them. Local news disproportionately reports crimes by strangers in public places, and that might distort viewers' perceptions on the nature of crime in their area.

Chiricos *et al.* (2000) conducted a similar study in Florida. In contrast to Romer *et al.*, they did find an effect of national media as well: the more one watches it, the more concerned one is about crime, but the local news media were found to be much more influential. The latter finding particularly applies to those who live in high-crime areas and those who have been victimised recently. It probably is these people with whom local crime stories have most resonance.

Is there more fear than crime? Should current crime levels have us more relaxed about our chances of becoming a victim? This is not always the case. An interesting counter-example concerns holidaymakers. Mawby *et al.* (2000) found that fear of crime was very low among British holidaymakers abroad, and yet crimes such as burglary, theft from a car and violence were much more common among holidaymakers and exceed the victimisation rates of the same people at home – and also of those who live in tourist areas. In fact, burglary at the holiday destination seems some 15 times more likely than at home. Mawby *et al.* found that personal experience of crime does enhance a sense of worry about crime on holiday, but not as much as we might expect. 'Victimization at home may be seen as symptomatic of the problems with British society; crime experiences abroad may be considered more a matter of bad luck' (Mawby *et al.* 2000: 477). Thus, it is not always true that people tend to overestimate their chances of becoming a victim. Maybe in certain situations, such as on holiday, we are actually not worried enough.

Deconstructing fear of crime

Thus far, we have discussed fear of crime and fear of becoming a victim as if they are homogeneous concepts. But of course they are not. It is not the same to be worried about, at some point, being burgled, as it is to live in constant fear of an abusive husband. Similarly, the constant threat of antisocial youngsters in your street will generate a different emotive response than the threat of identity theft. Some fears are highly localised and temporary, whereas others represent a continuous non-specific state of anxiety that affects people's sleeping patterns, daily movements and generally the quality of their life. In addition, when we talk about fear of crime, we need to distinguish between fear of personally becoming a victim, and fear about the general 'state of crime' in society.

Psychologists distinguish between states and traits. A person walking down the street who hears shouting and running behind them might experience a momentary state of fear. However, that feeling may well go once that person has arrived safely home. This is fear of crime in the guise of a state: it is temporary, and induced by a specific situation. People can also have a dispositional anxiety about crime. These people will be worried more often and will find many more situations worrying, and the worry will not subside as easily. Here fear is manifested as a trait. The two can obviously interact: if we regularly experience states of fear, that is not unlikely to seep into a disposition. But other factors are at play as well, such as self-efficacy and resilience (Gabriel and Greve 2003).

Fear is therefore made up of more than one component. First, there is a cognitive element: there must be awareness that a certain situation is risky or dangerous. Secondly, there is an affective component: we must experience a feeling of fear, or anxiety. Thirdly, there is a motivation or tendency to act (or not). Thus, the whole emotion of fear requires cognition, affect and an orientation in the area of motivation and action. It is, however, conceivable for a combination of components to occur that brings about a partial experience. For example, it is possible to experience a certain level of 'free-floating anxiety', without being in a situation appraised as dangerous. Similarly, a soldier or security officer could be frightened in a certain situation but remain composed and motionless.

Gabriel and Greve (2003) argue that we should disentangle these components in research. Rather than asking people whether they are fearful or worried, we should ask questions that tackle the cognitive, affective or motivational components of crime. That way, we can distinguish the prototypical taxi driver's response ('crime is totally out of control, but I'm not scared', in other words, a response to crime that is cognitively high but affectively low), from that of an elderly person whose life is very much affected by an ever-present dread of going outside the front door. Both involve concern about crime, but their subjective experience is radically different. We cannot view or treat them the same.

Getting to the causes

Just as fear of crime has various components, we also cannot assume that one single factor will universally explain levels of fear. Of course, we know that previous victimisation is a factor that helps explain levels of fear. But, in all likelihood, explanations will have be more sophisticated to capture the essence of fear of crime in society. Three theories are often mentioned in the literature. The first is the so-called *victimisation model*. This model stresses the role of victimisation, not so much on a personal as on an aggregate level: the more crime there is in society, the more people will be victims, the higher the level of concern about crime, and the more people will be afraid. However, we know that victimisation and fear do not seamlessly connect, so that we must conclude that victimisation and fear insufficiently explain each other.

In addition to the victimisation model, we need to look at the so-called *vulnerability model*, in which it is not the risk of victimisation but the consequences of victimisation that are the central element. Further to this perspective, we predict that the old and frail, rather than the young and fit, will be most afraid. Those that feel unable to defend themselves or recover financially, physically or psychologically from victimisation, are the most fearful. Thus, rather than risk, vulnerability is the key factor (European Crime Prevention Network 2004).

Finally, there is the factor of social disorganisation, which posits that fear of crime is highest in contexts where individuals feel that crime and disorder are not under control. Graffiti, clear evidence of drug abuse, noise pollution, and so forth make residents fearful. This became the inspiration for zero-tolerance policing, first in New York City and later elsewhere, as we will discuss later in this chapter. On the other side of the coin, the model suggests that fear of crime in quiet, affluent and well-maintained areas is low, but that is not necessarily the case. Indeed, many an area can be characterised as having residents with low rates of victimisation but high levels of worry about crime, as in so-called gated communities. Thus, in short, none of these models sufficiently pinpoint the relationship between personal characteristics, area characteristics, levels of actual crime, and levels of fear (European Crime Prevention Network 2004).

In policing circles, there is increased recognition that not only crime rates but also the relation between crime and fear should inform policing practices. Neighbourhood Watch (2006) in Britain discussed these factors in a so-called fear of crime matrix. Obviously, areas of low crime and low fear of crime are the least of our concerns. In areas of low crime but high fear of crime, it is worth devising a specific fear of crime strategy that might address the mismatch between fear and crime. In areas where crime is high but fear is low, education might be a way forward. Residents should perhaps be warned about the level of crime and advised of target hardening and other crime-prevention strategies. Finally, in areas of high crime and high fear of crime, both need to be addressed. Fear of crime in such contexts can work as an obstacle to crime reduction. In these neighbourhoods, many residents will be frightened to exercise informal social control. People will not intervene or speak out against antisocial behaviour but instead cross the road and look the other way. They are also more likely to be disappointed in the police and less likely to report crimes, or appear as witnesses. In addition, such neighbourhoods often lack the structures that enhance a sense of control and belonging. In sociological terms, that means that its *social capital* is low. 'Social capital' is a term used to describe a community's inner strength. It refers to strong social ties within the community, and its problem-solving capacity. It also refers to trust within the community and openness to other bodies such as the police (Portes 1998). In such areas, people's feelings are crucial; crime reduction cannot stand on its own if harnessing and empowering of neighbourhoods does not become part of the strategy.

Defensible space

A further way of reducing fear of crime is by environmental design. The concept of 'defensible space' was coined by Newman (1972), as was the phrase, crime prevention through environmental design (CPTED), (Newman 1996). This is an area where environmental psychology (e.g., Oliver 2002) and criminal psychology shake hands. Defensible space relates to outside or public spaces. Their layout can be vital for the extent that they deter crime, and allow local residents to acquire a sense of control over what goes on in these spaces.

Defensible space's best (and worst) example probably comes from Pruitt-Igoe in St. Louis in the USA. Pruitt-Igoe was a massive, high-rise (11 storeys) development of no fewer than 2,740 apartments, quite a prestigious project at the time when it was built. It was designed by Minoru Yamasaki, who would later design New York's World Trade Center. It was primarily built as affordable housing for low-income, single-parent families.

However,

> the design proved a disaster. […] The areas proved unsafe. The river of trees soon became a sewer of glass and garbage. The mail-boxes on the ground floor were vandalized. The corridors, lobbies, elevators, and stairs were dangerous places to walk. They became covered with graffiti and littered with garbage and human waste. (Newman 1996: 10)

Next to this development was a smaller area aimed at similar residents that did not seem to have the same level of crime, fear and disorganisation. It was called Carr Square. It led Newman to wonder why the one development was fully occupied and a pleasant place to live, whereas the other was, in fact, the exact opposite.

A key factor is territoriality. People must be able to feel a sense of ownership and responsibility for the area surrounding their property. In big, high-rise developments, this is a challenge: residents and visitors of hundreds of flats may be using the same spaces such as corridors, stairways, and lifts. Due to the size of these projects, these people will not know each other very well and might not be able to distinguish strangers and intruders from residents. That makes it difficult for spaces to become defensible. It is therefore best for such projects to feel smaller and more personalised to the residents. That can, for instance, be achieved by having dedicated entry points for the various parts of the complex. That can be achieved by having doors, lifts and corridors used by fewer people. If a lift is used by no more than 12 families, instead of by 80, strangers will be noticed quicker. If something is broken, it is more likely to be noticed. The members of the 12 households are more likely to view that lift as 'their' lift, and that makes a difference in how they behave and is a real deterrent to the development of crime and antisocial behaviour. That might set a virtuous circle in motion, in which crime as well as fear of crime both continuously decrease. This is of particular relevance in light of the broken-windows theory (Wilson and Kelling, 1982) that formed the inspiration for zero-tolerance policing.

Wilson and Kelling in 1982 wrote about the broken-windows theory after an experiment by Philip G. Zimbardo, who also had been involved in the famous Stanford prison experiment, which is a classic in psychology (Haney *et al.* 1973; see Chapter 10). In 1969, Zimbardo left abandoned cars in two neighbourhoods. The car was the same on each occasion and left in a similar state: licence plates removed, bonnet open and abandoned. One car was placed in the Bronx, at the time a crime-ridden area in New York City, whereas the other was left in pleasant and affluent Palo Alto in California. The car in the Bronx was soon stripped. Within 10 minutes, people started taking off bits of value such as the windscreen wipers. After that, the car became the object of both play and vandalism, and it was soon reduced to a pile of rubbish. The situation in Palo Alto was rather different. Nothing happened. After 1 week of waiting for something untoward to occur, Zimbardo himself set the ball rolling by doing some damage to the car with a sledge hammer. Then the Bronx scenario was soon repeated: the car was stripped, vandalised, and, bit by bit, destroyed. It soon ended up lying on its roof (Wilson and Kelling 1982).

The study offers an interesting insight into human nature. Vandalism seems to be fun. In addition, the environment can do a lot either to stimulate or deter it, and it seems that signs of previous vandalism rather invite others to do the same. Zimbardo, in the language of the 1960s, emphasises the role of the environment in human behaviour: 'One may be as readily moved to make war as to make love; the choice lies not within the disposition of the person but in the nature of the immediate situation' (Zimbardo 1978: 53).

An important lesson for crime prevention can be learnt from this: if the first signs of vandalism or disorganisation are not dealt with quickly, it gives the signal that vandalism is acceptable or that nobody cares. A situation with those characteristics can very quickly deteriorate (Wilson and Kelling 1982).

Notions of defensible space and the broken-windows theory have informed the 'crime prevention through environmental design' (CPTED). The following four principles underlie it:

1 *Surveillance.* People must be able to oversee public and communal spaces so that criminals cannot be safe in the knowledge that they cannot be spotted.
2 *Access management.* It is important to have measures in place to facilitate access to certain spaces and restrict access elsewhere.
3 *Territorial reinforcement.* Use must be made of physical and symbolic barriers to enhance residents' feeling of safety and ownership.
4 *Quality environments.* Communal spaces need to be pleasant and well maintained in order for residents to take responsibility for them.

Symbolic and physical measures must work together to make big projects feel small and intimate. That means that access to and from their local areas, as well as residents' ability literally to oversee them have become crucial. Older mass housing developments were often designed and built without much regard for such principles, but, since the 1960s, they have become of great importance as a secondary crime-prevention strategy.

If the CPTED principles are implemented successfully, we can tell a successful communal living environment by seven signs (Newman 1996). The first is access, such as safe movement and connections. It includes measures such as clear signposting, and avoiding wasted space that might be used by unwanted intruders, such as rough sleepers and drug addicts. The second is to do with surveillance and observation. It involves good lighting and building design that creates opportunities for informal surveillance, with fencing, landscaping and streetscape features that are designed to help visibility. In short, surveillance is all about 'to see and to be seen'. The third relates to the spatial layout, which has to be clear, logical and well signposted. The fourth factor of success is the concurrence of a variety of activities. Public spaces are better used and therefore safer when they are not only there for people to get to their homes. Shops can be helpful, as can other communal spaces. Legitimate activity, such as sport and social clubs, is a powerful deterrent to spatial disorganisation. The fifth factor is the aforementioned sense of ownership. This is, of course, not something designers and builders can impose, but it can be encouraged by community involvement in the designing process, and by ensuring that elements that delineate ownership boundaries are well designed. The sixth is quality environments, and this relies on good maintenance arrangements, so that materials and fixtures are vandal resistant. Finally, there is physical protection, which can include restricting access via use of intercoms and surveillance cameras (Newman 1996; New Zealand Ministry of Justice 2005).

In summary, environmental design can have a substantial impact on disorder and feelings of fear within an area. This might be at the very heart of residents' quality of life. The Pruitt-Igoe development bears witness to that: it never recovered from its flaws. Pruitt-Igoe was psychologically, not structurally, unsafe. In 1972, it was demolished, only 20 years after it was built (Newman 1996; New Zealand Ministry of Justice 2005).

Conclusion

Having established fear of crime as a social and psychological fact and identified various measures that can help tackle it, we conclude this chapter by mentioning a number of ways in which fear of crime can be reduced. It is essential in this regard that we must assess to what extent that fear is realistic and to what extent it has an adverse effect on people's lives. As we stated before, a certain level of wariness is helpful in order to be safe, and it is sensible to be afraid when there is immediate danger.

However, we have seen that high levels of fear regularly fail to correspond to high risks of being on the receiving end of a criminal offence. It is here that measures might be most required. Firstly, we can tackle fear by education. Education can occur in traditional establishments, but also via the media and via local community initiatives. Virtually everywhere, the 'stranger danger' is smaller than we think. There are far fewer monsters lurking in the undergrowth than most people imagine.

A further point worth emphasising is that the environment is a potent shaper of behaviour. Zimbardo's experiments show that the role that people assume and the behaviour of others affect us more than we like to think. From that perspective, there is a lot to gain from making crime difficult, and from establishing ownership and care for our social and physical environment.

Furthermore, isolation breeds fear. A variety of social contacts makes it easier to be convinced of the good nature of most people around us. That is something that we might forget when our television diet continually shows us otherwise. A chat on the doorstep does more than relay information or kill a bit of time. It helps us establish a feeling of belonging. That feeling is essential in establishing strong communities that experience little crime, and where no more than a proportionate level of wariness about crime is necessary.

On a more serious note, those who have been traumatised by crime are entitled to and should benefit from professional help. Organisations such as Victim Support offer a valuable service, which can be both practical and emotional (see www.victimsupport.org). In these cases, we must also be careful to avoid secondary victimisation as a result of the court experience (Williams 1984). This is something that the criminal justice system is intent on improving (e.g., Kelly *et al.* 2005), and there is no doubt that there still is plenty of room for improvement.

References

Abel, G.G., Becker, J.V. and Cunningham-Rathner, J. (1984) 'Complications, Consent and Cognitions in Sex Between Children and Adults', *International Journal of Law and Psychiatry*, 7: 89–103.

Acierno, R., Resnick, H.S. and Kilpatrick, D.G. (1997) 'Prevalence Rates, Case Identification, and Risk Factors for Sexual Assault, Physical Assault, and Domestic Violence in Men and Women', *Behavioral Medicine*, 23: 56–64.

Ainsworth, P. (2000) *Psychology and Policing*, Cullompton: Willan.

Ainsworth, P. (2001) *Offender Profiling and Crime Analysis*. Cullompton: Willan.

American Psychiatric Association (1994) *Diagnostic and Statistical Manual of Mental Disorders* (4th edition), Washington, DC: American Psychiatric Association.

Akhtar, N. and Bradley, E.J. (1991) 'Social Information Processing Deficits of Aggressive Children: Present Findings and Implications for Social Skills Training', *Clinical Psychology Review*, 11: 621–44.

Anderson, C.A. (2001) 'Heat and Violence', *Current Directions in Psychological Science*, 10: 33–8.

Anderson, C.A. and Bushman, B.J. (2002) 'Human Aggression'. *Annual Review of Psychology*, 53: 27–51.

Anderson, C.A., Anderson, K.B., Dorr, N., DeNeve, K.M. and Flanagan, M. (2000) 'Temperature and Aggression', *Advances in Experimental Social Psychology*, 32: 63–133.

Andrews, D.A. (2001) 'Principles of Effective Correctional Programs', in J. McGuire (ed.) *Offender Rehabilitation and Treatment: Effective Programmes and Policies to Reduce Re-offending*, Chichester: Wiley, 35–62.

Andrews, D.A. and Bonta, J. (1998) *The Psychology of Criminal Conduct* (2nd edition), Cincinnati, OH: Anderson.

Andrews, D.A., Bonta, J. and Hoge, R.D. (1990) 'Classification for Effective Rehabilitation: Rediscovering Psychology', *Criminal Justice and Behaviour*, 17: 19–52.

Appleby, L. (1999) *Safer Services: National Inquiry into Suicide and Homicide by People with Mental Illness*, London: Department of Health.

Archer, J. (2005) 'Testosterone and Human Aggression: A Review of the Challenge Hypothesis', *Neuroscience and Biobehavioural Reviews*, 30: 319–45.

Armstrong, T.A. (2005) 'Evaluating the Competing Assumptions of Gottfredson and Hirschi's (1990) A General Theory of Crime and Psychological Explanations of Aggression', *Western Criminology Review*, 6: 12–21.

Association of Therapeutic Communities (1999) 'Briefing Paper', available on: www.therapeuticcommunities.org

Audit Commission (2004) *Youth Justice 2004. A Review of the Reformed Youth Justice System*, London: Audit Commission.

Badger, D., Nursten, J., Williams, P. and Woodward, M. (1999) *CRD Report 15 – Systematic Review of the International Literature on the Epidemiology of Mentally Disordered Offenders*, available on: www.york.ac.uk/inst/crd/report15.htm

Bandura, A. (1965) 'Influence of Model's Reinforcement Contingencies on the Acquisition of Imitative Responses', *Journal of Personality and Social Psychology*, 36: 589–95.

Bandura, A. (1977) 'Self-Efficacy: Towards a Unifying Theory of Behaviour Change', *Psychological Review*, 84: 191-215.

Bandura, A. (1997) *Self Efficacy: The Exercise of Control*, New York: Freeman.

Bandura, A. (2004) 'Role of Selective Moral Disengagement in Terrorism and Counterterrorism', in F.M. Mogahaddam and A.J. Marsella (eds) *Understanding Terrorism: Psychological Roots, Consequences and Interventions*, Washington, DC: American Psychological Association Press, 121–50.

Bandura, A., Ross, D. and Ross, S.A. (1961) 'Transmission of Aggression through Imitation of Aggressive Models', *Journal of Abnormal and Social Psychology*, 63: 575–82.

Bandura, A., Ross, D. and Ross, S.A. (1963) 'Imitation of Film-Mediated Aggressive Models', *Journal of Abnormal and Social Psychology*, 6: 3–11.

Barber, J. (1995) *Social Work with Addictions*, Basingstoke: Macmillan.

Barker, M. and Morgan, R. (1993) *Sex Offenders: A Framework for the Evaluation of Community Based Treatment*, Faculty of Law, University of Bristol.

Bartol, C. and Bartol, A. (2004) *Introduction to Forensic Psychology*, Thousand Oaks, CA: Sage.

Bar-Yam, Y. (1997) *Dynamics of Complex Systems*, Reading, MA: Perseus Books.

Bateman, T. (2005) 'Reducing Child Imprisonment: A Systemic Challenge', *Youth Justice*, 5: 91–105.

Bates, A., Falshaw, L., Corbett, C., Patel, V. and Friendship, C. (2004) 'A Follow-Up Study of Sex Offenders Treated by Thames Valley Sex Offender

Groupwork Programme, 1995/1999', *Journal of Sexual Aggression*, 10 (1): 29–38.

BBC (2006) 'Quick Guide: UK Human Trafficking', 2 October 2006, available on: news.bbc.co.uk/1/hi/uk/5343036.stm

BBC (2006) Sex and Lies, available on: www.bbc.co.uk/bbcthree/tv/ sexandlies.shtml

BBC News (17 October 2006) 'Blunkett Gave Machine-Gun Order', available on: news.bbc.co.uk/1/hi/uk_politics/6057528.stm

Bean, P. and Mounser, P. (1993) *Discharged From Mental Hospital, Basingstoke, Hants, UK,* London: Macmillan Press

Becker, H. (1963) *Outsiders: Studies in the Sociology of Deviance*, New York: Free Press.

Becker, M., Love, C.E. and Hunter, M.E. (1997) 'Intractability Is Relative: Behaviour Therapy in the Elimination of Violence in Psychotic Patients', *Legal and Criminological Psychology*, 2: 89–101.

Beckett, R., Beech, A., Fisher, D. and Fordham, A.S. (1994) *Community-Based Treatment for Sex Offenders: An Evaluation of Seven Treatment Programmes. A Report for the Home office by The Step Team,* London: Home Office.

Beech, A., Fisher, D. and Beckett, R. (1999) *Step 3: An Evaluation of the Prison Sex Offender Treatment Programme,* London: HMSO.

Beech, A.R., Beckett, R. and Fisher, D. (2002) *Outcome Data of Representative UK Sex Offender Treatment Programmes: Short-Term Effectiveness and Some Preliminary Reconviction Data,* London: Sage.

Bensley, L. and Van Eenwyk, J. (2001) 'Video Games and Real-Life Aggression: Review of the Literature', *Journal of Adolescent Health*, 29: 144–257.

Berkowitz, L. (1989) 'Frustration-Aggression Hypothesis: Examination and Reformulation', *Psychological Bulletin*, 106: 59–73.

Berkowitz, L. (1990) 'On the Formation and Regulation of Anger and Aggression: A Cognitive-Neoassociationistic Analysis', *American Psychologist*, 45: 494–503.

Berkowitz, L. (1993) *Aggression: Its Causes, Consequences and Control*, New York: McGraw-Hill.

Bickel, W. and Potenza, M. (2006) 'The Forest and the Trees: Addiction as a Complex Self-Organizing System', in W.R. Miller and K. Carroll (eds) *Rethinking Substance Abuse: What the Science Shows and What We Should Do About It*, New York: Guilford Press, 8–21.

Bickley, J. and Beech, R. (2001) 'Classifying Child Abusers: Its Relevance to Theory and Clinical Practice', *International Journal of Offender Therapeutic Comparative Criminology*, 45: 51.

Bickley, J. and Beech, A.R. (2002) 'An Empirical Investigation of the Ward and Hudson Self-Regulation Model of the Sexual Offence Process with Child Abusers', *Journal of Interpersonal Violence*, 17: 371–93.

Blaauw, E., Winkel, F.W., Sheridan, L., Malsch, M. and Arensman, E. (2002) 'The Psychological Consequences of Stalking Victimisation', in J. Boon and L. Sheridan (eds) *Stalking and Psychosexual Obsession: Psychological Perspectives for Prevention, Policing and Treatment*, Chichester: Wiley, 23–34.

Blackburn, R. (2000) 'Treatment or Incapacitation? Implications of Research on Personality Disorders for the Management of Dangerous Offenders', *Legal and Criminological Psychology*, 5, 1–21.

Blackburn, R. (2004) '"What Works" with Mentally Disordered Offenders', *Psychology, Crime and Law*, 10: 297–308.

Blackburn, R., Logan, C., Donnelly, J. and Renwick, S. (2003) 'Personality Disorder, Psychopathy and Other Mental Disorders: Co-morbidity Among Patients at English and Scottish High Security Hospitals', *Journal of Forensic Psychiatry and Psychology*, 14: 111–37.

Blair, T. (1993) 'Why Crime Is a Socialist Issue', *New Statesman*, 29(12): 27–8.

Bletzer, K. and Koss, M. (2004) 'Narrative Constructions of Sexual Violence as Told by Female Rape Survivors' in Three Populations of the Southwestern United States: Scripts of Coercion, Scripts of Consent', *Medical Anthropology*, 23: 113–56.

Blumentahl, S., Gudjonsson, G. and Burns, J. (1999) 'Cognitive Distortions and Blame Attribution in Sex Offenders Against Adults and Children', *Child Abuse and Neglect*, 23: 129–43.

Blumstein, A., Cohen, J., Roth, J. and Visher, C. (1986) *Criminal Careers and 'Career Criminals'*, Washington, DC: Academic Press.

Boeringer, S.B. (1999) 'Associations of Rape-Supportive Attitudes with Fraternal and Athletic Participation', *Violence Against Women*, 5: 81–90.

Bornstein, R. (1996) 'Dependency', in C.G. Costello (ed.) *Personality Characteristics of the Personality Disordered*, New York: Wiley, 123–32.

Borum, R. (1996) 'Improving the Clinical Practice of Violence Risk Assessment: Technology, Guidelines and Training', *American Psychologist*, 51: 945–56.

Bottoms, A., Gelsthorpe, L. and Rex, S. (2001) *Community Penalties: Change and Challenges*, Cullompton: Willan.

Breakwell, G. and Rowett, C. (1982) *Social Work: A Social Psychological Perspective*, New York: Van Nostrand Reinhold.

Bretherick, D. (2006) *Crime from Below: An Examination of the Role of Popular Cultural Representations of Crime in Criminology*, Doctoral dissertation, Institute of Criminal Justice Studies, University of Portsmouth.

Brewer, K. (2000) *Psychology and Crime*, Oxford: Heinemann.

Brewster, M.P. (1997) *An Exploration of the Experiences and Needs of Former Intimate Stalking Victims: Final Report Submitted to the National Institute of Justice*, West Chester, PA: West Chester University.

Brewster, M.P. (2003) 'Power and Control Dynamics in Prestalking and Stalking Situations', *Journal of Family Violence*, 18: 207–17.

Briggs, D. (1998) *Assessing Men Who Sexually Abuse – A Practice Guide*. London: Jessica Kingsley.

British Crime Survey (2002) *British Crime Survey 2001/02*, available online: www.crimereduction.gov.uk/statistics/statistics18.htm

Britton, P. (1997) *The Jigsaw Man*, London: Corgi Books.

Brower, M.C. and Price, B.H. (2001) 'Neuropsychiatry of Frontal Lobe Dysfunction in Violent and Criminal Behaviour: A Critical Review', *Journal of Neurology, Neurosurgery and Psychiatry*, 71: 720–6.

Brown, H. (2000) *Stalking and Other Forms of Harassment: An Investigator's Guide*, London: Metropolitan Police.

Brunner, H.G., Nelen, M., Breakefield, X.O., Ropers, H.H. and Van Oost, B.A. (1993) 'Abnormal Behavior Associated with a Point Mutation in the Structural Gene for Monoamine Oxidase A', *Science*, 262: 578–80.

Bryant, J. and Zillmann, D. (1979) 'Effect of Intensification of Annoyance Through Unrelated Residual Excitation on Substantially Delayed Hostile Behavior', *Journal of Experimental Social Psychology*, 15: 470–80.

Buchanan, A. (2006) 'Quantifying the Contributions of Three Types of Information to the Prediction of Criminal Conviction Using The Receiver Operating Characteristic', *British Journal of Psychiatry*, 188: 472–8.

Budd, T. and Mattinson, J. with Myhill A. (2000) *The Extent and Nature of Stalking: Findings from the 1998 British Crime Survey*, Home Office Research Study 210, London: Home Office.

Burt, M. (1980) 'Cultural Myths and Supports for Rape', *Journal of Personality and Social Psychology*, 38: 217–30.

Bushman, B.J. and Cooper, H.M. (1990) 'Effects of Alcohol on Human Aggression: An Integrative Research Review', *Psychological Bulletin*, 107: 341–54.

Canter, D. (1994) *Criminal Shadows: Inside the Mind of the Serial Killer*, London: HarperCollins.

Canter, D. (1995) 'Psychology of Offender Profiling', in R. Bull and D. Carson (eds) *The Handbook of Psychology in Legal Contexts*, Chichester: Wiley.

Canter, D. and Alison, L. (1999) *Profiling in Theory and Practice*, Aldershot: Ashgate.

Canter, D. and Fritzon, K. (1998) 'Differentiating Arsonists: A Model of Firesetting Actions and Characteristics', *Legal and Criminological Psychology,* 3: 73–96.

Canter, D. and Heritage, R. (1990) 'A Multivariate Model of Sexual Offence Behaviour' *Journal of Forensic Psychiatry*, 1, 185–212.

Canter, D. and Larkin, P. (1993) 'The Environmental Range of Serial Rapists', *Journal of Environmental Psychology*, 13: 63–9.

Carroll, J. and Weaver, F. (1986) 'Shoplifters' Perceptions of Crime Opportunities: A Process-Tracing Study', in D.B. Cornish and R.V. Clarke (eds) *The Reasoning Criminal: Rational Choice Perspectives on Offending*, New York: Springer, 19–38.

Chapman, T. and Hough, M. (1998) *HM Inspectorate of Probation, A Guide to Effective Practice, Evidence Based Practice*, London: Home Office Publications Unit.

Chick, J. (2002) 'Evolutionary Psychobiology: Any Relevance for Therapy?', *Addiction* 97: 473–4.

Chiricos, T., Padgett, K. and Gertz, M. (2000) 'Fear, TV News and the Reality of Crime', *Criminology*, 38: 755–86.

Christiansen, K.O. (1977) 'A Review of Studies of Criminality Among Twins', in S.A. Mednick and K.O. Christiansen (eds) *Biosocial Bases of Criminal Behaviour*, New York: Gardiner Press, 45–88.

CJS (2006) Press Release 20 July 2006, available on: www.cjsonline.gov.uk

Clancy, A., Hough, M., Aust, R. and Kershaw, C. (2001) *Crime, Policing and Justice: The Experience of Ethnic Minorities. Findings from the 2000 British Crime Survey*, Home Office Research, Development and Statistics Directorate.

Commission for Racial Equality (2003) *Race Equality in Prisons: A Formal Investigation by the Commission for the Racial Equality into HM Prison Service of England and Wales*, Part II, available on: www.cre.gov.uk/publs/cat_fi.html

Connor, M.O., Phillips, L., Quirk, R. and Rosenfeld, B. (2004) 'Is It Stalking? Perceptions of Stalking among College Undergraduates', *Criminal Justice and Behavior,* 31(1): 73–96.

Connor, T. (n.d.) Untitled, available on: www. faculty.ncwc.edu/toconnor. Accessed 19 May 2006.

Cooper, C.L., Murphy, W.D. and Haynes, M.R. (1996) 'Characteristics of Abused and Non-Abused Adolescent Sexual Offenders', *Sexual Abuse: A Journal of Research and Treatment*, 8: 105–19.

Copson, G. (1995) *Coals to Newcastle? A Study of Offender Profiling*, Part 1; Police Research Group: Special Interest Paper Series, 7. London: Home Office Police Department.

Coyle, A. (2005) *Understanding Prisons: Key Issues in Policy and Practice,* Maidenhead: Open University Press/McGraw-Hill Education.

Cozens, C. (2003) 'Tabloids Stoke Fear of Crime', *Guardian*, 17 July 2003.

Craig, L.A., Browne, K.D. and Stringer, I. (2004) 'Comparing Sex Offender Risk Assessment Measures on a UK Sample', *International Journal of Offender Therapy and Comparative Criminology*, 48: 7–27.

Crawley, E. (2004) *Doing Prison Work: The Public and Private Lives of Prison Officers*, Cullompton: Willan.

Crick, N.R. and Dodge, K.A. (1994) 'A Review and Reformulation of Social Information-Processing Mechanisms in Children's Social Adjustment', *Psychological Bulletin*, 115: 74–101.

Crisp, Q. (1968) *The Naked Civil Servant*, London: Cape.

Crow, I. (2001) *The Treatment and Rehabilitation of Offenders*, London: Sage.

Dalgaard, O.S. and Kringlen, E. (1976) 'A Norwegian Study of Criminality', *British Journal of Criminology*, 16: 213–33.

Davies, A. (1997) 'Specific Profile Analysis; A Data-Based Approach To Offender Profiling', in J.L. Jackson and D. Bekerian (eds) *Offender Profiling: Theory, Research And Practice,* Chichester: Wiley, 191–208.

Davies, A. and Dale, A. (1995) *Locating the Stranger Rapist*, Police Group Special Interest Series, London: HMSO.

Davison, G.C., Neale, J.M. and Kring, A.M. (2004) *Abnormal Psychology* (9th edition), Hoboken, NJ: Wiley.

Dean, J. and Hastings, A. (2000) *Challenging Images: Housing Estates, Stigma and Regeneration*, Bristol: Joseph Rowntree Foundation/Policy Press.

de Clérambault, G. (1942) *Les Psychoses passionelles*, Paris: Presses Universitaire de France.

Department of Health/Mental Health Strategies (2005) *The 2004/05 Survey of Investment in Mental Health Services*, London: DOH.

Dhawan, S. and Marshall, W.L. (1996) 'Sexual Abuse Histories of Sexual Offenders', *Sexual Abuse: A Journal of Research and Treatment*, 8: 7–15.

DiClemente, C. and Prochaska, J. (1998) 'Toward a Comprehensive Transtheoretical Model of Change', in W.R. Miller and N. Heather (eds) *Treating Addictive Behav* (2nd edition), New York: Plenum Press, 3–24.

Dodd, V. (2006) 'Prison Whistleblower Lifts Lid on "Regime of Torture"', 13 November 2006, available on: www.guardian.co.uk

Dollard, D., Doob, L., Miller, N., Mowrer, O. and Sears, R. (1939) *Frustration and Aggression*, New Haven, CT: Yale University Press.

Douglas, J. and Olshaker, M. (1997) *Mindhunter. Inside the FBI Elite Serial Crime Unit*, London: Arrow Books.

Dowden, C. and Andrews, D. (2004) 'The Importance of Staff Practice in Delivering Effective Correctional Treatment: A Meta-Analytic Review of Core Correctional Practice', *International Journal of Offender Therapy and Comparative Criminology*, 48: 203–14.

Driscoll, M. (1994) *Psychology of Learning for Instruction*, Boston: Allyn and Bacon.

Dunn, P.C., Vail-Smith, K. and Knight, S.M. (1999) 'What Date/Acquaintance Rape Victims Tell Others: A Study of College Students Recipients of Disclosure', *Journal of American College Health*, 47: 213–19.

Dutton, D.G. (1998) *The Abusive Personality: Violence and Control in Intimate Relationships*, New York: Guildford Press.

Dweck, C.S. (2000) *Self Theories: Their Role in Motivation, Personality and Development*, Lillington: Taylor and Francis.

Dwyer, D. (2001) *Angles on Criminal Psychology*, Cheltenham: Nelson Thornes.

Dye, M.L. and Davis, K.E. (2003) 'Stalking and Psychological Abuse: Common Factors and Relationship-Specific Characteristics', *Violence and Victims*, 18: 163–80.

Edwards, G. (2004) *Matters of Substance*, London: Penguin.

Eldridge, H.J. (1992) *Relapse Prevention and Its Application to Patterns of Adult Male Sex Offending; Implications for Assessment*, NOTA Conference, Dundee University.

Emler, N. (2001) *Self Esteem: The Costs and Causes of Low Self Worth*, York: Joseph Rowntree Foundation.

European Crime Prevention Network (2004) *A Review of Scientifically Evaluated Good Practices for Reducing Feelings of Insecurity or Fear of Crime in the EU Member States*, European Commission, available on: ec.europa.eu/justice_home/eucpn/docs/review_reducing_feelings_insecurities_fear_crime_en.pdf

Eysenck, H.J. and Eysenck, S.B.G. (1975) *The Eysenck Personality Questionnaire*, London: Hodder and Stoughton.

Eysenck, H.J. and Eysenck, S.B.G. (1976) *Psychoticism as a Dimension of Personality*, London: Hodder and Stoughton.

Eysenck, H. and Eysenck, M. (1985) *Personality and Individual Differences: A Natural Science Approach*, New York: Plenum.

Eysenck, H. and Gudjonsson, G. (1989) *The Causes and Cures of Criminality*, New York: Plenum Press.

Falshaw, L., Friendship, C., Travers, R. and Nugent, F. (2003) *Searching for 'What Works': An Evaluation of Cognitive Skills Programmes*, Findings 206, London: Home Office.

Farrington, D. (1991) 'Anti-Social Personality from Childhood to Adulthood', *Psychologist*, 4: 389–94.

Farrington, D.P. (1986) 'Age and Crime', in M. Tonry and N. Morris (eds) *Crime and Justice*, vol. 7, Chicago: University of Chicago Press.

Farrington, D.P. (1989) *The Origins of Crime: The Cambridge Study of Delinquent Development*, Home Office Research and Planning Unit, Research Bulletin No. 27. London: HMSO.

Farrington, D.P. (1996) *Understanding and Preventing Youth Crime*, York: Joseph Rowntree Foundation/York Publishing Services.

Farrington, D.P. (2000) 'Explaining and Preventing Crime: The Globalization of Knowledge', *Criminology*, 38: 1–24.

Farrington, D.P. and Welsh, B. (2002) 'Developmental Prevention Programmes: Effectiveness and Benefit-Cost Analysis', in J. McGuire (ed.) *Offender Rehabilitation and Treatment: Effective Programmes and Policies to Reduce Re-Offending*, Chichester: Wiley, 143–66.

Farrington, D.P. and West, D.J. (1990) *The Cambridge Study in Delinquent Development: A Prospective Longitudinal Study of 411 Males*, New York: Springer.

Fennell, P. (2000) 'Radical Risk Management, Mental Health and Criminal Justice', in N. Gray, J. Laing and L. Noaks (eds) *Criminal Justice, Mental Health and the Politics of Risk*, London: Cavendish, 69–97.

Ferraro, K. (1995) *Fear of Crime*, Albany, NY: State University of New York.

Finkelhor, D. (1986) *Sourcebook on Child Sexual Abuse*, Beverly Hills, CA: Sage.

Finkelhor, D. (1993) 'Epidemiological factors in the Clinical Identification of Child Sexual Abuse', *Child Abuse and Neglect*, 17: 67–70.

Finn, J. (2004) 'A Survey of Online Harassment at a University Campus', *Journal of Interpersonal Violence*, 19: 468–83.

Fisher, B., Cullen, F.T. and Daigle, L.E. (2005) 'The Discovery of Acquaintance Rape: The Salience of Methodological Innovation and Rigor', *Journal of Interpersonal Violence*, 20: 493–500.

Fisher, D. and Mair, G. (1998) *A Review of Classification Systems for Sex Offenders*, Edinburgh: Scottish Office.

Fitzgerald, N. and Riley, K. (2000) 'Drug-Facilitated Rape: Looking for the Missing Pieces', *National Institute of Justice Journal*, April, 8–15.

Fitzgerald, P. and Seeman, M.V. (2002) 'Erotomania in Women', in J. Boon and L. Sheridan (eds) *Stalking and Psychosexual Obsession: Psychological Perspectives for Prevention, Policing and Treatment*, Chichester: Wiley, 165–79.

Foucault, M. (1977) *Discipline and Punish: The Birth of the Prison*, Harmondsworth: Penguin Books.

France, A. and Homel, R. (2006) 'Societal Access Routes and Developmental Pathways: Putting Social Structure and Young People's Voice into the Analysis of Pathways into and out of Crime', *Australia and New Zealand Journal of Criminology*, 39: 295–398.

Friendship, C., Falshaw, L. and Beech, A. (2003) 'Measuring the Real Impact of Accredited Offending Behaviour Programmes', *Legal and Criminal Psychology*, 8: 115–27.

Furstenberg, F.F., Brooks-Gunn, J. and Morgan, S.P. (1987) 'Adolescent Mothers and Their Children in Later Life', *Family Planning Perspectives*, 19: 142–51.

Gable, R.S. (2004) 'Acute Toxic Effects of Club Drugs', *Journal of Psychoactive Drugs*, 36: 303–13.

Gabriel, U. and Greve, W. (2003) 'The Psychology of Fear of Crime: Conceptual and Methodological Issues', *British Journal of Criminology*, 43: 600–14.

Gardner, D.G. and Pierce, J.L. (1998) 'Self-Esteem and Self-Efficacy within the Organizational Context', *Group and Organization Management*, 23: 48–70.

Garmezy, N. (1985) 'Stress-Resistent Children: The Search For Protective Factors' in J.E. Stevenson (ed.) *Recent Research in Developmental Psychopathology*. Book Supplement to *Journal of Child Psychology and Psychiatry*, 213-33.

Geary, D.C. (1998) *Male, Female: The Evolution of Human Sex Differences*, Washington, DC: American Psychological Association.

Giddens, A. (2001) *Sociology* (5th edition), Cambridge: Polity Press.

Gifford, E. and Humphreys, K. (2007) 'The Psychological Science of Addiction', *Addiction*, 102: 352–261.

Glueck, S. and Glueck, E. (1950) *Unraveling Juvenile Delinquency*, Cambridge, MA: Harvard University Press.

Goerner, S. (1995) 'Chaos, Evolution and Deep Ecology', in R. Robertson and A. Combes (eds) *Chaos Theory in Psychology and the Life Sciences*, Mahwah, NJ: Lawrence Erlbaum Associates, 17–38.

Goffman, E. (1963) *Stigma*, Englewood Cliffs, NJ: Prentice-Hall.

Goffman, E. (1968) *Asylums*, Harmondsworth: Penguin Books.

Goldson, B. (1997) 'Children, Crime, Policy and Practice: Neither Welfare nor Justice', *Children and Society*, 2: 77–88.

Goldson, B. (2002) *Vulnerable Inside: Children in Secure and Penal Settings*, London: Children's Society.

Goldson, B. (2006) 'Penal Custody: Intolerance, Irrationality and Indifference', in B. Goldson and J. Muncie (eds) *Youth Crime and Justice*, London: Sage, 139–53.

Goldson, B. and Coles, D. (2005) *In the Care of the State? Child Deaths in Penal Custody in England and Wales*, London: INQUEST.

Goldstein, A. (2001) *Addiction: From Biology to Drug Policy* (2nd edition), New York: Oxford University Press.

Goldstein, A. (2002) 'Low-Level Aggression: Definition, Escalation, Intervention', in J. McGuire (ed.) *Offender Rehabilitation and Treatment: Effective Programmes and Policies to Reduce Re-Offending*, Chichester: Wiley, 169–92.

Goldstein, A., Kaizer, S. and Whitby, O. (1969) 'Psychotropic Effects of Caffeine', *Clinical Pharmacology and Therapeutics*, 10: 489–97.

Gordon, D.A. (2002) 'Intervening with Families of Troubled Youth', in J. McGuire *Offender Rehabilitation and Treatment: Effective Programmes and Policies to Reduce Re-Offending*, Chichester: Wiley, 193–221.

Gossop, M., Marsden, J., Stewart, D. and Kidd, T. (2003) 'The National Treatment Outcome Research Study (NTORS): 4-5 Year Follow Up Results', *Addiction*, 98: 291–303.

Gottfredson, M.R. and Hirschi, T. (1990) *A General Theory of Crime*, Stanford, CA: Stanford University Press.

Gould, S.J. (1981) *The Mismeasure of Man*, New York: Norton.

Grafman, J., Schab, K. and Warden, D. (1996) 'Frontal Lobe Injuries, Violence and Aggression: A Report of the Vietnam Head Injury Study', *Neurology*, 46: 1231–8.

Graham, J. (1988) *Schools, Disruptive Behaviour and Delinquency. A Review of Research*, Home Office Research Study 96, London: HMSO.

Graham, J. and Bowling, B. (1995) *Young People and Crime*, Home Office Research Study 145, London: Home Office.

Greenwald, A., Banaji, M., Rudman, L., Farnham, S., Nosek, B. and Mellott, S. (2002) 'A Unified Theory of Implicit Attitudes, Stereotypes, Self-Esteem, and Self-Concept', *Psychological Review* 109: 3–25.

Gross, K, and Aday, S. (2003) 'The Scary World in Your Living Room and Neighborhood: Using Local Broadcast News, Neighborhood Crime Rates, and Personal Experience to Test Agenda Setting and Cultivation', *Journal of Communication*, 53: 411–26.

Groth, A.N. (1979) *Men Who Rape: The Psychology of the Offender*, New York: Plenum Press.

Groth, A.N., Burgess, A. and Holmstrom, L. (1977) 'Rape, Power, Anger, and Sexuality', *American Journal of Psychiatry*, 134: 12–39.

Grubin, D. (1998) *Sex Offending Against Children: Understanding the Risk*, Police Research Series Paper 99, London: Home Office.

Grubin, M. and Madsen, L. (2006) 'Accuracy and Utility of Post-Conviction Polygraph Testing of Sex Offenders', *British Journal of Psychiatry*, 188: 479–83.

Gudjonsson, G.H. and Copson, G. (1997) 'The Role of the Expert in Criminal Investigation', in J.L. Jackson and D. Bekerian (eds) *Offender Profiling: Theory, Research and Practice*, Chichester: Wiley, 61–76.

Guerrero, L.K. (1998) 'Attachment-Style Differences in the Experience and Expression of Romantic Jealousy', *Personal Relationships*, 5: 273–91.

Gutheil, T. and Appelbaum, P. (2000) *Clinical Handbook of Psychiatry and the Law* (3rd edition), Baltimore: Williams and Wilkins.

Hale, C. (1996) 'Fear of Crime: A Review of the Literature', *International Review of Victimology*, 4: 79–150.

Hall, D.M. (1998) 'The Victims of Stalking', in J. Reid Meloy (ed.) *The Psychology of Stalking: Clinical and Forensic Perspectives*. San Diego, CA: Academic Press, 113–37.

Hall, G. (1996) *Theory-Based Assessment, Treatment, and Prevention of Sexual Aggression*, Oxford: Oxford University Press.

Hamilton, B. (n.d.) *Getting Started in AA*, available on: http://books.google.co.uk/books?id=mopszni8cqec&dq

Hamm, M., Coupez, T., Hoze, F. and Weinstein, C. (1994) 'The Myth of Humane Imprisonment: A Critical Analysis of Severe Discipline in U.S. Maximum Security Prisons, 1945-1990', in M. Braswell, R. Montgomery Jr, and L. Lombardo (eds) *Prison Violence in America* (2nd edition), Cincinnati, OH: Anderson Publishing, 167–200.

Haney, C., Banks, W.C. and Zimbardo, P.G. (1973) 'A Study of Prisoners and Guards in a Simulated Prison', *Naval Research Review*, 30: 4–17. Washington, DC: Office of Naval Research.

Hanson, R.F. (2002) 'Adolescent Dating Violence: Prevalence and Psychological Outcomes', *Child Abuse and Neglect*, 26: 447–51.

Hanson, R.K. (2000) *The Effectiveness of Treatment for Sexual Offenders*, Report of the Association for the Treatment of Sexual Abusers Collaborative Data Research Committee. Presentation at the Association for the Treatment of Sexual Abusers 19th Annual Research and Treatment Conference, San Diego, California.

Hanson, R.K. and Bussiere, M.T. (1998) 'Predicting Relapse: A Meta-Analysis of Sexual Offender Recidivism Studies', *Journal of Consulting and Clinical Psychology*, 66: 348–62.

Hare, R.D. (1991) *Manual for the Revised Psychopathy Checklist*, Toronto: Multi-Health Systems.

Hare, R.D. (1993) *Without Conscience: The Disturbing World of the Psychopaths Among Us*, New York: Pocket Books.

Hare, R.D. (1996) 'Psychopathy: A Clinical Construct Whose Time Has Come', *Criminal Justice and Behaviour*, 23: 25–54.

Hare, R.D. (2002) 'Psychopathy and Risk for Recidivism', in N. Gray, J. Laing and L. Noaks (eds) *Criminal Justice, Mental Health and the Politics of Risk*, London: Cavendish, 27–47.

Harrington, R., Bailey, S., Chitsabesan, P., Kroll, L., Macdonald, W., Sneider, S., Kenning, C., Taylor, G., Byford, S. and Barrett, B. (2005) *Mental Health Needs and Effectiveness of Provision for Young Offenders in Custody and in the Community*, London: Youth Justice Board for England and Wales.

Harris, J. (2000) *The Protection From Harassment Act 1997 – An Evaluation of Its Use and Effectiveness*, Home Office: Research, Development and Statistics Directorate, Research Findings 130, London: Home Office.

Harrison, K. (2005) 'The High-Risk Sex Offender Strategy in England and Wales: Is Chemical Castration an Option?', *Howard Journal*, 46: 16–37.

Harrower, J. (1998) *Applying Psychology to Crime*, Abingdon: Hodder Arnold.

Hawkins, J.D., Catalano, R.F. and Miller, J.Y. (1992) 'Risk and Protective Factors for Alcohol and Other Drug Problems in Adolescence and Early Adulthood: Implications for Substance Abuse Prevention', *Psychological Bulletin*, 112: 64–105.

Hawkins, J.D., Lishner, D.M., Jenson, J.M. and Catalano, R.F. (1987) 'Delinquents and Drugs: What the Evidence Says About Prevention and Treatment Programming', in B.S. Brown and A.R. Mills (eds) *Youth at High Risk for Substance Abuse*, Rockville, MD: US Department of Health and Human Science, 81–131.

Hazan, C. and Shaver, P.R. (1987) 'Romantic Love Conceptualized as an Attachment Process', *Journal of Personality and Social Psychology*, 52: 511–24.

Hazelwood, R.R. (1983) 'The Behavior-Oriented Interview of Rape Victims: The Key to Profiling', *FBI Law Enforcement Bulletin*, September: 8–15.

Hazelwood, R.R. and Burgess, A.E. (eds) (1995) *Practical Aspects of Rape Investigation*, Boca Raton, FL: CRC Press.

Healthcare Commission and Commission for Social Care inspection (CSCI) (2007), available on: www.csci.org.uk/registeredservicesdirectory/

Heather, N. and Robertson, I. (1997) *Problem Drinking* (3rd edition), Oxford: Oxford University Press.

Heilbrun, K. and Peters, L. (2000) 'Community-Based Treatment Programmes', in S. Hodgins and R. Muller-Isberner (eds) *Violence, Crime and Mentally Disordered Offenders: Concepts and Methods for Effective Treatment and Prevention*, Chichester: Wiley, 193–215.

Hensley, L. (2003) 'GHB Abuse Trends and Use in Drug-Facilitated Sexual Assault: Implications for Prevention', *NASPA Journal*, 40: 17–28.

Her Majesty's Chief Inspector of Prisons (1999) *Suicide Is Everyone's Concern: A Thematic Review by HM Chief Inspector of Prisons for England and Wales*. London: Home Office.

Herzog, T. (2005) 'When Popularity Outstrips the Evidence: Comment on West', *Addiction*, 100: 1040–1.

Hindman, J. and Peters, J.M. (2001) 'Polygraph Testing Leads to Better Understanding of Adult and Juvenile Sex Offenders', *Federal Probation*, 65: 8–15.

Hindmarch, I. and Brinkmann, R. (1999) 'Trends in the Use of Alcohol and Other Drugs in Cases of Sexual Assault', *Human Psychopharmacology*, 14: 225–31.

Hirschi, T. (1969) *Causes of Delinquency*, Berkeley, CA: University of California Press.

HM Inspectorate of Probation (2006) *An Independent Review of a Serious Further Offence Case: Damien Hanson and Elliot White*, London: HMIP.

Hodgins, S. (2000) 'Offenders with Major Mental Disorders', in C. Hollin (ed.) *Handbook of Offender Assessment and Treatment*, Chichester: Wiley, 433–51.

Hodgins, S. and Muller-Isberner, R. (2000) 'Evidence-Based Treatment for Mentally Disordered Offenders', in S. Hodgins and R. Muller-Isberner (eds) *Violence, Crime and Mentally Disordered Offenders: Concepts and Methods for Effective Treatment Prevention,* Chichester: Wiley 7–38.

Hoge, R.D. (1999) 'An Expanded Role for Psychological Assessment in Juvenile Justice Systems', *Criminal Justice and Behaviour*, 26: 251–66.

Hoge, R.D. (2002) 'Standardized Instruments for Assessing Risk and Need in Youthful Offenders', *Criminal Justice and Behaviour*, 29: 380–96.

Hoge, R.D. (n.d.) *Position Paper: Responses to Youth Crime*, available on: www.cpa.ca/documents/youth_crime.pdf

Holder, H. (1998) *Alcohol and the Community: A Systems Approach to Prevention*, Cambridge: Cambridge University Press.

Hollin, C., Palmer, E., McGuire, J., Hounsome, J. *et al.* (2004) 'Pathfinder Programmes in the Probation Service: A Retrospective Analysis', Home Office Online Report 66/04, available on: www.homeoffice.gobv.uk/rds/

Holmes, R. and Holmes, S. (2002) *Sex Crimes: Patterns and Behaviors*, Thousand Oaks, CA: Sage.

Home Office (1998) *Tackling Drugs Together to Build a Better Britain,* London: Home Office Publications.

Home Office (2002) *Updated Drug Strategy*, London: Home Office Publications.

Home Office (2003) *Prison Statistics of England and Wales, 2001*, RDS Paper 195, London: Home Office.

Home Office (2005) 'Prison Population', available on: www.homeoffice.gov.uk/press-releases.

Home Office (2006) 'Scared to Travel on Public Transport?', available on: www.homeoffice.gov.uk/crime-victims/worried-about-crime/too-scared-for-public-transport/

Home Office Press Release (2005) 'Why Do the Young Turn to Crime? Early Findings Turn Some Theories on Their Heads', ESRC Society Today, available on: www.esrc.ac.uk/esrcinfocentre/po/releases/2005/

Hood, R., Shute, S., Feilzer, M. and Wilcox, A. (2002) 'Sex Offenders Emerging from Long-Term Imprisonment: A Study of Their Long-Term Reconviction Rates and of Parole Board Members' Judgments of Their Risk', *British Journal of Criminology*, 42: 371–94.

Hope, T. (1996) 'Communities, Crime and Inequality in England and Wales', in T. Bennett (ed.) *Preventing Crime and Disorder. Targeting Strategies and Responsibilities*, Cambridge: Institute of Criminology (Cropwood Series).

Hough, M. (1995) *Anxiety About Crime: Findings From the 1994 Home Office Research Study No. 147*, London: Home Office.

House, J.C. (1997) 'Towards a Practical Application of Offender Profiling: The RNC's Criminal Suspect Prioritization System', in J.L. Jackson and D. Bekerian (eds) *Offender Profiling: Theory, Research and Practice*, Chichester: Wiley, 177–90.

House of Commons (14 June 2005) 'Fiona Mctaggart Responds to Question on Prisoners put by Steve Webb', available on: www.publications.parliament. uk

House of Commons (2006) *Report of the Zahid Mubarek Inquiry*, London: Stationery Office.

House of Commons Select Committee of Inquiry (1828) *Report into the Cause of the Increase in the Number of Commitments and Convictions, and into the State of the Police of the Metropolis*, Sessional Papers, available on: www. bopcris.ac.uk/cgi-bin/swish-cgi.pl?query=Juveniles&field=all&daterange= &series=&series=sess&recout=20&style=long

Howard, D.E. and Wang, M.Q. (2003) 'Risk Profiles of Adolescent Girls Who Were Victims of Dating Violence', *Adolescence*, 38: 1–14.

Hucker, S. (2005) *Psychiatric Aspects of Risk Assessment*, available on: www. violence-risk.com

Hudson, S.M., Ward, T. and McCormack, J.C. (1999) 'Offence Pathways in Sexual Offenders', *Journal of Interpersonal Violence*, 14: 779–98.

Huesmann, L.R., Moise-Titus, J., Podolski, C.L. and Eron, L. (2003) 'Longitudinal Relations Between Children's Exposure to TV Violence and Their Aggressive and Violent Behavior in Young Adulthood: 1977–1992', *Developmental Psychology*, 39: 201–21.

Hughes, G., Leisten, R. and Pilkington, A. (1998) 'Teetering On The Edge: The Futures of Crime Control and Community Safety', in G. Hughes, E. McLaughlin and J. Muncie (eds) *Crime Prevention and Community Safety: New Directions*, London: Sage, 318–40.

Iggulden, A. (2006) 'Pilfering Stars Make Wimbledon Throw in the Towel', *The Daily Telegraph*, 6 July 2006, available on: www.telegraph.co.uk/news/ main.jhtml?xml=/news/2006/07/08/nwimb08.xml.

Jackson, J.L. and Bekerian, D. (eds) (1997) *Offender Profiling: Theory, Research and Practice*, Chichester: Wiley.

Jackson, S.M., Cram, F. and Seymour, F.W. (2000) 'Sexual Violence and Sexual Coercion in High School Students' Dating Relationships, *Journal of Family Violence*, 15: 23–36.

Jaffee, S.R., Caspi, A., Moffitt, T.E., Dodge, K.A., Rutter, M., Taylor, A. and Tully, L.A. (2005) 'Nature X Nurture: Genetic Vulnerabilities Interact with Physical Maltreatment to Promote Conduct Problems', *Development and Psychopathology*, 17: 67–84.

James, E. (2006) 'Shut Up Blair? Hear, Hear', available on: http:// commentisfree.guardian.co.uk/erwin_james/2006/06/yes_shut_up_mr_ blair.html

Jasinski, J.L. and Dietz, T.L. (2003) 'Domestic Violence and Stalking Among Older Adults: An Assessment of Risk Markers', *Journal of Elder Abuse and Neglect*, 15(1): 3–18.

Jones, S. (2003) *Spiked!* London: Essjay Films.

Källmén, H. and Gustafson, R. (1998) 'Alcohol and Disinhibition', *European Addiction Research*, 4: 150–62.

Kalus, O., Bernstein, D. and Siever, L. (1995) 'Schizoid Personality Disorder', in J.W. Livesley (ed.) *The DSM-IV Personality Disorders*, New York: Guilford Press, 58–70.

Kantor, M. (1992) *Diagnosis and Treatment of the Personality Disorder*, St. Louis, Tokyo: Ishiyaku Euroamerica.

Katz, J. (1988) *Seductions of Crime: Moral and Sensual Attractions in Doing Evil*, New York: Basic Books.

Keith, B. (2006) *Report of the Zahid Mubarek Inquiry*, House of Commons, 29th June 2006, London: Stationery Office.

Kelly, L. and Radford, J. (1987) 'The Problem of Men: Feminist Perspectives on Sexual Violence', in P. Scraton (ed.) *Law, Order, and the Authoritarian State: Readings* in *Critical Criminology*, Buckingham: Open University Press, 237–53.

Kelly, L., Lovett, J. and Child, L.R. (2005) *A Gap or a Chasm? Attrition in Reported Rape Cases*, Home Office Research Study 293, London: HMSO.

Kemshall, H., Marsland, L., Boeck, T. and Dunkerton, L. (2006) 'Young People, Pathways and Crime: Beyond Risk Factors', *Australian and New Zealand Journal of Criminology*, 30: 354–70.

Kenrick, D.T. and MacFarlane, S.W. (1984) 'Ambient Temperature and Horn-Honking: A Field Study of the Heat/Aggression Relationship', *Environment and Behaviour*, 18: 179–91.

Kersting, K. (2004) 'New Hope for Sex Offender Treatment', in J. Lafond (ed.) *Preventing Sexual Violence: How Society Should Cope with Sex Offenders*, Washington, DC: American Psychological Association.

Knight, R. and Prentky, R. (1987) 'The Developmental Antecedents and Adult Adaptations of Rapist Subtypes', *Criminal Justice and Behavior*, 14: 403–26.

Knight, R. and Prentky, R. (1990) 'Classifying Sexual Offenders: The Development and Corroboration of Taxonomic Models', in W. Marshal, D. Laws and H. Barbaree (eds) *Handbook of Sexual Assault*, New York: Plenum Press, 23–52.

Knust, S. and Stewart, A.L. (2002) 'Risk-Taking Behaviour and Criminal Offending: An Investigation of Sensation Seeking and Eysenck Personality Questionnaire', *International Journal of Offender Therapy and Comparative Criminology*, 46: 586–602.

Koob, G. (2006) 'The Neurobiology of Addiction: A Neuroadaptational View Relevant for Diagnosis', *Addiction,* 101 (Suppl. 1): 23–30.

Lader, D., Singleton, N. and Meltzer, H. (1999) *Psychiatric Morbidity Among Young Offenders in England and Wales*, London: Office of National Statistics.

Lange, J.S. (1931) *Crime as Destiny*, London: Allen and Unwin.

Le Blanc, M., Ouimet, M. and Tremblay, R.E. (1988) 'An Integrative Control Theory of Delinquent Behaviour: A Validation of 1976–1985', *Psychiatry*, 51: 164–76.

Lee, M. (2001) 'The Genesis of "Fear of Crime"', *Theoretical Criminology*, 5: 467–85.

Lees, J., Manning, N. and Rawlings, B. (1999) *A Systematic International Review of Therapeutic Community Treatment for People with Personality Disorders and Mentally Disordered Offenders*. CRD Report 17, Therapeutic Community Effectiveness: Centre for Reviews and Dissemination, available on: www.york.ac.uk

Lende, D.H. and Smith, E.O. (2002) 'Evolution Meets Biopsychosociality: An Analysis of Addictive Behaviour', *Addiction*, 97: 447–58.

Lewis, D.O., Pincus, J.H., Feldman, M. *et al.* (1986) 'Psychiatric, Neurological and Psychoeducational Characteristics of 15 Death Row Inmates in the United States', *American Journal of Psychiatry*, 143: 838–45.

Li, J., Stokes, S.A. and Woeckener, A. (1998) 'A Tale of Novel Intoxication: A Review of the Effects of Gamma-Hydroxybutyric Acid with Recommendations for Management', *Annals of Emergency Medicine*, 31: 729–36.

Liebling, A. (1992) *Suicides in Prison*, London: Routledge.

Liebling, A. and Price, D. (2001) *The Prison Officer*, Leyhill: HM Prison Service.

Lindstrom, L. (1992) *Managing Alcoholism: Matching Clients to Treatments*, Oxford: Oxford University Press.

Linhhan, M. (1993) *Cognitive-Behavioral Treatment of Borderline Personality Disorder*, New York: Guilford Press.

Lipsey, M.W. (1992) 'Juvenile Delinquency Treatment: A Meta-Analytic Inquiry into the Variability of Effect', in T.D. Cook, H. Cooper, D.S. Cordray, H. Hartmann, L.V. Hedges, R.J. Light, T.A. Louis and F. Mosteller (eds) *Meta-Analysis for Explanation: A Casebook*, New York: Russell Sage Foundation, 83–127.

Lipsey, M.W. (1995) 'What Do We Learn from 400 Research Studies on the Effectiveness of Treatment with Juvenile Delinquents?', in J. McGuire (ed.) *What Works: Reducing Reoffending Guidelines from Research and Practice*, Chichester: Wiley, 63–78.

Lipsey, M.W. and Wilson, D.B. (1998) 'Effective Intervention for Serious Juvenile Offenders: A Synthesis of Research', in R. Loeber and D.P. Farrington (eds) *Serious and Violent Juvenile Offenders: Risk Factors and Successful Intervention*, Thousand Oaks, CA: Sage, 313–45.

Lishman, W.A. (1968) 'Brain Damage in Relation to Psychiatric Disability After Brain Injury', *British Journal of Psychiatry*, 114: 373–410.

Loeber, R. and Farrington, D.P. (eds) (1998) *Serious and Violent Offenders: Risk Factors and Successful Interventions*, Thousand Oaks, CA: Sage.

Loeber, R. and Hay, D.F. (1996) 'Key Issues in the Development of Aggression and Violence from Childhood to Early Adulthood', *Annual Review of Psychology*, 48: 371–410.

Loeber, R. and Stouthamer-Loeber, M. (1986) 'Family Factors as Correlates and Predictors of Juvenile Conduct Problems and Delinquency', in M. Tonry and N. Morris (eds) *Crime and Justice: Annual Review*, vol. 7, Chicago: University of Chicago Press, 29–149.

Lombroso, C. (1911) *Crime: Its Causes and Remedies*, Boston: Little Brown.

Lonsway, K.A. and Fitzgerald, L.F. (1994) 'Rape Myths: In Review', *Psychology of Women Quarterly*, 18: 133–64.

Luthar, S.S. (ed) (2003) *Resilience and Vulnerability: Adaptation in the Context of Childhood Adversities*, Cambridge: Cambridge University Press.

Ly, L. and Howard, D. (2004) *Statistics of Mentally Disordered Offenders 2003, England and Wales*, Home Office Statistical Bulletin, London: HMSO.

MacFarlane, B.A. (1997) 'People Who Stalk People', *USB Law Review*, 31: 37–103.

Maguin, E. and Loeber, R. (1996) 'Academic Performance and Delinquency', in M. Tonry (ed.) *Crime and Justice: A Review of Research*, vol. 20, Chicago: University of Chicago Press.

Malamuth, N.M., Linz, D., Heavey, C.L., Barnes, G. and Acker, M. (1995) 'Using the Confluence Model of Sexual Aggression to Predict Men's Conflict with Women: A 10-Year Follow-Up Study', *Journal of Personality and Social Psychology*, 69: 353–69.

Man, L.H., Best, D., Marshall, J., Godfrey, C. and Budd, T. (2002) *Dealing With Alcohol-Related Detainees in the Custody Suite*, Home Office Research Development and Statistics Directorate, Paper No. 178, London: Home Office.

Mann, R.E. and Shingler, J. (1999) *'Working with Cognitive Schemas'*, Workshop Presented at the National Organisation for the Treatment of Abusers (NOTA) Annual Conference, Pontypridd, Wales.

Marlatt, G.A. and Gordon, J.R. (eds) (1985) *Relapse Prevention: Maintenance Strategies in the Treatment of Addictive Behaviours*, New York: Guilford Press.

Marlatt, G.A., Baer, J.S. and Quigley, L.A. (1995) 'Self-Efficacy and Addictive Behaviour', in A. Bandura, (ed.) *Self Efficacy in Changing Societies*, Cambridge: Cambridge University Press, 289–315.

Marshall, W.L. and Barbaree, H. (1990) *An Integrated Theory of the Etiology of Sexual Offending*, New York: Plenum Press.

Marshall, W.L., Hamilton, K. and Fernandez, Y. (2001) 'Empathy Deficits and Cognitive Distortions in Child Molesters', *Sexual Abuse: A Journal of Research and Treatment*, 13: 123–30.

Martinson, R. (1974) 'What Works? Questions and Answers About Prison Reform', *Public Interest*, 35: 22–54.

Martinson, R. (1979) 'New Findings, New Views: A Note of Caution Regarding Sentencing Reform', *Hofstra Law Review*, 7: 243–58.

Mawby, R.I., Brunt, P. and Hambly, Z. (2000) 'Fear of Crime Among British Holidaymakers', *British Journal of Criminology*, 40: 468–79.

Mazur, A. and Booth, A (1998) 'Testosterone and Dominance in Men', *Behavioral and Brain Sciences*, 21: 353–97.

McCord, J. (1979) 'Some Child-Rearing Antecedents of Criminal Behavior in Adult Men', *Journal of Personality and Social Psychology*, 37: 1477–86.

McCord, W.M. and McCord, J. (1964) *The Psychopath: An Essay on the Criminal Mind*, New York: Van Nostrand.

McGuire, J. (ed.) (1995) *What Works: Reducing Re-offending: Guidelines from Research and Practice*, Chichester: Wiley.

McGuire, J. (2000) *Treatment Approaches for Offenders with Mental Disorder*, Correction Services Canada, available on: www.csc-scc.gc.ca

McGuire, J. (ed.) (2002) *Offender Rehabilitation and Treatment: Effective Practice and Policies to Reduce Re-offending*, Chichester: Wiley.

McGuire, J. (2004) *Understanding Psychology and Crime: Perspectives on Theory and Action*, Buckingham: Open University Press.

McGuire, J. (2005) 'Is Research Working? Revisiting the Research and Effective Practice Agenda', in J. Winstone and F. Pakes (eds) *Community Justice: Issues for Probation and Criminal Justice*, Cullompton: Willan, 257–83.

Mennell, J. and Shaw, I. (2006) 'The Future of Forensic and Crime Scene Science. I. A UK Forensic Science User and Provider Perspective', *Forensic Science International*, 157, S7–S12.

Merton, R.K. (1957) *Social Theory and Social Structure*, New York: Free Press.

Michael, G., McGrath, M.D. and Eoghan, C. (2002) 'Forensic Psychiatry and the Internet: Practical Perspectives on Sexual Predators and Obsessional Harassers in Cyberspace', *Journal of American Academy of Psychiatry and Law*, 30: 81–94.

Milgram, S. (1963) 'Behavioral Study of Obedience', *Journal of Abnormal and Social Psychology*, 67: 371–8.

Miller, N. (2001) *Stalking Laws and Implementation Practices: A National Review for Policymakers and Practitioners*, Alexandra, VA: Institute for Law and Justice.

Miller, W.R. (2006) 'Motivational Factors in Addictive Behaviors', in W.R. Miller and K. Carroll (eds) *Rethinking Substance Abuse: What the Science Shows and What We Should Do About It*, New York: Guilford Press, 134–50.

Miller, W.R. and Carroll, K. (eds) (2006) *Rethinking Substance Abuse: What the Science Shows and What We Should Do About It*, New York: Guilford Press.

Miller, W.R. and Rollnick, S. (1991) *Motivational Interviewing: Preparing People to Change Addictive Behavior*, New York: Guilford Press.

Millon, T. and Davis, R. (1996) *Disorders of Personality: DSM-IV and Beyond*, New York: Wiley.

Moffitt, T.E. (1993) 'Adolescence-Limited and Life-Course Persistent Antisocial Behaviour: A Developmental Taxonomy', *Psychological Review*, 100: 674–701.

Moffitt, T.E. and Caspi, A. (2001) 'Childhood Predictors Differentiate Life-Course Persistent and Adolescence-Limited Antisocial Pathways Among Males and Females', *Development and Psychopathology*, 13: 355–75.

Monahan, J., Steadman, H.J., Silver, E., Appelbaum, P.S., Clark Robbins, P., Mulvey, E.P., Roth, L.H., Grisso, T. and Banks, S. (2001) *Rethinking Risk*

Assessment: The MacArthur Study of Mental Disorder and Violence, Oxford: Oxford University Press.

Moran, P. and Hagell, A. (2001) *Intervening to Prevent Antisocial Personality Disorder: A Scoping Review,* Home Office Research Study 225, London: HMSO.

Morrall, P. (2002) *Madness, Murder and Media: A Realistic Critique of the Psychiatric Disciplines in Post-Liberal Society,* available on: www.critpsynet. freeuk.com

Mruk, C. (1999) *Self-Esteem: Research, Theory and Practice,* London: Free Association Books.

Mueser, K.T., Bond, G.R., Drake, R.E. and Resnick, S.G. (1998) 'Models of Community Care for Severe Mental Illness: A Review of Research on Case Management', *Schizophrenia Bulletin,* 24: 37–47.

Mullen, P.E., Pathé, M., Purcell, R. and Stewart, G.W. (1999) 'A Study of Stalkers', *American Journal of Psychiatry,* 156: 1244–9.

Mullins, M.E. (1999) 'Laboratory Confirmation of Flunitrazepam in Alleged Cases of Date Rape', *Emergency Medicine,* 6: 966–8.

Muncie, J. (1999) *Youth and Crime: A Critical Introduction,* London: Sage.

Muncie, J. (2006) *Youth and Crime* (2nd edition), London: Sage.

Murdoch, D., Pihl, R.O. and Ross, D. (1990) 'Alcohol and Crimes of Violence: Present Issues', *International Journal of Addiction,* 25: 1059–75.

Murray, D.J. (1989) *Review of Research on Re-offending of Mentally Disordered Offenders,* Research and Planning Unit Paper, 55, London: Home Office.

NACRO (2003) *A Failure of Justice: Reducing Child Imprisonment,* London: NACRO.

Neighbourhood Watch (2006) 'How to Reduce Fear of Crime in the Community', available on: www.crimereduction.gov.uk/neighbourhoodwatch/ nwatch03e.htm

Nellis, M. (2005) 'Dim Prospects: Humanistic Values and the Fate of Community Justice', in J. Winstone and F. Pakes (eds) *Community Justice: Issues for Probation and Criminal Justice,* Cullompton: Willan, 33–52.

Nesse, R. (2001) 'Evolution and Addiction', *Addiction,* 97: 470–1.

Neville, H.A., Heppner, M.J., Oh, E., Spanierman, L.B. and Clark, M. (2004) 'General and Culturally Specific Factors Influencing Black and White Rape Survivors' Self-Esteem', *Psychology of Women Quarterly,* 28: 83–94.

Newman, O. (1972) *Defensible Space,* New York: Macmillan.

Newman, O. (1996) *Creating Defensible Space,* Washington, DC: US Department of Housing and Urban Development Office of Policy Development and Research

Newman, O. and Franck, K. (1980) *Factors Influencing Crime and Instability in Urban Housing Developments,* Washington, DC: US Department of Justice.

New Scientist (2006) 'Timeline Drugs and Alcohol', September, available on: www.http://www.newscientist.com/article.ns?id=dn9924

New Zealand Ministry of Justice (2005) *National Guidelines for Crime Prevention Through Environmental Design in New Zealand. Part 1. Seven Qualities of Safer Places,* Wellington: Ministry of Justice.

NHS (n.d.) *National Electronic Library for Health: Mental Health*, available on: www.nelmh.org/

Nicholas, S., Povey, D., Walker, D. and Kershaw, C. (2005) *Crime in England and Wales 2004/5*. London: Home Office, available on: www.homeoffice. gov.uk/rds/pdfs05/hosb1105.pdf

Nicholas, S., Povey, D., Walker, A. and Kershaw, C. (2005) *Crime in England and Wales 2004/2005,* Home Office: Research, Development Statistics, available on: www.homeoffice.gov.uk/rds/crimeew0405.html

NOMS (2005) *Probation Bench Handbook* (Edition One), London: Home Office.

NOMS (2006) 'Estate Planning and Development Unit: Prison Population and Accommodation Briefing for 14 July 2006', available on: www. hmprisonserice.gov.uk/resourcecentre/publicationsdocuments/

Nurius, P.S., Norris, J., Macy, R.J. and Huang, B. (2004) 'Women's Situational Coping with Acquaintance Sexual Assault: Applying an Appraisal-Based Model', *Violence Against Women*, 10: 450–78.

Nurius, P.S., Norris, J., Young, D., Graham, T.L. and Gaylord, J. (2000) 'Interpreting and Defensively Responding to Threat: Examining Appraisals and Coping with Acquaintance Sexual Aggression', *Violence and Victims*, 15: 187–208.

O'Connor, D.B., Archer, J. and Wu, F.C.W. (2004) 'Effects of Testosterone on Mood, Aggression and Sexual Behavior in Young Men: A Double-Blind, Placebo-Controlled, Cross-Over Study', *Journal of Clinical Endocrinology and Metabolism*, 86: 2837–45.

Offender Health Care Strategies (OHCS) (2005) 'Improving Services for Offenders in the Community', available on: www.ohcs.co.uk/pdf/ guides/000101_hop_report.pdf

Offending Behaviour Programmes (2005) Available on: www. prisonmentalhealth.org

Oldham, J. (1990) *The Personality Self-Portrait, Why You Think, Work, Love, and Act the Way You Do*, New York: Bantam Books.

Oliver, K. (2000) *Psychology and Everyday Life*, London: Hodder and Stoughton.

Olsson, C.A., Bond, L., Burns, J.M., Vella-Brodrick, D.A. and Sawyer, S.M. (2003) 'Adolescent Resilience: A Concept Analysis', *Journal of Adolescence*, 26: 1–11.

Orford, J. (1990) 'Looking for a Synthesis in Studying the Nature of Dependence: Facing Up to Complexity', in G. Edwards and M. Lader (eds) *The Nature of Drug Dependence*, Oxford: Oxford University Press, 41–62.

Orford, J. (2001) *Excessive Appetites: A Psychological View of Addictions*, Chichester: Wiley.

Osborn, S.G. and West, D.J. (1979) 'Conviction Records of Fathers and Sons Compared', *British Journal of Criminology*, 19: 120–33.

Osofsky, M.J., Bandura, A. and Zimbardo, P.G. (2005) 'The Role of Moral Disengagement in the Execution Process', *Law and Human Behavior*, 29: 371–93.

Paine, M. and Hansen, D. (2002) 'Factors Influencing Children to Self-Disclose Sexual Abuse', *Clinical Psychology Review*, 22: 271–95.

Palmer, E.J. (2003) *Offending Behaviour: Moral Reasoning, Criminal Conduct and the Rehabilitation of Offenders*, Cullompton: Willan.

Palmer, E.J. and Hollin, C.R. (2000) 'The Inter-Relations of Sociomoral Reasoning, Perceptions of Own Parenting and Attribution of Intent with Self-Reporting Delinquency', *Legal and Criminological Psychology*, 5: 201–18.

Palmer, E.J. and Hollin, C.R. (2001) 'Sociomoral Reasoning, Perceptions of Parenting and Self-Reported Delinquency in Adolescents', *Applied Cognitive Psychology*, 15: 85–100.

Pathé, M. and Mullen, P.E. (1997) 'The Impact of Stalkers on Their Victims', *British Journal of Psychiatry*, 170: 12–17.

Patrick, S., Dorman, P. and Marsh, R. (1999) 'Simulating Correctional Disturbances: The Application of Organization Control Theory to Correctional Organizations via Computer Simulation', *Journal of Artificial Societies and Social Simulation*, 2(1).

Patterson, F.R., Forgatch, M.S., Yoerger, K.L. and Stoolmiller, M. (1998) 'Variables that Initiate and Maintain an Early-Onset Trajectory for Juvenile Offending', *Development and Psychopathology*, 10: 531–47.

Perkins, D., Hammond, S., Coles, D. and Bishopp, D. (1998) *Review of Sex Offender Treatment Programmes*, High Security Psychiatric Services Commissioning Board (HSPSCB), available on: www.ramas.co.uk/report4.pdf

Pew Center for the People and the Press (1998) *Event-Driven News Audiences: Internet News Takes Off*, available on: www.people-press.org/questionnaires/med98que.htm

Plant, M., Plant, M. and Thornton, C. (2002) 'People and Places: Some Factors in the Alcohol–Violence Link', *Journal of Substance Use*, 7: 207–13.

Portes, A. (1998) 'Social Capital: Its Origins and Applications in Modern Sociology', *Annual Review of Sociology*, 24: 1–24.

Power, A. and Tunstall, R. (1997) *Dangerous Disorder, Riots and Violent Disturbances in Thirteen Areas of Britain, 1991–92*, York: Joseph Rowntree Foundation/York Publishing Services.

Prentky, R. (1996) 'Community Notification and Constructive Risk Reduction', *Journal of interpersonal Violence*, 11: 295–8.

Prime, J. (2002) *Progress Made Against Home Office Public Service Agreement No. 10*, Home Office online Report 16/02, available on: www.homeoffice.gov.uk/rds.

Prison Reform Trust (October 2006) 'Seven Point Plan to End Jail Overcrowding', available on: www.prisonreformtrust.org.uk/

Prison Reform Trust (January 2007) *Making Sentencing Clearer: A Consultation and Report of a Review by the Home Secretary, Lord Chancellor and Attorney General. A Response by the Prison Reform Trust*, available on: www.prisonreformtrust.org.uk/uploads/documents/makingsentencingclearerjan07.doc

Project Match Research Group (1997) 'Matching Alcoholism Treatments to Client Heterogeneity. Project Match Post Treatment Drinking Outcomes', *Journal of Studies on Alcohol*, 58: 7–29.

Psychnet-UK (n.d.) *Mental Health,* available on: www.psychnet-uk.com

Pycroft, A. (2005) 'A New Chance for Rehabilitation: Multi Agency Provision and Potential Under NOMS', in J. Winstone and F. Pakes (eds) *Community Justice: Issues for Probation and Criminal Justice*, Cullompton: Willan, 130–41.

Quayle, E. and Taylor, M. (2003) 'Model of Problematic Internet Use in People with a Sexual Interest in Children', *Cyberpsychology and Behavior*, 6: 93–106.

Quinsey, V.L. (1988) 'Assessment of the Treatability of Forensic Patients', *Behavioural Sciences and the Law*, 6: 443–52.

Quinsey, V.L., Harris, G.T., Rice, M.E. and Cormier, C.A. (1998) *Violent Offenders: Appraising and Managing Risk*, Washington, DC: American Psychological Association.

Radkey-Yarrow, M. and Sherman, T. (1990) 'Children Born at Medical Risk: Factors Affecting Vulnerability and Resilience', in J. Rolf, A.S. Masten, D. Cicchetti., K.H. Neuchterlein and S. Weinraub (eds) *Risk and Protective Factors in the Development of Psychopathology*, Cambridge: Cambridge University Press.

Raistrick, D., Heather, N. and Godfrey, C. (2006) *Review of the Effectiveness of Treatment for Alcohol Problems*, National Treatment Agency for Substance Misuse.

Reid, J. (2006) 'Where Next for Penal Policy?' Home Secretary Speech to the Prison Reform Trust 06.05.06, available on: www.homeoffice.gov.uk/speeches

Ressler, R.K. and Shachtman, T. (1988) *Whoever Fights Monsters,* London: Simon and Schuster.

Rice, M.E. and Harris, G.T. (1997) 'The Treatment of Mentally Disordered Offenders', *Psychology, Public Policy and Law*, 3: 126–83.

Rodgers, J. Ashton, C.H. Gilvarry, E. and Young, A.H. (2004) 'Liquid Ecstasy: A New Kid on the Dance Floor', *British Journal of Psychiatry*, 184: 104–11.

Romer, D., Jamieson, H.K. and Aday, S. (2003) 'Television News and the Cultivation of Fear of Crime', *Journal of Communication*, 53: 88–104.

Roosevelt, F.D. (1933) 'Inaugural Address', 4 March, 1933, in S. Rosenman, (ed) (1938) *The Public Papers of Franklin D. Roosevelt, Volume Two: The Year of Crisis, 1933*, New York: Random House, 11–16.

Rosenfeld, B. (2004) 'Violence Risk Factors in Stalking and Obsessional Harassment: A Review and Preliminary Risk Assessment', *Criminal Justice and Behavior*, 2004, 9–36.

Ross, R., Fabiano, E. and Ewles, C. (1998) 'Reasoning and Rehabilitation', *International Journal of Offender Therapy and Comparative Criminology*, 32: 29–33.

Rossow, I. (2001) 'Alcohol and Homicide: A Cross-Cultural Comparison of the Relationship in 14 European Countries', *Addiction*, 96 (Suppl. 1), S77–92.

Royal College of Psychiatrists (RCP) (2005) *New Ways of Working for Psychiatrists: Enhancing Effective, Person-Centred Services Through New Ways of Working in Multidisciplinary and Multi-Agency Contexts*, London: Department of Health Publications.

Rutter, M. (1971) 'Parent–Child Separation: Psychological Effects on the Children', *Journal of Child Psychology and Psychiatry*, 12: 233–60.

Rutter, M., Giller, H. and Hagell, A. (1998) *Antisocial Behaviour by Young People*, Cambridge: Cambridge University Press.

Safety First (2001) *Safety First: Five-Year Report of the National Confidential Inquiry in the Suicide and Homicide by People with Mental Illness*, London: Department of Health.

Salisbury, H. and Upson, A. (2004) *Ethnicity, Victimisation and Worry about Crime: Findings from the 2001/02 and 2002/03 British Crime Surveys*, Home Office Findings 237, London: HMSO.

Salter, A. (1998) *Truth, Lies and Sex Offenders*, Thousand Oaks, CA: Pal Video, Sage.

Sampson, R.J. (1986) 'Crime in Cities: The Effects of Formal and Informal Social Control', in A.J. Reiss and M. Tonry (eds) *Crime and Justice*, vol. 8, Chicago: University of Chicago Press, 271–311.

Sampson, R.J. (1997) 'Collective Regulation of Adolescent Misbehaviour: Validation Results From Eight Chicago Neighborhoods', *Journal of Adolescent Research*, 12: 227–44.

Sampson, R.J. (2000) *Acquaintance Rape of College Students: Problem-Oriented Guide for Police Services, No. 17*, US Department of Justice: Office of Community Oriented Policing Services.

Sarler, C. (2006) 'The Anti-rape Ads Mean Well, But Making Men Entirely Responsible for Sex Implies that Women are Incompetent', *Guardian*, 16 March.

Sawyer, R.G., Thompson, E.E. and Chicorelli, A.M. (2002) 'Rape Myth Acceptance Among Intercollegiate Student Athletes: A Preliminary Examination', *American Journal of Health Studies*, 18: 19–25.

Schachter, S. and Singer, J.E. (1962) 'Cognitive, Social and Physiological Determinants of Emotional State', *Psychological Review*, 69: 379–99.

Scharf, P. (1983) 'Empty Bars: Violence and the Crisis of Meaning in Prison', *Prison Journal*, 63: 114–24.

Schubot, D.B. (2001) 'Date Rape Prevalence Among Female High School Students in a Rural Midwestern State During 1993, 1995, and 1997', *Journal of Interpersonal Violence*, 16: 291–6.

Schumacher, J. (1993) *Falling Down*, Los Angeles: Warner Brothers.

Scott, H. (2003) 'Stranger Danger: Explaining Women's Fear of Crime', *Western Criminology Review*, 4(3), available on: http://wcr.sonoma.edu/v4n3/scott.html.

Scott-Ham, M. and Burton, F.C. (2005) 'Toxicological Findings of Alleged Drug Facilitated Sexual Assault over a 3-Year Period', *Journal of Clinical Forensic Medicine*, 12: 175–86.

Scottish Office (1997) *A Commitment to Protect; Supervising Sex Offenders – Proposals for More Effective Practice*, Scottish Office.

Serin, R.C., Peters, R. and Barbaree, H.E. (1990) 'The Prediction of Psychopathy and Release Outcome in a Criminal Population', *Psychological Assessment: A Journal of Consulting and Clinical Psychology*, 2: 419–22.

Sharp, C., Aldridge, J. and Medina, J. (2006) *Delinquent Youth Groups and Offending Behaviour: Findings from the 2004 Offending, Crime and Justice Survey*, Home Office Online Report 14/06, available on: www.homeoffice. gov.uk/rds/pdfs06/rdsolr1406.pdf

Sheridan, L. and Davies, G.M. (2001) 'Stalking: The Elusive Crime', *Legal and Criminological Psychology*, 6: 133–47.

Sheridan, L. and Boon, J. (2002) 'Stalker Typologies: Implications for Law Enforcement', in J. Boon and L. Sheridan (eds) *Stalking and Psychosexual Obsession*, Chichester: Wiley, 63–82.

Sheridan, L., Davies, G.M. and Boon, J. (2001) 'The Course and Nature of Stalking: A Victim Perspective', *Howard Journal*, 40: 215–34.

Sheridan, L., Gillett, R. and Davies, G.M. (2003) '"There's No Smoke Without Fire": Are Male Ex-Partners Perceived as More "Entitled" to Stalk than Acquaintance or Stranger Stalkers?', *British Journal of Psychology*, 94: 87–98.

Sherman, L., Denise, C., Gottfredson, D., Mackenzie, J., Reuter, P. and Bushway, S. (1997) *Preventing Crime: What Works, What Doesn't, What's Promising*, Washington, DC: US Department of Justice.

Shkolnikov, V.M. and Nemtsov, A. (1997) 'The Anti-Alcohol Campaign and Variations in Russian Mortality', in J.L. Bobadilla, C.A. Costello and F. Mitchell (eds) *Premature Death in the New Independent States*, Washington, DC: National Academy Press, 239–61.

Singleton, N., Meltzer, H. and Gatward, R. (1998) *Psychiatric Morbidity Among Prisoners in England and Wales*, London: Office for National Statistics.

Singleton, N., O'Brien, M., Lee, A. and Meltzer, H. (2000) 'Psychiatric Morbidity Among Adults Living in Single Households', *International Review of Psychiatry*, 15: 63–73.

Skogan, W.G. (1995) 'Crime and Racial Fears of White Americans', *Annals of the American Academy of Political and Social Science*, 539: 59–71.

Slaughter, L. (2000) 'Involvement of Drugs in Sexual Assault', *Journal of Reproductive Medicine*, 45: 425–30.

Smith, R. (2003) *Youth Justice: Ideas, Policy, Practice*, Cullompton: Willan.

Social Exclusion Unit (2006a) *What Is Social Exclusion?* London: SEU, available on: www.socialexclusionunit.gov.uk/page.asp?id=213

Social Exclusion Unit (2006b) *Reaching Out: An Action Plan on Social Exclusion*, HM Government, available on: www.cabinetoffice.gov.uk/social_exclusion_ task_force/documents/reaching_out/reaching_out_full.pdf

Spence-Diehl, E. (2003) 'Stalking and Technology: The Double-Edged Sword', *Journal of Technology in Human Services*, 22: 15–18.

Spencer, A. (1999) *Working with Sex Offenders in Prisons and Through Release to the Community: A Handbook*, London: Jessica Kingsley.

Sperry, L. (1995) *Handbook of Diagnosis and Treatment of the DSM-IV Personality Disorders*, New York: Brunner/Mazel.

Spitzberg, B.H. and Cadiz, M. (2002) 'The Media Construction of Stalking Stereotypes', *Journal of Criminal Justice and Popular Culture*, 9: 128–49.

Stanko, B. (2000) 'The Day to Count: A Snapshot of the Impact of Domestic Violence in the UK', *Criminal Justice*, 1(2).

Stanko, E.A. (1992) 'The Case of Fearful Women: Gender, Personal Safety and Fear of Crime', *Women and Criminal Justice*, 4: 117–35.

Stanko, E.A. (1996) 'The Commercialisation of Women's Fear of Crime', in C. Sumner, M. Israel, M. O'Connell, and R. Sarre (eds) *International Victimology: Selected Papers from the 8th International Symposium Held 21–26 August 1994*, Canberra: Australian Institute of Criminology, 79–85.

Stone, N. (2003) *A Companion Guide to Mentally Disordered Offenders* (2nd edition), Crayford: Shaw.

Sutherland, D.H. (1974) *Criminology*, Philadelphia: Lippincott.

Swanson, J., Estroff, S., Swartz, M., Borum, R., Lachicotte, W., Zimmer, C. and Wagner, R. (1997) 'Violence and Severe Mental Disorder in Clinical and Community Populations: The Effects of Psychotic Symptoms, Comorbidity, and Disaffiliation from Treatment', *Psychiatry*, 60: 1–22.

Sykes, S. and Matza, D. (1957) 'Techniques of Neutralization: A Theory of Delinquency', *American Sociological Review*, 22: 664–73.

Tajfel, H. (1982) 'Social Psychology of Intergroup Relations', *Annual Review of Psychology*, 33: 1–39.

Taylor, G. (2002) *Castration. An Abbreviated History of Western Manhood*, London: Routledge.

Taylor, P.J. and Gunn, J. (1999) 'Homicides by People with Mental Illness: Myth and Reality', *British Journal of Psychiatry*, 174: 9–14.

Taylor, R. (2000) *A Seven-Year Reconviction Study of HMP Grendon Therapeutic Community*, Research Findings No. 115, Home Office Development and Statistics Directorate, available on: www.homeoffice.gov.uk/rds/pdfs/r115.pdf

Tewksbury, R. (2005) 'Collateral Consequences of Sex Offender Registration', *Journal of Contemporary Criminal Justice*, 21: 82–90.

This Is Worcestershire (2003) *The Price of Violence*, 17 June 2003, available on: http://archive.thisisworcestershire.co.uk/2003/6/17/196624.html

Thornton, D. (1997) *Structured Anchor Clinical Judgment Risk Assessment (SACJ): Proceedings of the NOTA Conference*, September, Brighton, UK.

Thornton, D. (2002) 'Constructing and Testing a Framework for Dynamic Risk Assessment', *Sexual Abuse: A Journal of Research and Treatment*, 14: 137–51.

Thornton, D., Mann, R., Webster, S., Blud, L., Travers, R., Friendship, C., *et al.* (2003) 'Distinguishing and Combining Risks for Sexual and Violent Recidivism', *Annals of the New York Academy of Sciences*, 989, 225–35.

Tjaden, P. and Thoenness, N. (1998) *Stalking in America: Findings from the National Violence Against Women Survey*, Washington, DC: US Department of Justice, National Institute of Justice.

Tonin, E. (2004) 'The Attachment Styles of Stalkers', *Journal of Forensic Psychiatry and Psychology*, 15: 584–90.

Townley, L. and Ede, R. (2004) *Forensic Practice in Criminal Cases*, London: The Law Society.

Tremblay, R.E., Masse, B., Perron, D., Le Blanc, M., Schwartzman, A.E. and Ledingham, J.E. (1992) 'Early Disruptive Behaviour, Poor School Achievement, Delinquent Behaviour and Delinquent Personality: Longitudinal Analysis', *Journal of Consulting and Clinical Psychology*, 60: 64–72.

Tulloch, M. (2000) 'The Meaning of Age Differences in the Fear of Crime', *British Journal of Criminology*, 40: 451–67.

Turvey, B. (2002) *Criminal Profiling: An Introduction to Behavioural Evidence Analysis* (2nd edition), San Diego, CA: Academic Press.

Utting, D. (1996) *Reducing Criminality Among Young People: A Sample of Relevant Programmes in the United Kingdom*, Home Office Research Study 161, London: Home Office

Utting, D., Bright, J. and Henricson, C. (1993) *Crime and the Family. Improving Child-Rearing and Preventing Delinquency*, London: Family Policy Studies Centre.

Van Dam, C. (2006) *The Socially Skilled Child Molester*, Binghamton, NY: Haworth.

Vizard, E., Monck, E. and Misch, P. (1995) 'Child and Adolescent Sex Abuse Perpetrators: A Review of the Research Literature', *Journal of Child Psychology and Psychiatry*, 36: 731–7.

Von Hirsch, A. (1976) *Doing Justice: The Choice of Punishments. Report of the Committee for the Study of Incarceration*, New York: Hill and Wang.

Vrij, A., Van Der Steen, H. and Koppelaar, J. (1994) 'Aggression of Police Officers as a Function of Temperature: An Experiment with the Fire Arms Training System', *Journal of Community and Applied Social Psychology*, 4: 365–70.

Wadsworth, M. (1979) *Roots of Delinquency*, London: Martin Robertson.

Walby, S. and Allen, J. (2004) *Domestic Violence, Sexual Assault and Stalking: Findings from the British Crime Survey*, Home Office Research Study 276, London: HMSO.

Walker, A., Kershaw, C. and Nicholas, S. (2006) *Crime in England and Wales 2005/2006*, available on: www.homeoffice.gov.uk/rds/pdfs06/hosb1206.pdf

Ward, T. and Hudson, S.M. (1998) 'A Model of the Relapse Process in Sexual Offenders', *Journal of Interpersonal Violence*, 13: 700–25.

Ward, T. and Hudson, S.M. (2001) 'A Critique of Finkelhor's Precondition Model of Sexual Abuse', *Psychology, Crime and Law*, 7: 333–50.

Ward, T., Fon, C., Hudson, S.M. and McCormack, J. (1998) 'A Descriptive Model of Dysfunctional Cognitions in Child Molesters', *Journal of Interpersonal Violence*, 13: 129–55.

Warr, M. (1993) 'Parents, Peers and Delinquency', *Social Forces*, 72: 247–64.

Watson J.B. (1913) 'Psychology as a Behaviourist Views It', *Psychological Review*, 20: 158–77.

Werner, E.E. and Smith, R.S. (1992) *Overcoming the Odds: High Risk Children from Birth to Adulthood*, New York: Cornell University Press.

West, D. and Farrington, D. (1973) *Who Becomes Delinquent?* London: Heinemann.

West, D.J. (1982) *Delinquency: Its Roots, Careers and Prospects*, London: Heinemann.

West, R. (2001) 'Theories of Addiction', *Addiction*, 96: 3–13.

West, R. (2005) 'Time for a Change: Putting the Transtheoretical (Stages of Change) Model to Rest', *Addiction*, 100: 1036–39.

West, R. (2006) *Theory of Addiction*, Oxford: Addiction Press, Blackwell.

Westerberg, V.S. (1998) 'What Predicts Success', in W.R. Miller and N. Heather (eds) *Treating Addictive Behaviors* (2nd edition), New York: Plenum Press, 301–16.

Whiting, E. and Cuppleditch, L. (2006) *Re-offending of Juveniles: Results from the 2004 Cohort*, Reconviction Analysis Team, RDS-NOMS, London: Home Office.

Willan, V.-J. and Pollard, P. (2003) 'Likelihood of Acquaintance Rape as a Function of Males' Sexual Expectations, Disappointment, and Adherence to Rape Conducive Attitudes', *Journal of Social and Personal Relationships*, 20: 637–61.

Williams, J.E. (1984) 'Secondary Victimisation: Confronting Public Attitudes about Rape', *International Journal of Victimology*, 9: 66–81.

Williams, R. and Johnson, P. (2005) 'Inclusiveness, Effectiveness and Intrusiveness: Issues in the Developing Uses of DNA Profiling in Support of Criminal Investigations', *Journal of Law and Medical Ethics*, 33: 545–58.

Wilson, C. and Seaman, C. (1990) *The Serial Killers*, London: Virgin.

Wilson, J.Q. and Kelling, G.L. (1982) 'Broken Windows: The Police and Neighbourhood Safety', *Atlantic Monthly* (March): 29–38.

Winkel, F.W., Sheridan, L., Malsch, M. and Arensman, E. (2002) 'The Psychological Consequences of Stalking Victimisation', in J. Boon and L. Sheridan (eds) *Stalking and Psychosexual Obsession*, Chichester: Wiley, 23–33.

Winstone, J. and Pakes, F. (2005) 'Marginalised and Disenfranchised: Community Justice and Mentally Disordered Offenders', in J. Winstone and F. Pakes (eds) *Community Justice: Issues for Probation and Criminal Justice*, Cullompton: Willan, 219–37.

Winstone, J. and Pakes, F. (in press) 'The Mentally Disordered Offender: Disenablers for the Delivery of Justice', in D. Carson, R. Milne, F. Pakes, K. Shalev and A. Shawyer (eds) *Applying Psychology in Criminal Justice*, Chichester: Wiley.

Wolf, S.C. (1985) 'A Multi-Factor Model of Deviant Sexuality', *Victimology: An International Journal*, 10 (1–4): 359–74.

Woolf, Lord Justice (1991) *Prison Disturbances April 1990: Report of an Inquiry by The Rt Hon Lord Justice Woolf (Parts I and II) and His Honour Judge Stephen Tumim (Part II)*, Cm. 1456, London: HMSO.

World Wide Ages of Consent (2006) 'World Wide Ages of Consent', available on: www.ageofconsent.com

Yalom, I. (1995) *The Theory and Practice of Group Psychotherapy* (4th edition), New York: Basic Books.

Young, J. (1986) 'The Failure of Criminology: The Need for a Radical Realism', in J. Young and R. Matthews (eds) *Confronting Crime*, London: Sage, 4–30.

Young, J. (1997) 'Left Realist Criminology: Radical in its Analysis, Realist in its Policy', in M. Maguire, R. Morgan and R. Reiner (eds) *The Oxford Handbook of Criminology*, Oxford: Oxford University Press, 473–98.

Young, J. (n.d.) 'Risk of Crime and Fear of Crime: The Politics of Victimisation Studies' available on: www.malcolmread.co.uk/jockyoung/

Young, J. and Matthews, R. (2003) 'New Labour, Crime Control and Social Exclusion', in R. Matthews and J. Young (eds) *The New Politics of Crime and Punishment*, Cullompton: Willan, 1–32.

Youth Justice Board (YJB) (2001) *Risk and Protective Factors Associated with Youth Crime and Effective Interventions to Prevent It*, London: Youth Justice Board for England and Wales.

Youth Justice Board (YJB) (2003) *Mental Health: Key Elements of Effective Practice*, London: Youth Justice Board for England and Wales.

Youth Justice Board (YJB) (2004) *Youth Justice Annual Statistics 2003/04*, London: Youth Justice Board, available on: www.youth-justice-board.gov.uk

Youth Risk Behavior Surveillance (YRBS) – United States 2003 (2004) Atlanta, GA: Department of Health and Human Services, available on: www.cdc.gov/healthyyouth/yrbs/index.htm

Zevitz, R. and Farkas, M. (2000) 'Sex Offender Community Notification: Managing High Risk Criminals or Exacting Further Vengeance?', *Behavioral Sciences and the Law*, 18: 375–91.

Zillmann, D., Hoyt, J.L. and Day, K.D. (1974) 'Strength and Duration of the Effect of Aggressive, Violent and Erotic Communications on Subsequent Aggressive Behaviors', *Communication Research*, 1: 286–306.

Zillmann, D., Katcher, A.H. and Milavsky, B. (1972) 'Excitation Transfer from Physical Exercise to Subsequent Aggressive Behavior', *Journal of Experimental Social Psychology*, 8: 247–59.

Zimbardo, P.G. (1978) *'Deindividuation'*, in B.B. Woman (ed) *International Encyclopedia of Psychiatry, Psychology, Psychoanalysis and Neurology*, vol. 4, New York: Human Sciences Press, 52–53.

Zimring, F. and Hawkins, G. (1993) *The Scale of Imprisonment*, Chicago: University of Chicago Press.

Index